Endorsements From Charitable Givers and Philanthropists

"Chris Gabriel has written an inspiring call to action that defines generosity and delivers a masterful explanation of what it is, why it matters, and how to make it happen. *WISEgenerosity* is a must-read for everyone from professional philanthropists to young people seeking meaning and purpose in their lives."

- Rodney Bullard, CEO of The Safe House and former head of The Chick fil-A Foundation

"Chris has been instrumental in helping our family foundation become more intentional in our giving and more engaged as a Board. Thanks to his guidance, we have gained a deeper understanding of the issues we care about most and are now able to focus our giving in a more targeted and effective way. Chris helped us to come together as a family and to engage purposefully and practically as we look to continue our tradition of productive giving into a fifth and sixth generation. We highly recommend Chris's *WISEgenerosity* materials to anyone who wants to make a real difference in the world."

-Thompson Turner, Bradley-Turner Foundation

"Chris and his principles on W.I.S.E. generosity set a foundation for our family's way of sharing resources. His guidelines have opened opportunities to give enthusiastically and generously."

- Susan Marshall, community leader

"No other book combines inspiration and implementation like *WISEgenerosity*. Having supported community revitalization efforts in my city and around the world, Chris's work illuminates what successful giving is and how to make it happen."

- David Allman, owner and chairman of Regent Partners

Endorsements From Entrepreneurs and Business Leaders

"*WISEgenerosity* is a powerful platform. Chris brings to life the 'Why' behind giving and then connects that motivation to each person's unique 'How,' 'What,' 'Where,' and 'When.' The resulting outcomes are meaningful and effective."

- *Randy Street,* vice chairman of ghSMART,
coauthor of *Who: The A Method for Hiring*

"The world needs more people willing to band together, to break down barriers, and to unite to help their neighbors. *WISEgenerosity* explains why giving matters and how it delivers transformative power for individuals, communities, and society. Read this book and live out what it offers!"

- *Blake Canterbury,* cofounder and CEO of Purposity

"Many entrepreneurs see their ventures as a social operation—meeting a social need first and then generating profits as a result of meeting that need. For any entrepreneur who cares about leveraging their venture, energy, and resources to maximize their impact, *WISEgenerosity* is THE platform to produce optimal outcomes for your business, your family, and your community."

- *Michael Blake,* High Score Strategies

Endorsements From Nonprofit Leaders

"In working with Chris for nearly twenty years, I've seen first-hand his passion for generosity and his commitment to excellence in giving. The ideas and resources in *WISEgenerosity* offer transformational potential to donors and nonprofits alike."

- Bruce Deel, founder and CEO of City of Refuge

"Chris Gabriel's *WISEgenerosity* succinctly connects the dots around the WHY, the HOW and the LASTING IMPACT of giving. The creation of legacy can feel complex. *WISEgenerosity* shows it is not. It is doable, necessary, and instrumental to a purposeful life lived with wisdom, impact, and satisfaction."

- Bryan K. Clontz, founder and president of
Charitable Solutions, creator of National Gift Annuity
Foundation, and guest columnist with *Forbes*

"Chris has trained leaders, development officers, and donors for our organization at national programs and in local chapters across the country. He is one of the most productive advocates I've ever seen at providing giving tools that deliver results. *WISEgenerosity* is the source of those principles and practices."

- Terry Balko, director of Resource Development Club
Services for Boys & Girls Clubs of America (Retired)

"I have waited decades for a book to provide the valuable and much-needed wisdom in these pages. *WISEgenerosity* is the first and most comprehensive resource I have seen on such an important subject. Chris Gabriel writes from a position of experience and expertise. His authentic and compelling words will move the reader to make life-changing and life-improving actions."

- Wayne Olson, international keynote speaker
and author of *Fundraising for Nonprofit Board Members,*
The Disney Difference, and *Words of Encouragement*

Endorsements From Professional Advisors

"Buying and taking action on this book will change your life! Chris has provided the blueprints to build happiness, enlightenment, and fulfillment for you and those around you. True success is defined by thriving relationships and productive resources, and *WISEgenerosity* is an amazing guide to achieving both."

- Syd Walker, founder and CEO of Prosperis Partners

"As a CPA, I value rigorous analysis. As a nonprofit volunteer, I appreciate commitment to meaningful and effective community service. Chris combines a systematic head for doing good with a compassionate heart for purposeful impact. *WISEgenerosity* is a platform that professional advisors should understand and use."

- Ellen Siegfried, principal with Jones and Kolb

"Working with special needs families, I appreciate the levels of generosity needed to navigate possessional, personal, social, emotional, and relational needs. *WISEgenerosity* points towards the things that matter most and prompts people to act in ways that benefit their loved ones, themselves, and others around them."

- Kristen M. Lewis, special needs planning attorney in Atlanta, GA

Endorsements From Thought and Faith Leaders

"As humans, we are meant to give in service to something higher than ourselves, but our inherent generosity is threatened by dangers, deficiencies, difficulties, and distractions that also undermine our own happiness and fulfillment. *WISEgenerosity* offers a framework of protection, provision, power, and peace that transforms individuals, relationships, society, and the world."

- Ryan West, founder and president of Paro Communities

"We live in a broken world. When you sense that the wind, waves, and current are against you, you need a wise guide to help you navigate those difficult waters. Chris Gabriel is just such a guide, and I believe the insights he shares through *WISEgenerosity* will help you discover the considerate, caring, and compassionate help you need to experience a life that matters."

- Bill Britt, senior minister at Peachtree Road UMC

"*WISEgenerosity* is both a guide to living a meaningful life as well as an invitation to a life of abundance, kindness, and joy. I LOVE that Chris shares a view of generosity that makes it readily accessible to everyone! — YOU have something to share that somebody needs! Chris illuminates the path for you to be the person you long to be and live the life you most long to live — a life characterized by generosity...and overflowing with gratitude."

- Kevin Monroe, founder of Gratitude Consulting,
The Grateful App, and The Global Gratitude Society

"Hope and opportunity are the antidotes to despair and division in our society. Chris Gabriel delivers a powerful dose of these much-needed medicines. *WISEgenerosity* will help you to live more meaningfully and effectively as you serve your personal purpose, your family, your community, and the world at large."

- Randy Hicks, president and CEO of
Georgia Center for Opportunity

WISE
generosity

A Guide to Purposeful and Productive
Living and Giving

CHRIS GABRIEL

Forefront
BOOKS

Published by Forefront Books.
Distributed by Simon & Schuster.

Library of Congress Control Number: 2023918129

Print ISBN: 978-1-63763-193-5
E-book ISBN: 978-1-63763-194-2

Cover Design by Bruce Gore, Gore Studio, Inc.
Interior Design by Bill Kersey, KerseyGraphics

Dedication

To Courtenay for being my guiding star.

To Ellie and Reed for providing inspiration and hope for the future.

To my family for sharing a lifetime of giving examples

and loving encouragement.

To the many friends who have shone light and shared support.

To all of those who have made this generosity

journey possible: past, present, and future.

Table of Contents

SECTION 1
Living Generously—
The Path to a Purposeful Life

SECTION 2
Giving Wisely—
The Path to a Productive Life

SECTION 3

Experiencing WISEgenerosity—
The Path to Your Best Life

Introduction

————————————————————————————————→

WHERE DID THIS BOOK COME FROM? "Midlife crisis" would be the simplest first answer. Some people try to rewind their personal life odometer by buying a sports car (I'm too practical) or diving into vigorous youthful pursuits (I'm too uncoordinated).

Instead, I began to reflect some time ago on the most fundamental personal question we can ask ourselves: *Why am I here?* As the years went by, an outline to that answer started to take shape.

There are four pillars on which my life rested both then and now: *spiritual* (seeking good), *relational* (family and friends), *professional* (work and career), and *communal* (volunteer service). While they differed in levels of engagement, all four were important. Moreover, I wanted to be intentional about aligning these four pillars in a balanced way to find the life I was seeking.

This was progress, but I had traded one question for another: *How do you live an aligned life?*

I was drawn to the pursuit of meaning. It was important that the things I was doing mattered in some way. I also felt responsible for having a positive impact on others, based on the opportunities that had been given to me. I had been blessed abundantly in all four pillars of my life, and I wanted to share these blessings with others. This was a puzzle to solve involving purpose and productivity, and I struggled to see how the pieces fit together.

On March 28, 2013, the picture of an aligned life first took shape for me while I was driving home to Atlanta from Orlando. I know the date because, as the significance of the resulting quest became clearer over time, I went back to my calendar and looked up exactly when the proverbial light bulb came on.

In an effort to align my professional and communal interests, I was working pro bono for a national nonprofit organization, drawing on my prior career as a charitable fundraiser and my current one as a financial advisor. Having been invited by the local leaders in central Florida to consult with them, the visit focused on educating and inspiring successful entrepreneurs and the advisors who serve them. How could these business owners realize the full benefits of giving personally and financially for the betterment of their companies, their families, and their communities? That question related directly to my own quest to live an aligned life.

Long, solo car rides are good opportunities for me to clear my head and listen to audiobooks, podcasts, and other content I typically am too distracted to absorb fully. Traveling up I-75 that day, I played a message titled "Be Rich,"[1] which talked about harnessing things that have *transient* significance (like money) in service to things that have more *permanent* significance (like changing lives for the better).

In the way a machine engages when the gears finally are aligned, a flood of thoughts and emotions started coursing through me. I felt a wave of gratitude for my loved ones—my wife, my children, my family, and my friends. Images of other people who had helped me throughout my life rushed into my mind: teachers, mentors, and others who had provided me with inspiration and support. Places bubbled up in my mind as well: the community groups where I'd volunteered, the schools I had attended, the youth organizations of which I had been a part, all the way back to the nonprofit hospital where I had been born.

It became clear in the moment that there was a common thread tying together all the important elements of my life: *generosity*. Generosity fulfilled my spiritual desire to seek good. Generosity defined my best role in the relationships I cared about. Generosity gave purpose to my professional work that previously had been missing. Generosity was at the heart of the community service I enjoyed and from which I had benefitted so richly.

At a rest area along the highway, I pulled off the road, overcome by these ideas and feelings and needing a moment to gather my thoughts. Extracting a pad of paper from the briefcase lying on the seat next to me, I started writing a stream of consciousness—page after page.

As my mind began to clear and I started to breathe more normally, a realization emerged. When asking, "What am I supposed to do in life?" the answer was, "Be generous."

Your Connection to WISEgenerosity

Before going any further, you should know what to expect from this book.

WISEgenerosity synthesizes years of experience and exploration on the topic of giving across all dimensions of life. It is intended as a guidebook that you read, digest, and reference over and over again as you consider how to live your own best life of meaning and impact. I hope that you keep it readily accessible on a bookshelf or elsewhere where you can get to it easily when you need it. I also hope that you share this material with others who can benefit from the ideas and inspirations presented in it.

The book's format is based on a method that has been developed to produce purposeful and practical giving. We will explore a series of questions—why, how, what, when, and where—and the answer to each question will result in a more refined understanding of your most generous life.

Your WISEgenerosity journey is meant to be interactive. In the book's afterword, there are links to a journal in which you can make notes while you read, as well as links to study guides designed to help you make productive use of the material presented.

Above all, I hope that throughout these pages, you are drawn into the stories of the amazingly generous people who have touched me deeply. This project has changed my life, and I hope that it will be richly beneficial to you as well.

Let's begin...

SECTION 1

Living Generously— The Path to a Purposeful Life

Section 1, Part 1

Presenting WISEgenerosity

THE ROADMAP TO WISEGENEROSITY IN THIS BOOK IS DIVIDED INTO THREE SECTIONS:

1. Living Generously
2. Giving Wisely
3. Experiencing WISEgenerosity

In the first section, we will explore how generosity applies to all areas of our lives and gives us purpose, meaning, and impact.

In the second section, we will look at ways in which giving is done wisely and well. We'll also talk about where we should give, what we should give, and when we should give.

The third section explores meaningful and effective generosity. Each of us gives in accordance with our own unique abilities and interests. We also give alongside others who share complementary perspectives and priorities.

Along the way, we will encounter inspiration and guidance from some of the most generous people I know.

One of my favorite quotes related to giving is from the Roman philosopher Seneca:

> The wise will give wealth either to good people or to those whom it may make into good people. He or she will give it after having taken the utmost pains to choose those who are fittest to receive it, as becomes one who bears in mind that they ought to give an account of what they spend as well as of what they receive. They will give for good and commendable reasons, for a gift ill bestowed counts as a shameful loss: they will have an easily opened pocket, but not one with a hole in it, so that much may be taken out of it, yet nothing may fall out of it.[2]

I especially love the line, "an easily opened pocket, but not one with a hole in it, so that much may be taken out of it, yet nothing may fall out of it." This suggests freely sharing but with good sense and a commitment to the best outcomes for all involved. Such an approach to all aspects of life is meaningful and effective. In the pages to come, I will define this type of sharing with others as *wise* and will show how living and giving in this way is the optimal path to purpose and productivity—and to WISEgenerosity.

CHAPTER 1

→

WISEgenerosity Is Key to a Meaningful and Effective Life

THINK ABOUT THE MOST SUCCESSFUL PEOPLE YOU KNOW— those with wealth, power, and status.

Are they happy? Do they radiate confidence and joy?

Are they enlightened? Do they seem illuminated by positivity and unburdened by cares and concerns?

Are they fulfilled? Are they grounded and able to navigate life's ups and downs with poise?

Perhaps you answered yes, but it's likely you answered no. "Success" seems to create its own pressures and problems. Especially in the social media age, those who seem to "have it all" may be struggling deeply in ways we can't see.

Now think about the most generous people you know: relatives, neighbors, mentors, and friends.

Chances are these people are happier, more enlightened, and more fulfilled than anyone else in your life. It likely makes you smile just to think about them. Regardless of age or circumstances, they exhibit traits you admire—traits that you may wish you had more of.

It's not a coincidence that successful people often struggle and generous people are usually fulfilled. The attributes that our society embraces and rewards are ultimately empty if they don't serve a genuine purpose beyond merely satisfying ourselves. Celebrities, moguls, and titans frequently implode in spectacular self-destruction. Others closer to home can do likewise, or at least can damage connections and reputations when harmful selfishness bubbles to the surface.

In contrast, centuries of science, philosophy, and spiritual teachings affirm that generosity is an essential virtue of a life well-lived. Ultimate meaning and impact are measured not in dollars or followers or position or fame but in serving and supporting others in ways large and small.

We Are What We Give

True generosity is active, not passive. It is thoughtful and effective. It engages the emotions and the intellect. It builds up rather than tears down.

Genuine generosity nurtures the giver and elevates the receiver. It ripples out into our relationships and into our communities. It produces positive change unlike anything else in human existence, and it's the primary antidote for whatever distress, division, and destruction negatively affects our lives.

It has been more than ten years since I started on my generosity journey. I have been led by inspiring guides, learned incredible lessons, had moving experiences, and dealt with more personal discovery and growth than I ever could have imagined. As the result, I have found a calling to harness the power of generosity myself and to support others who are doing likewise.

What about you? Perhaps you are in the middle of life, asking yourself questions similar to the ones I was asking myself: *Why am I here? What really matters in life, and how can I pursue my most important goals purposefully and effectively?*

Perhaps you are a few laps closer to the finish of your life, and you're reflecting maturely on your legacy: *What good am I leaving behind to benefit those close to me and in the world beyond?*

Perhaps you are closer to the starting line, and you're seeking direction as your life takes shape: *What will define my life and steer me toward success in my relationships and with my resources?*

Whatever your age and stage of life, generosity leads toward *purpose* and *productivity*—allowing you to be the best you can be while helping others be the best they can be.

Engaged generosity is one of the only universally positive human behaviors. When done wisely and well, there can't be too much of it. Whether you are young or old, rich or poor, healthy or sick, happy or sad, secure or teetering on the edge, you benefit by giving and from giving. So does everyone around you.

Ultimately, what matters most is the meaning we share with others and the impact that radiates from ourselves out into the world. Nothing we own, nothing we accomplish, and nothing we care about will outlive us, except by how these elements of life affect others now and in years to come.

Generosity is essential and existential. *We are what we give.*

WISEgenerosity Is Key to Effective Living and Giving

Purposeful and effective generosity is the healthiest and most helpful approach to life. It is not a vague aspiration but is attainable through specific attitudes and actions unique to you. This book is a guide for living your optimal life of WISEgenerosity, which will help to transform our world in the process.

WISEgenerosity Combines Purpose and Practice

Philosophers from ancient times have recognized that life is relational; that is, our personal virtue is expressed largely in terms of how it affects others. We thrive when we enable others to do so as well. Likewise, virtuous behavior doesn't happen on its own. It requires conscious effort combined with discipline. It requires asking the two most essential questions:

- *Why are we here?*
- *And what do we do about it?*

Wisdom is the combination of values and experience. It is produced by asking these questions and discovering the purpose (why) and the practice (what) that work best for you.

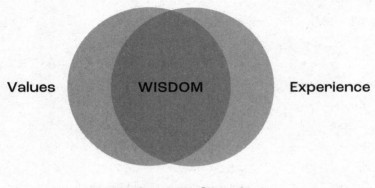

Wisdom Defined

Wisdom is applied virtue and values. Wise living reflects what you believe combined with how you behave. Both elements are needed. A meaningful life without effective action is unproductive. An active life without underlying meaning is pointless.

Wisdom can be acquired by assimilation or absorption. You can learn from the experiences of others, or you can be taught by your own experiences. The former is easier; the latter is more powerful. This book provides both avenues for learning: inspiring stories and useful tools combined with opportunities for you to build your own generous experiences.

Generosity is a way of living. It infuses itself into our lives and has the potential to affect everything we do for the better. The means by which living a generous life happens are attitude and action. A considerate attitude and caring actions enable the generous part of ourselves to be developed and expressed.

WISEgenerosity combines purpose (attitude) and practice (action) and is based on the answer to two other fundamental questions:

- *What human attribute leads to the best life, regardless of situation or circumstances?*

- *What human behavior is surest to produce happiness, enlightenment, and fulfillment?*

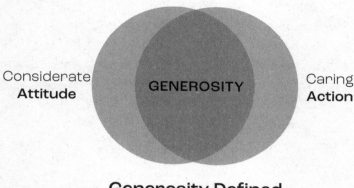

Generosity Defined

Based on years of research, reflection, observation, and engagement as a philosopher ("lover of wisdom") and financial advisor, I suggest that the answer to both questions is *generosity*.

WISEgenerosity provides understanding and guidance about how best to live our lives. WISEgenerosity is also direct and engaging. You can explore the most important aspects of life in ways that illuminate and activate.

This book and its related materials are intended to inspire and engage readers of all ages and at all stages of life. My hope is that you find the ability to live with even greater meaning and impact when it comes to the things most important to you—family, friends, favorite activities, work, your community, and society at large.

WISEgenerosity is designed to lead you on a journey to discover and enjoy the practical expressions of your underlying purpose. Accordingly, WISEgenerosity combines the elements that bring generosity fully to life. It is a simple concept with infinite potential:

- WISEgenerosity believes that abundance triumphs over scarcity.

- WISEgenerosity celebrates individual goodness and collective greatness.
- WISEgenerosity is radically optimistic and relentlessly realistic.
- WISEgenerosity sees potential in adversity and opportunity in need.
- WISEgenerosity reflects on small acts that can produce limitless impact.
- WISEgenerosity appreciates that what is inside each of us radiates out to all of us.
- WISEgenerosity celebrates the best of who we are and sees the even better people we can become.
- WISEgenerosity understands that bright light can overcome vast darkness.
- Most importantly, WISEgenerosity invites you to experience a force for good that underlies every positive relationship, strong community, and successful society in the past, present, and future.

WISEgenerosity Is W.I.S.E. Giving

It's clear by now that I consider generosity essential to a good life. There is exhaustive evidence to prove this point: study after study and volume after volume of writings back me up.

Even so, generosity is not as widespread or as productive as it could and should be. In the pages to come, we will explore key questions related to maximizing the benefits of generosity—why, how, what, where, and when. For now, just remember this important idea: the best giving is W.I.S.E.:

- **W**ell-grounded
- **I**nspired
- **S**atisfying
- **E**ffective

Think back to our definition of generosity as considerate attitude + caring action.

Two dimensions of W.I.S.E. giving are internal, and they relate to the attitude of the giver: *Inspired, Satisfying*.

Two dimensions of W.I.S.E. giving are external, and they relate to the actions of the giver: *Well-grounded, Effective*.

An ideal gift can be considered in this same way. Imagine a scenario in which you have an opportunity to serve or support someone else:

- Your circumstances are *Well-grounded*.
  The resources and capabilities you need are solid and readily available.
- As you consider potential options, an *Inspired* choice comes to mind.
  Your plans will align perfectly with the needs of the receiver.
- When you receive great appreciation after you make the gift, the result is *Satisfying*.
  You take pleasure in having provided a meaningful resource.
- Ultimately, your generosity proves to be *Effective*.
  The item or experience shared is used well by the receiver and your goal has been accomplished.

Here is another way of mapping out a W.I.S.E. gift:

	Internal Factor	External Factor
Before the Gift	Inspired	Well-grounded
After the Gift	Satisfying	Effective

Let's consider an example to illustrate the point.

Imagine a child whose parent is seriously ill. This young daughter desperately wants to support her mother. The girl takes on odd jobs and puts aside the money earned. She dedicates time to combing through family photos, selecting snapshots that reflect special memories and happy moments. She then assembles the pictures into an album that she purchases with her savings and hand-decorates with her own drawings and writings.

The mother appreciates the kindness of this special gift and draws inspiration from it during her most difficult moments. The daughter is comforted by the acts of sharing her efforts and expressing her love.

This gift was *Well-grounded* (it involved both preparation and commitment), *Inspired* (genuine concern was reflected, as well as an understanding of what the recipient wanted), *Satisfying* (both the giver and the receiver appreciated the present), and *Effective* (support was provided for both the receiver and the giver).

Hopefully, W.I.S.E. giving is beginning to resonate with you, and you're starting to realize how it is a useful guide for understanding healthy, productive generosity. In that vein, now is a good time to make a note about this book. As you'll see, there are many frameworks and formulas offered as part of WISEgenerosity. Please know that these are meant as useful tools and not as rigid rules to follow.

Good giving is an expression of who you are: carefree or careful, structured or spontaneous, low-key or loud—even perhaps all of these things at one time or another. My hope is that you refer to these perspectives as inspiration and encouragement as you pursue a life of meaningful and effective service and support for others. Use what makes sense to you and pass over what does not.

For instance, the order of letters in the acronym "W.I.S.E." is not prescriptive in the sense that "E" must follow "S" must follow "I" must follow "W." You may be Inspired to give even before you are sure that a gift is Well-grounded. You also may wait to see if a gift is Effective before being fully Satisfied that it's what you intended.

Any approach that works given the situation is fine. That said, since putting the letters in a different order—like IWSEgenerosity, WIESgenerosity, or IWES-generosity—doesn't have quite the same ring, we'll stick with WISEgenerosity.

WISEgenerosity Is Transformational

Generosity is the most powerful force for positive transformation in the world. Properly understood and implemented, generosity improves everything it touches.

Generosity is a universal trait that is at the heart of humanity. It is evident throughout all of history.

Unfortunately, while generosity is *normal*, it is not *natural*. Altruism and compassion define us at our best, but past episodes and our own experience offer ample evidence that we often treat each other poorly and suffer as a result. For every selfless act of caring, there can seem to be many cases of human cruelty.

The seeds of generosity are rooted deep inside us, but the weeds of selfishness and the floods of fear can overwhelm them. Giving effectively and serving others is learned behavior, built over time through conscious decisions and deliberate effort.

The rewards of giving are evident. Our life circumstances can be marvelous or miserable, but generosity improves our condition regardless of anything else. Good giving makes us happier, more enlightened, and more fulfilled. It generates positivity everywhere and for everyone.

A generous life is built on a combination of self-awareness and concern for others. When we are living generously, we are committed to our own wholeness and dedicated to the wellness of those around us. We are loving others as we love ourselves.

Generous relationships are built on mutual affection and connection. Dedicating ourselves to the welfare of others is both energizing and elevating.

A generous society is built on shared opportunity and mutual respect. We care for each other and create conditions where all people can flourish to their full potential.

A generous world is built on commonality *and* difference. We connect through the beliefs that unite us rather than focusing on what divides us. Together we honor the past, engage constructively in the present, and work toward an even better future. We celebrate our distinctions and consider our disagreements as potential fuel for mutual improvement.

Here's what generosity looks like when done wisely and well:

Giving changes
the world for the
better

Giving changes
society for the
better

Giving changes
the receiver for
the better

Giving changes
the giver for
the better

Transformational Generosity

The rest of this book is dedicated to exploring how to be generous and to understanding what generosity will produce in terms of blessings and benefits.

Section 1, Part 2

Why You Should Be Generous

LET'S START WITH "WHY?"

Simon Sinek delivered one of the most-watched TED Talks of all time in 2009.[3] He presented a basic but powerful idea: great results come from prioritizing *purpose*. The concept is expressed in a diagram he refers to as "The Golden Circle":[4]

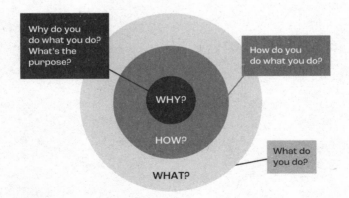

Why do you do what you do? What's the purpose?

How do you do what you do?

WHY?

HOW?

WHAT?

What do you do?

Start With Why: The "Golden Circle"

Idea Credit: Simon Sinek

Sinek's talk became a book (*Start with Why: How Great Leaders Inspire Everyone to Take Action*) and then a consulting practice focused on helping organizations answer the seemingly simple but often elusive question: "*Why* do we do what we do?" From there, it makes sense to consider, "*How* do we do what we do?" and then, "*What* do we do?"

As we consider WISEgenerosity, I suggest that asking the same questions in the same order—*Why? How? What?*—are important for us as well.

First, let's tackle the question of "Why?"

The "Why" of Generosity: To Find Fruitful Purpose

WHAT IS OUR PURPOSE IN LIFE? Much of philosophy boils down to four competing views: *Futility* (that is to say, no meaningful purpose), *Happiness*, *Enlightenment*, or *Fulfillment*:

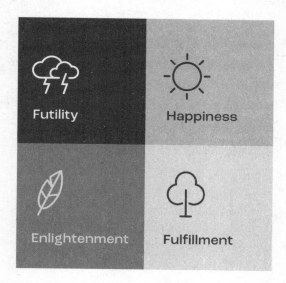

Four Potential Life Purposes

Futility does not relate well to giving. The other three perspectives all connect fundamentally with generosity, although each in different ways:

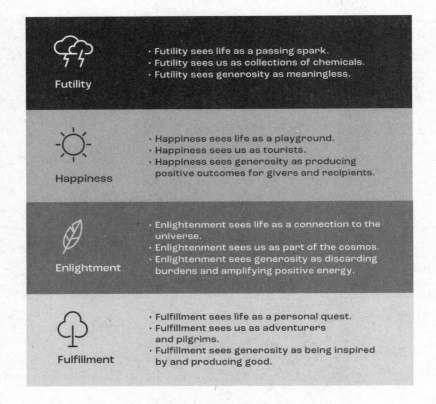

Futility	· Futility sees life as a passing spark. · Futility sees us as collections of chemicals. · Futility sees generosity as meaningless.
Happiness	· Happiness sees life as a playground. · Happiness sees us as tourists. · Happiness sees generosity as producing positive outcomes for givers and recipients.
Enlightment	· Enlightenment sees life as a connection to the universe. · Enlightenment sees us as part of the cosmos. · Enlightenment sees generosity as discarding burdens and amplifying positive energy.
Fulfillment	· Fulfillment sees life as a personal quest. · Fulfillment sees us as adventurers and pilgrims. · Fulfillment sees generosity as being inspired by and producing good.

Four Potential Life Purposes Expressed

Futility

Futility argues that the universe is an accidental combination of forces. This worldview is entirely materialistic and is based on the belief that what we observe is all that exists. There is no larger purpose or meaning to life.

Likewise, existence is pointless. Each of us is a randomly assembled collection of space dust, here today and gone tomorrow. Eventually, we all are "annihilated" and returned to the void from which we came.

Futility Progression

Nihil is Latin for "nothing," and the philosophy of futility is known as *nihilism*.[5] While I suspect few people fully believe this ultimately bleak view of life, the influence of nihilism is evident in our society and is hostile to a culture of caring, compassion, and giving.

From a nihilist's perspective, there is little or nothing we can or should do to promote or encourage generosity.

Happiness

Happiness also is grounded in the material world. While futility is inherently negative, happiness is inherently positive, and a person prioritizing happiness will aspire to make the best of what is around them.

Happiness is self-referential. Nonetheless, a life of thoughtful happiness recognizes others. Relationships are a critical component of life and a main driver of happiness.

Like many things in life, happiness tends to be sequential. We don't instantly go from "zero" to "happy." Happiness builds. With this in mind, here is a "Happiness Progression":

Happiness Progression

Pleasure is a common and, hopefully, everyday emotion. It comes and goes quickly: a smile from a loved one, a burst of laughter stemming from a good joke, the satisfaction of a tasty meal, and myriad other small delights are the building blocks of happiness.

Satisfaction comes from combining pleasure with purpose. Accomplishing a task or reaching a goal is meaningful, and rewarding work produces satisfaction.

Joy is the ultimate form of happiness, but it is rare and, when achieved, is hard to keep. It is the laser beam of multiple pleasures and satisfactions amplified together. We treasure each moment of joy we experience.

Giving is a ready route to happiness. This is the meaning behind the biblical adage: "It is better to give than to receive."[6] Our own happiness depends on those around us. Generosity enables us to lift up others and allows us to avoid the truth in the expression, "Misery loves company."[7]

Happiness is good to experience but can be fleeting. It is shallow and finite. It is also linear in nature in that is has a beginning and an end. There is an ancient fable in which a great ruler asked for a phrase that would be true at all times and in all circumstances. The wise reply was, "This too shall pass."[8] Everything in the material world will end. This truth comforts affliction but threatens satisfaction.

Adam Smith was a professor of moral philosophy in eighteenth-century Scotland. He wanted to understand why people behaved the way they did, and he wrote down his observations and reflections. Most famous for the book *Wealth of Nations*, Smith's first book of philosophy was the slimmer yet broader *Theory of Moral Sentiments*. In its very first line Smith says, "How selfish soever man may be supposed, there are evidently some principles in his nature, which interest him in the fortune of others, and render their happiness necessary to him, though he derives nothing from it, except the pleasure of seeing it."[9]

In other words, it makes us happy to see the people we care about happy. Economics has been called "the dismal science,"[10] but here the person considered its founder saw the connection between generosity and happiness.

Enlightenment

We can understand enlightenment from two perspectives: Western or Eastern. Western enlightenment relates to illumination. We seek light, not darkness, in life. Eastern enlightenment is about shedding unnecessary and unwanted possessions, behaviors, and attitudes in search of alignment with forces that exist inside of and beyond the self.

Western enlightenment emerged during the "Age of Reason," from the late 1600s to the early 1800s. Western philosophers and scientists like Voltaire, Locke, Kant, and Newton elevated logic and individualism. One of the era's lasting influences is the idea that history is positive and progressive. Generations build upon the knowledge and accomplishments of those who have come before them.

In personal life, Western enlightenment champions freedom. From the perspective of generosity, supporting others comes not from obligation or tradition but from recognizing in each other a shared humanity and a desire to improve the state of others alongside improving one's own condition. These concepts are ingrained in Western culture to this day.

Because Western enlightenment is so familiar to us, we're going to spend a little more time focusing on the less familiar Eastern perspective of *purpose.* Eastern enlightenment sees the universe as interconnected—both material and immaterial. There are things we can see and things we cannot see. Our individual lives are part of a larger whole. Perspective is situational and relative.

Buddha taught that a critical step in the path to enlightenment is giving.[11] Life should be cooperative and not antagonistic.

The Buddhist concept of *metta* recognizes that every living creature seeks to experience good and to avoid feeling bad.[12] In this understanding, people naturally want to produce positive outcomes for themselves and everything around them. *Metta* reflects an open heart seeking general goodwill and relates to the holistic concept of generosity that we are exploring.

There are many words for generosity in Buddhism. Two of them are *dana* and *caga.*[13] *Dana* can translate as "distribution of gifts." It is an action and relates to cause-and-effect expressed in the idea of "karma." In Western terms, a similar idea is that "we reap what we sow."[14]

Caga can translate as "a heart set toward giving." It is an expression of *metta*.[15] *Caga* describes the state of mind of the person who is doing the giving. Like our earlier reference to attitude and action being the basis of generosity, *caga* is an essential part of producing a positive impact for both the giver and the receiver.

The other positive purpose perspectives—happiness and fulfillment—understand individual life experience as linear. We pass through a series of stages, including childhood, youth, adulthood, and old age, as part of a singular existence. In contrast, enlightenment involves an ongoing cyclical process known as *samsara*:[16]

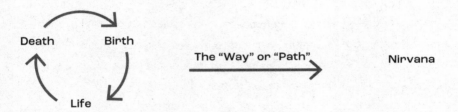

Eastern Enlightenment Progression

In samsara, birth leads to life leads to death leads to rebirth. There are levels to this cycle, and a disciple on "The Path" seeks to move higher and higher over many lifetimes.

In Buddhism, the ultimate goal of this spiritual climb is *nirvana*, when the basic cycle of self ends. Nirvana liberates the disciple from suffering and ends the cycle of rebirth. Giving away and unburdening are essential to the disciple's progress toward enlightenment.

Fulfillment

A purpose viewpoint toward fulfillment sees individuals as unique combinations of material and immaterial. It seeks positive engagement in both the physical world and the spiritual world. Fulfillment recognizes values and beliefs that supersede our individual selves.

The word *fulfillment* implies a final state, and fulfillment by nature is both orderly and progressive. It believes in cause-and-effect, the connection of the past to the present to the future, and the idea that there is another life after this one. Meanwhile, our individual time on earth is more of a journey than a destination. In the earlier diagrams, fulfillment is represented by a tree—a living, growing object with great substance and usefulness that grew from a tiny seed. This is a good analogy for WISEgenerosity.

The Fulfillment Progression

In fulfillment mode, generosity provides the means for our values to produce actions that, in turn, have the potential to create positive outcomes for ourselves and for other people. These actions can grow far beyond their small beginnings.

Fulfillment comes from orienting ourselves toward a purpose that is outside of ourselves; it also strongly opposes the futility perspective of life. In contrast to the happiness perspective, fulfillment does not always seek or produce self-oriented positive outcomes (although it can be the surest road to happiness in the right circumstances). Likewise, fulfillment does not pursue enlightenment by trying to shed the unwanted or the negative. Fulfillment can involve taking on burdens in pursuit of a higher goal or purpose.

The last point is an important one. This book is largely positive and shares many inspiring examples of generosity. At the same time, we know that life is not always sunshine and roses. In fact, one of the most powerful examples of fulfillment I've come across was inspired by profound suffering rather than by happiness.

Viktor Frankl was a successful Jewish physician in Vienna prior to World War II. He and his family were sent to concentration camps, where his parents, brother, and beloved first wife were exterminated by the Nazis. Dr. Frankl survived to write a truly remarkable book, *Man's Search for Meaning*.

Prior to the war, Dr. Frankl had been developing a new form of psychology that he came to call *logotherapy*. The approach took its name from the Greek word *logos*, defined as "meaning."[17]

Using his own story as an example, Dr. Frankl made the case in his book that "meaning" is an essential element of life. In the first half of *Man's Search for Meaning*, "Experiences in a Concentration Camp," Frankl described in awful detail what it was like in hell on earth. In the second half, he presented "Logotherapy in a Nutshell," explaining how being in the camps provided lessons that later enabled him to make positive use of what was otherwise overwhelmingly dark and terrible.

Dr. Frankl's life purpose in psychology was refined and amplified by his experiences as a survivor. In turn, his ideas and their impact were magnified many times over by the powerful and personal story he used to present them.

Dr. Frankl later added a postscript to the book called, "The Case for a Tragic Optimism." In it, he suggests that there is a "human capacity to creatively turn life's negative aspects into something positive or constructive. In other words, what matters is to make the best of any given situation."[18] I take this as another way of describing what it means to have an abundance mentality, even in the worst possible circumstances.

The ultimate message of *Man's Search for Meaning* is that humanity "always allows for: (1) turning suffering into a human achievement and accomplishment; (2) deriving from guilt the opportunity to change oneself for the better; and (3) deriving from life's transitoriness an incentive to take responsible action."[19] These all are measures of fulfillment.

Dr. Frankl looks at the half-empty glass and wants us to decide what else to put in it to benefit ourselves and those around us. The original book ends with a striking description of humanity at both its worst and its best: "Our generation is realistic, for we have come to know man as he really is. After all, man is that being who invented the gas chambers of Auschwitz; however, he is also that being who entered those gas chambers upright, with the Lord's Prayer or the *Shema Yisrael* on his lips."[20] He understood that the ability to make good even from evil is at the heart of generosity.

Dr. Frankl endured real-life nightmares almost beyond imagining, and I am amazed by the purpose he derived from those experiences. I see his determination to share his sufferings with the world and to find meaning in them as fundamentally generous.

Purposes Expressed

At this point, I'm sure that professional philosophers are shaking their heads at the audacity of an amateur "lover of wisdom" trying to distill the idea of *purpose* into four broad categories. So allow me to double down on my hubris by offering a different way of organizing the four presented purposes:

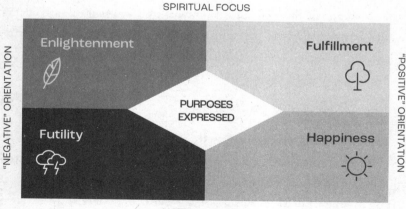

The Four Purposes Expressed

In this matrix, purpose aligns across two dimensions: spiritual versus material, and "positive" versus "negative." Using such a tool, we can place ourselves somewhere on this grid in terms of our own orientation.

The matrix suggests that futility and happiness are material in nature. Each focuses on the physical world and our own direct experience with it. Enlightenment and fulfillment are spiritual in nature. They each recognize forces at work beyond the physical world and seek to engage meaningfully with them.

Meanwhile, futility and enlightenment are "negative" in orientation. The word *negative* is not ideal, because it gives connotations of something subpar or unwelcome. That's not what I mean by negativity, particularly in regard to enlightenment. Instead, I think of enlightenment as about shedding unwanted or unneeded burdens and becoming lighter—less heavy or weighed down—in the process.

Fulfillment, on the other hand, is "positive" in that it is willing to take on burdens for the sake of a larger calling. Likewise, the word *positive* doesn't necessarily mean that fulfillment is "better"; rather, it suggests the idea of stepping toward difficulties rather than away from them—adding elements to our lives rather than subtracting them. Meanwhile, seeking happiness clearly is a more positive approach than futility to living in the material world.

As you can tell, these are ideas I continue to wrestle with. I imagine that you do likewise, and I welcome your thoughts and feedback. In the meantime, perhaps the professional philosophers do have job security after all.

Further Reflections on Purpose

If happiness is the mayfly of purpose—here one minute and gone the next—fulfillment is the elephant—weighty and lasting. Meanwhile, Eastern enlightenment is more botanical—organic and growing and interconnected. Futility, in contrast to the other views, is the cancer of purpose. If invited in, it eats away at everything else.

My own perspective on purpose, as it relates to generosity and to life overall, tends toward seeking fulfillment. Much of modern American life relates to the "pursuit of happiness," so here I offer a few thoughts about happiness versus fulfillment, in particular.

Fulfillment is produced by accumulated effort and experience. Unlike happiness, it is not purely circumstantial. As Dr. Frankl demonstrated, fulfillment and meaning are closely connected. Fulfillment can exist in good times and bad, in joy and in suffering. In this, it is more fully connected to life with its inevitable ups and downs.

The pursuit of happiness may include fulfillment, or it may not. The pursuit of fulfillment might result in happiness, or it might not. The best moments of our lives involve a combination of happiness and fulfillment. Moreover, joy (the highest expression of happiness) is produced only when meaning and circumstances align. Thus, we are most likely to experience joy in the course of pursuing fulfillment than we are in any other realm of purpose.

There is an essential tension at work here. In terms of daily living, we might choose to focus either on happiness or fulfillment. If we seek happiness, however, we are unlikely to find and retain it in isolation. Pursuit of our own agenda separated from others is self-defeating.

Why is it self-defeating? Life is not lived in isolation. We are "relational" creatures. There is a reason why solitary confinement is considered a higher level of punishment than being deprived of freedom on its own.

How do we pursue our own happiness while being surrounded by other people who are all doing the same thing? In any positive relationship, we care about more than just our own needs and goals. We recognize that our own happiness is tied to the other person's. In order for relationships to thrive, there must be giving involved. In order for there to be optimal giving, there must be an interest in mutual fulfillment. Our purpose must include not only our own agenda but the agendas of others as well.

A Powerful Example of Fulfilled Giving

Reflecting on these ideas made me think of "The Gift of the Magi," fiction by American writer O. Henry.[21] If you are not familiar with the short story, it is powerfully bittersweet. Two poor newlyweds live together in a small apartment. It is Christmas. Seeking perfect gifts for each other, each spouse gives up something central to their own identity for the sake of the other. The young wife cuts off her beautiful hair and sells it to buy a platinum chain for her husband's prized pocket watch, while the young husband sells his watch to give his wife a set of expensive and elaborate combs for her hair. Even though the resulting presents no longer have any practical use, the demonstrations of unselfish generosity reinforce the couple's love for each other. The author ends the story as follows:

> And here I have lamely related to you the uneventful chronicle of two foolish children in a flat who most unwisely sacrificed for each other the greatest treasures of their house. But in a last word to the wise of these days let it be said that of all who give gifts these two were the wisest... They are the magi.[22]

Rather than being an example of futility, as a nihilist would have anticipated, the couple ends up happy in their relationship because of their sacrifices.

Consider this story from the standpoint of W.I.S.E. giving. The resource each partner used was *Well-grounded*—valuable and readily accessible. The choice of each present was *Inspired*—selected sacrificially to benefit the other person.

What about *Satisfying* and *Effective*? A cynic would argue that the result was neither. Such a negative perspective does not account for the definition of generosity, however. The attitude of each giver was pure, and the actions of each giver were noble. O. Henry viewed the exchange as a beautiful success because it furthered the couple's loving relationship in ways well beyond any material benefit.

Along these same lines, it seems to me that the pursuit of fulfillment in generosity can lead to happiness. I see no evidence to the contrary—that the pursuit of happiness outside of generosity leads to fulfillment. In fact, it strikes me clearly that a life lived selfishly and divorced from fulfillment undermines the pursuit of happiness as well.

Final Thoughts on Purpose

Both fulfillment and happiness are common objectives in American life, but they are not always aligned. The good news is that generosity can connect happiness and fulfillment through the relationships that are central to our lives. Making those connections is the focus of the later section on the "How" of generosity.

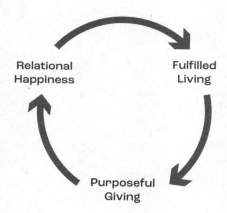

The Virtuous Cycle of Giving

Living in pursuit of fulfillment involves giving that is connected to purpose. That purpose can be internally generated or, more commonly, tied to an outside force like social justice or religious experience. Our purpose, in turn, can lead to happiness as we support the needs of other people in our lives and reinforce our own fulfillment in the process.

As noted in the introduction to this book, my initial reason for beginning this project was to find purpose and meaning. Understanding generosity to be at the center of my own experience has indeed produced more fulfillment and more happiness in my life. It also has led to enlightenment, as a clearer focus about priorities and pursuits has emerged in my spiritual walk, my personal life with family and friends, and in my professional and community service work. It has become easier for me to identify what is important and what is not, and to make both everyday and life-changing decisions using the tools and perspectives that follow. My sincere hope is that WISEgenerosity provides similar direction and support for you.

Considering purpose and meaning is weighty, and I hope that these thoughts and ideas resonate with you as well. As we move on from the philosophical to the practical aspects of giving, we will explore concepts that can help us to live generously.

CHAPTER 3

---→

The "Why" of Generosity: Abundance, Meaning, and Impact

FINDING A FRUITFUL PURPOSE is not the only reason we should pursue a life of generosity. There are several other "why" factors that move WISEgenerosity from merely a philosophical concept to an actual way to live our lives. Three of these practical *whys* are:

- Abundant Living
- Adding Inward Meaning
- Building Outward Impact

Let's consider these ideas as we strive to better understand what "generosity in action" means.

Abundant Living

The original working title of this book was *The Abundance Imperative*. The tension between abundance and scarcity struck me then—and still does now—as central to understanding generosity.

A central choice we make in life is how we decide to view ourselves in relation to everything around us. Do we seek to serve or to be served? Are we comfortable with what we have or are we always seeking more? Such questions are at the heart of our attitude and our actions.

If we are lifted up by abundance, we always will have enough, no matter how little we own. If we are weighed down by scarcity, we will never have enough, no matter how much we own. Our alignment with abundance or scarcity affects the way we live and determines our ability and willingness to give.

An abundance mentality embraces positive change. It focuses on making the most of what is available. It is humble and considerate. Abundance offers an open hand extended from an open heart.

In contrast, a scarcity mentality is wary and skeptical. It focuses on taking advantage of what is available. It is dismissive and self-absorbed. Scarcity holds a closed fist that protects a closed heart.

Abundance is not connected to material wealth. In fact, there can be an inverse relationship between having possessions and living abundantly. The endless striving of materialism is a primary driver for a scarcity mindset.

If we are wealthy, abundance encourages benevolence. If we are poor, abundance promotes sharing. On the other hand, if we are wealthy, scarcity prompts hoarding. If we are poor, scarcity tempts stealing.

"Life gives to the giver and takes from the taker" is an ancient proverb.[23] Jesus similarly taught: "Give, and you will receive. Your gift will return to you in full—pressed down, shaken together to make room for more, running over, and poured into your lap. The amount you give will determine the amount you get back."[24]

Other spiritual traditions hold that giving taps into a rich vein of abundance flowing through the universe. Kindness multiplies itself with benefits for giver and receiver alike.

Abundance leads to a virtuous cycle of generosity, strong relationships, and fulfillment.

Scarcity leads to anxiety, alienation, and emptiness.

Living abundantly involves recognizing the reality of good or bad circumstances, but also seeking to harness whatever resources are available—time, talent, treasure, social connections, emotional engagement, relational opportunities—in service to positive engagement. An abundance mindset seeks to overcome difficulties and to take advantage of opportunities. Likewise,

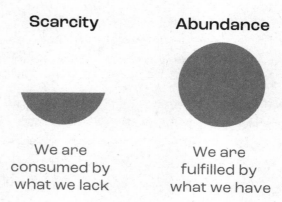

Scarcity	Abundance
We are consumed by what we lack	We are fulfilled by what we have

Scarcity Mindset vs. Abundance Mindset

WISEgenerosity seeks to build on the potential of any situation and make it better.

Adding Inward Meaning

At first, it may not seem obvious why giving is beneficial to the giver. After all, parting with things of value can be costly—literally and figuratively.

"The Gift of the Magi" story we just considered suggests that giving is a paradox, "a seemingly absurd or contradictory statement or proposition which when investigated may prove to be well-founded or true."[25] What in material terms seemed to be a pair of costly mistakes for a poor young couple ended up being a blessing for them instead.

How can this be true? How can giving away add to our lives rather than subtract from them? As it happens, there is a lot of research to support the truth that giving is good for us.

Along these lines, academics Christian Smith and Hilary Davidson of the University of Notre Dame wrote a book called *The Paradox of Generosity: Giving We Receive, Grasping We Lose*, which contains detailed research on this topic. Their work argues strongly that generosity is essential to a meaningful and effective life, and it's worth reflecting on their message for a moment.

The introduction to *The Paradox of Generosity* makes the following points (with my notes in brackets):

[**Generosity is good for us.**]

- "First, the more generous Americans are, the more happiness, health, and purpose in life they enjoy. This association between generous practices and personal well-being is strong and highly consistent across a variety of types of generous practices and measures of well-being."

[**Generosity makes us better people.**]

- "Second, we have excellent reason to believe that generous practices actually create enhanced personal well-being. The association between generosity and well-being is not accidental, spurious, or simply an artifact of reverse causal influence. Certain well-known, explicable causal mechanisms explain to us the specific ways that generous practices shape positive well-being outcomes."

[**Evidence of generosity's benefits are all around us.**]

- "Third, the way Americans talk about generosity [by applauding and valuing it] confirms and illustrates the first two points. The paradox of generosity is evident in the lives of Americans."

[**Generosity is not as fully adopted as it could be or should be.**]

- "Fourth, despite all of this, it turns out that many Americans fail to live generous lives. A lot of Americans are indeed very generous—but even more are not. And so the latter are deprived, by their lack of generosity, of the greater well-being that generous practices would likely afford them."

[**Generosity is an answer to age-old questions about living a meaningful and effective life.**]

- "Finally...many wise writers, philosophers, religious teachers, sages, and mystics have been teaching us about the paradox of generosity for thousands of years. What today's empirical social-science research tells us only confirms what we might have known all along, had we trusted the traditional teachers."[26]

In summary, the white coats (scientists) and the white robes (sages) agree—generosity is essential to a life well-lived.

WISEgenerosity Example: What We Do with What Happens to Us

Paraphrasing British author and futurist Aldous Huxley, experience isn't what happens to us; it's what we *do* with what happens to us.[27]

In the same vein, a critic of generosity might say it is easy to give from a place of abundance. It is much harder to give abundantly from a position of difficulty or distress. As evidence of the inward benefits that come from living out the positive paradox of generosity, I offer the story of Ross Mason.

Ross is a true Renaissance man. He received his bachelor's degree in industrial and systems engineering from Georgia Tech and his MBA from the Wharton School at Penn. He studied literature and history at Oxford University and Russian at Middlebury College.

Ross started and sold a healthcare technology company in San Francisco. He created a real estate investment and development company in Moscow. He worked in private banking for a Wall Street investment firm.

Volunteering at an AIDS hospital in Zambia made Ross passionate about healthcare. He has since led numerous public and private efforts to deliver quality healthcare to people who need it most. In 2004, he created HINRI (High Impact Network of Responsible Innovators),[28] which is "a venture philanthropy that focuses on solving today's most difficult healthcare challenges."[29]

Prior to 2007, Ross was a top-level amateur athlete. He competed in triathlons and was a shipwreck-, cave-, and ice-diver, a surfer, a rock climber, and a NASCAR-certified driver.

The "prior to 2007" is significant. Ross was on a routine bike ride that summer when a bee flew into his helmet. While trying to get it out, his elbow hit the handlebars and sent him careening down a hill and into a tree. His neck was broken in the accident, paralyzing him from the collarbone down. Ross's response to such a life-changing situation? "I've grown up in one of the richest societies on earth with a tremendous amount of opportunities. What in the world do I have to complain about?"[30]

Ross is realistic about his situation but, more importantly, his attitude and actions demonstrate abundance—and a positive and forward-looking outlook on life. Interviewed by his hometown newspaper about a charity event he hosted for others experiencing similar challenges he said, "I think there is a sense of freedom and control loss that people with paralysis experience, a sense of independence that kind of goes away. They realize life won't be the same, but we want them to feel encouraged rather than discouraged. We want them to come out, have a great time, and see the impact that they can have on others."[31]

It is hard to imagine someone more dedicated to having an impact on others than Ross. In fact, he is legendarily generous. Ross and I both live in Atlanta, but we had not crossed paths until 2015. I was introduced to him by someone who lived across the country in California. This individual told me if I was writing a book on generosity, I needed to talk to Ross Mason. He was right.[32]

Living the Generosity Paradox: Inverted Cause and Effect

I first met Ross in his Atlanta home one afternoon. The place was a whirlwind of activity. Adults and kids ran in and out of the house. There were too many people there to meet them all—the house seemed to be the hub of the whole neighborhood. A variety of conversations were happening throughout the rooms, as people discussed personal and community activities, both large and small. Ross rolled back and forth in his wheelchair, popping in on different groups and managing to chat with everyone, like the choreographer of an elaborate dance. The atmosphere was purposeful, lively, and fun.

Sitting together at the table in a front room while people swirled around us, Ross and I had one of the most far-reaching conversations I've ever enjoyed. We covered faith, philosophy, charity, and philanthropy. I took nine pages of notes.

Ross shared his vision for the way in which he wanted his different efforts to unify around a common theme of empowerment. He told me he appreciates that his personal story amplifies his ability to be a messenger for good, and he takes full advantage of those opportunities. I left energized and grateful for his intelligence, wisdom, energy, and commitment to others.

Ross also confirmed something that this project has helped me to realize. The foundation for a generosity mentality is an inversion of the normal cause-and-effect in life. We seek blessings and good fortune, but we tend to misunderstand the means by which these positive aspects of life are produced.

A scarcity mentality believes that contentment, gratitude, and giving are reactive. When we *have*, then we can *give*. This accounts for one of the major barriers to generosity. It is self-fulfilling that if we feel like we don't have enough, then we won't share with others. Scarcity becomes a negatively constraining force across every dimension of life.

In contrast, an abundance mentality believes that we should be kind, charitable, and philanthropic no matter what. We don't give because we are blessed; we are blessed because we give.

Along the same lines, psychologists confirm that gratitude has amazing powers.[33] Ross expresses thanks for what he has rather than lamenting what he does not have. We may imagine that good things happening to us produce happiness that leads to gratitude, when in fact, more often, the reverse is true. Gratitude leads to happiness, which leads to good things happening.

I asked Ross what most bothers him in life. He answered passionately: "People who don't or can't realize their potential."[34] Then he went on to explain how his greatest joy comes from enabling others to thrive. I can imagine a million self-directed things Ross could have said. Yet instead of focusing inward on any of his own challenges, he chooses to look relentlessly outward in service—something we'll discuss in more detail shortly. Without a doubt, Ross is one of the most powerfully connective and amplifying forces for good I ever have met.

Living abundantly is the basis for substantial and sustained generosity. Ross Mason is proof of this proposition and a wonderful example of

WISEgenerosity. Moving past what others would have viewed as a catastrophic situation, he leads a happy and fulfilled life. He takes full advantage of his prodigious talents and capabilities. He refuses to give his limitations power over his expectations and activities. He embodies living with meaning and purpose, and he inspires me to want to do the same.

Building Outward Impact

Lynne Twist, an accomplished international aid worker and nonprofit fundraiser, published a thoughtful book in 2003 called *The Soul of Money*. She set up a contrast between the soul, where "generosity is natural,"[35] and the domain of money, where we "race to 'get what is ours.'"[36]

One of Twist's chapter titles is a clever play on words: "What You Appreciate Appreciates."[37] In finance, *appreciation* means growth. An appreciating asset gets larger—potentially much larger as compounding takes hold. *Appreciation* also can refer to things that we admire, value, and celebrate.

The chapter ends with a lesson from Buddha, who taught that each of our lives and the world as a whole are like a garden. In the garden are seeds of compassion, forgiveness, love, commitment, courage, and "all the qualities that affirm and inspire us."[38] Referring back to the prior pages, these are abundant outcomes. Also in the garden are seeds of hatred, prejudice, vengeance, violence, and "all other destructive ways of being."[39] These are scarcity outcomes.

Twist explains this well in her book:

> Our attention is like water and sunshine, and the seeds we cultivate will grow and fill our garden. If we choose to invest . . . in the seeds of scarcity—acquisition, accumulation, greed, and all that springs from those seeds—then scarcity is what will fill the space of our life and the world. If we tend the seeds of sufficiency with our attention and use our money like water to nourish them with soulful purpose, then we will enjoy that bountiful harvest.[40]

These metaphors help to express the reality that giving is not just good for us but good for those around us, even under extreme conditions, as in the following example.

WISEgenerosity Case Study: Turning Tragedy into Redemption

Rais Bhuiyan's story started as a classic immigrant's tale.[41] He had been successful in his home country of Bangladesh, graduating from a prestigious military school and training to become a fighter pilot. He had a different vision for his life, however, and the call of opportunity pushed him to leave his family and then fiancée to move to America in 1999.

Rais started out in New York, then moved to Dallas, where the cost of living was lower. He wanted to take computer classes, find his dream job in technology, and save money toward buying a house for himself and his intended wife. Making many sacrifices along the way to pursue his goals, he worked at a gas station convenience store to supplement his strained income.

Covering for a coworker, Rais was behind the counter on September 21, 2001, ten days after the tragic events of 9/11. There, he was shot in the face at point-blank range by a troubled and violent assailant who imagined himself an "Arab Slayer" who was taking revenge on Muslims.[42] Rais was fortunate in one respect—he survived. The shooter, Mark Stroman, killed the two other men he shot—one a few days before and one a few days after wounding Rais. The last murder was recorded on a security camera, and Stroman was arrested and eventually sentenced to die for his crime.

Rais's world was shattered. He lost his right eye and endured surgery after surgery to repair damage from the thirty-eight shotgun pellets embedded in his head. His father had a stroke when he heard the news of his son's injuries. His wife-to-be broke off their relationship. Rais couldn't work and had to rely on others for shelter and support while his medical bills piled up. He was afraid and lonely, and it would have been entirely understandable for him to withdraw forever into disappointment, bitterness, and anger.

But Rais persisted. After years of struggle and recovery, he found the IT job for which he'd originally come to America. A devout Muslim, he worked hard and saved enough money to take his mother on a *Hajj*, a pilgrimage to the holy city of Mecca, in November 2009. They stayed there for a month.

During the prayers and rituals said and performed on their pilgrimage, Rais "felt his heart soften; he felt the pouring forth of something warm, something invigorating. He felt something leaving his body. He felt forgiveness. What had been pure fear, pent up for years, was now compassion. He didn't hate Mark Stroman. He pitied him. Thinking of this man sitting in a prison cell, counting down the days he has left on this planet, [Rais] wondered if he could help him in some way."[43]

Describing this spiritual journey, Rais later said, "In my faith, in Islam, it says that saving a life is like saving…mankind."[44] So motivated, he dedicated himself to saving Mark Stroman.

It was a powerful story that got a lot of attention. Stroman awaited lethal injection in the summer of 2011. During the weeks beforehand, Rais and a team of attorneys tried to stay the execution in order to give the two men the chance to meet in person, as stipulated in a Texas law providing such an opportunity for crime victims. Rais further hoped that their reconciliation would prompt the authorities to set aside the death penalty for Stroman.

Media outlets in the US and abroad told the story of how the assailed had forgiven the assailant and now was trying to save his life. That the former was a clean-cut Muslim immigrant and the latter was a professed white supremacist covered in hateful tattoos added to the drama.

Stroman found out about Rais's efforts in prison, and they had a strong impact on him. In early letters from jail, Stroman was not at all remorseful. He described his actions as "not a crime of hate but…an act of retribution and recompense." He imagined himself to be the "first American to retaliate and take a stand" in response to the terrorist attacks.[45]

Touched by Rais's efforts on his behalf, Stroman wrote to him with a far different attitude in 2011:

Dear Rais. My death is slotted in Huntsville July 20th...and that means I need to get some things straight with the world.... With many emotions flowing like clouds in the sky ... it's better late than never. So let's go. I was completely and utterly wrong and I hope you can forgive me.[46]

Ultimately, the campaign to prolong Stroman's life was unsuccessful. On the day he was executed, Stroman put Rais on a list of people with whom he wanted to speak in his last hours. Rais told the story of their brief phone call:

As soon as he came on the phone, I said, "Mark, you should know that I never hated you. I forgave you." And he said, "Rais, I love you bro." The same person, 10 years back, his heart was filled with hate and ignorance. But when he came to know me, he saw me as a human being. He was able to tell me that he loved me, and he called me "brother."[47]

Today, Rais is an executive for a global technology company. He also founded a nonprofit organization called World Without Hate, which has the goal of "educating people about the transformational power of mercy and forgiveness based on the hope that we can build a better world."[48] In living out his organization's mission, Rais offers a remarkable and powerful example of generosity.

The Normative Impact of Generosity

Rais's story further suggests what I will call the "normative impact of generosity." *Normative* is a term from social science meaning, to establish or derive a behavioral standard. It is a fancy way of saying that people tend to adapt based on what they observe and experience from others. Positivity breeds positive behavior. Negativity breeds negative behavior.

The surest path to good relationships is to think the best of other people. Behaving generously toward others has two positive effects: We ourselves behave better when we think well of others. In turn, treating other people posi-tively steers them toward behaving better.

Rais's story offers an extreme model of this phenomenon. His generosity changed the trajectory of his own life from victimization to empowerment. In turn, he offered an extraordinary example for others about how to treat those who harm us.

In one jailhouse correspondence, Stroman said about Rais: "His deep Islamic Beliefs Have [given] him strength to Forgive the Unforgiveable...that is truly Inspiring to me, and should be an Example for us all."[49] Stroman's last words were: "I am at total peace. God bless America. God bless everyone."[50]

This story ultimately is about redemption. Of course, tragedy does not *always* produce redemption. Nonetheless, if there is any hope for good arising from evil, it is through generosity of the kind demonstrated in this story.

Likewise, we all have an opportunity to bend the arc of the lives around us for the better when we choose to treat others with kindness and generosity. In Rais's words, "All the good things I was taught inspired me—go and do the right thing."[51] In attitude and action, Rais Bhuiyan is amazingly generous.

Section 1, Part 3

How Generosity Works: Expressions and Examples

This book aims to enhance our understanding of generosity in order to show that giving is a uniquely constructive force in every aspect of life.

Here are three essential points about generosity:

- Generosity is *comprehensive*.
  Generosity can and should apply across the entirety of our lives.
- Generosity is *universal*.
  Giving is not just the province of the wealthy, gifted, or secure. Generosity is essential to a life well-lived and is necessary for everyone, since we all are both givers and receivers at different times.

- Generosity *takes effort.*

  While essential, generosity is not *natural.* The rewards may be great for all involved, but generosity doesn't happen on its own. It is deliberate behavior.

CHAPTER 4

Three Expressions of Generosity: Kindness, Charity, and Philanthropy

GENEROSITY IS GIVING. We share things of value with other people. These things can be money, time, skills, connections, emotions, and relationships.

There are three primary means of expressing generosity:
- Kindness
- Charity
- Philanthropy

In this chapter, we will expand our definition of generosity and learn more about the application of these vital behaviors.

Most people would say that kindness relates to small good deeds, charity reflects help given to needy strangers, and philanthropy involves efforts toward broad social improvement. These statements all are true, but the common understandings are too narrow.

Kindness is not just temporary and superficial; it's a powerful force for building sustainable and positive relationships and social engagement. Charity can go beyond a fleeting act and instead be a determined and ongoing process that improves the lives of people in need. Philanthropy is not just the province of the rich, the powerful, or the professional, but rather, it can be for any of us willing to take a thoughtful approach to aligning ourselves with forces that will produce positive changes in our society.

Kindness

Kindness is the most common form of generosity. You can see kindness happening everywhere, although it may not always be appreciated as much as it should be. Acts of kindness are ways of expressing appreciation and affection for, or connection with, another person.

Sharing expressions of love and gifts with loved ones for special occasions is kindness. Reaching out to help friends in need with an errand or making time for conversation when they are feeling down is kindness. Most generosity expressed to people we know is kindness.

Kindness also extends to people we don't know or don't know well. These are smaller generous gestures that happen when someone recognizes a situational need and provides support. Opening the door for a person carrying a cumbersome package, letting another car in front of you in traffic, and flashing a smile at a stranger with whom you make eye contact are acts of kindness.

Charity

Charity works to alleviate pain, suffering, and disadvantage. It is individually focused and most often relates to people we don't know. It focuses directly on a particular person or need. Donating money to an organization that helps the poor or needy is charitable. Volunteering time to mentor at a local after-school program is charitable. Advocating for local conservation efforts is charitable.

Charity can also be the act of giving major gifts to people we know. If you pay college tuition for the child of a neighbor or a relative who has fallen on hard times, that would go beyond the bounds of kindness and into the realm of charity.

Kindness and charity both are *people-focused*. Whether they are given person-to-person or through an intermediary like a charitable organization, the goal is to improve someone else's quality of life in the here and now.

Philanthropy

In contrast, philanthropy is *cause-* or *problem-focused*. Philanthropy applies tools and resources to address broader social issues. It is institutional and involves giving to improve a situation that affects multiple people.

Kindness	Charity	Philanthropy
Gifts to people we know.	Gifts to people we don't know.	Gifts for causes.
Small efforts for people we don't know.	Significant efforts for people we do know.	Efforts to problem-solve.

Expressing Generosity: Kindness, Charity, and Philanthropy

Attraction Toward Generosity

Kindness attracts *People Helpers*, those who are attentive to others and want to be connected directly to their giving.

Charity attracts *Neighbor Savers*, those who are concerned about improving lives, being engaged with others in need, etc.

Philanthropy attracts *Problem Solvers*, those who are more focused on big-picture needs and strategy.

All of these expressions of generosity are important. Which is most appealing and relevant to you? In considering that question, let's take a look at the potential advantages and disadvantages of each:

Kindness
- Potential Advantages
  - ▸ Simple and accessible to all

- ▸ Immediate gratification that can transform into lasting relational benefits
- • Potential Disadvantages
  - ▸ Can be superficial
  - ▸ Limited impact and duration if not thoughtful and repeated

Charity
- • Potential Advantages
  - ▸ Addresses immediate needs
  - ▸ Potential direct satisfaction and personal engagement
- • Potential Disadvantages
  - ▸ Inefficient—giving tends to be to one person or group at a time
  - ▸ Inadequate to "solve" the entire scope of whatever root problems are involved

Philanthropy
- • Potential Advantages
  - ▸ Coordinated efforts and economies of scale
  - ▸ Can "teach people to fish" rather than "give them a fish"
- • Potential Disadvantages
  - ▸ Disconnected from emotion and empathy; can be impersonal and bureaucratic
  - ▸ Much more difficult to fix a systemic issue than to improve a specific one

The Primacy of Kindness

If only one aspect of this book resonates with you, I hope that it is the amazing power of kindness. Much of what we will explore in the coming pages comes back to this simple but powerful virtue. Along the same lines, I believe the vast majority of contentment and goodwill we experience in life comes from kindness. Providing and accepting comfort and support, giving and receiving presents large and small, and enjoying the many ways in which we engage positively with one another are central aspects of a life well-lived.

Jewish teaching includes the concept of *hesed* or "loving-kindness" as a fundamental principle: "This is the generic term for a whole variety of actions including hospitality, visiting the sick, dowering a bride, providing interest-free loans, redeeming captives, burying the dead, and comforting mourners."[52]

The Babylonian Talmud is a central text of Jewish law dating back to around the year 500.[53] It observes:

> Our Rabbis taught, in three respects *g'milut hasadim* (acts of kindness) are superior to *tz'dakah* (charity): *Tz'dakah* can only be done with one's money, but *g'milut hasadim* can be done with one's person and one's money. *Tz'dakah* can be given only to the poor, while *g'milut hasadim* can be done both for the rich and the poor. *Tz'dakah* can be given to the living only, while *g'milut hasadim* can be done both to the living and to the dead.[54] [BT *Sukkah* 49b]

More recently, social researcher, author, and speaker Shaunti Feldhahn published a book in 2016 called *The Kindness Challenge*. Feldhahn, who has spent years researching what makes us grounded and successful, wrote:

> I've seen what makes us miserable and what lights us up, and as you might guess, it makes a big difference when our needs are being met and when others know how to avoid hurting us. It makes a big difference when we experience fulfillment at work, and love and appreciation at home.
>
> But above all that is one greater factor: *whether we thrive depends far more on how we choose to treat others than on how we ourselves are treated* [italics in original]. In fact, when handled well, that one factor often leads to those other things that light us up. When handled poorly, it often leads to misery.

The path to our happy place starts with one choice: whether or not to be kind. Especially when we really don't want to be.[55]

This insight is central to generosity and reinforces that kindness is a "superpower."[56] It is behavior we control that works for good in nearly every circumstance. We will revisit Feldhahn's work when exploring relationships later in this section. Meanwhile, we can conclude that kindness is beneficial and important.

Charity vs. Philanthropy

Let's spend a further moment on charity vs. philanthropy. We each may not be as charitable or philanthropic as we could or should be. Moreover, we might not be sure which approach—charity or philanthropy—better suits us. Yet if uncertainty is a barrier to heightened generosity, we should try to eliminate it.

The words *charity* and *philanthropy* sometimes are used interchangeably. I suggest, however, that they are distinct.[57] Differences emerge upon consideration. Charity is more about caring; philanthropy is more about curing. Charity may be more heart-driven; philanthropy may be more head-driven.

One other difference comes in terms of impact. Philanthropists may argue that problem-solving is superior, since it reduces the need for future charity. That certainly can be true. On the other hand, the larger the problem, the more difficult it is to solve and the more likely that an intended solution will not work as planned. Charity may be small-scale, but you usually can tell right away if it is effective. For example, providing a single meal to a hungry family feeds them for that night, giving them an immediate benefit. A full philanthropic plan to address the hunger crisis in the community, on the other hand, could make a bigger impact and help more people long-term, but it won't deliver any results immediately—if it delivers them at all.

My observation is that philanthropy has become much more celebrated in our world than simple acts of charity. While charity is much more common, its small personal scale means that it receives little widespread attention except in extreme cases. That is fine, of course—most people aren't generous because they are seeking recognition but because they genuinely want to help others.

Even so, I worry that the mechanics of philanthropy have redefined what we as a society consider to be generous. If I am not financially capable of giving millions, or even thousands, I may feel that my contributions aren't worthy or even necessary. I'm left thinking, *What kind of difference can I really make?* This can lead to an unintended crowding-out effect.

Philanthropy also seems neat and well-organized. Solving big problems is the realm of charts and statistics. There is a related movement in the nonprofit sector to quantify and assess everything in the name of evaluating "impact." As a result, civic projects that defy neat categorization become harder to fund than ones with specific goals.

In contrast, charity is messy but essential. The Judeo-Christian value system that has driven most generosity in Western history addresses charity far more than philanthropy. This moral message pushes its followers to engage directly with people in need, person-to-person, as much as they can.

I confess that I am playing devil's advocate here to a degree. Most would agree that charity and philanthropy both are important. To be truthful, I am more philanthropically minded myself. I tend to engage in big picture questions and strategic considerations rather than being down in the trenches of small-scale charity work.

Still, if there is a pendulum in terms of attention and resources in our society, I think it may have swung too far in the direction of philanthropy. Given that there is no shortage of immediate needs in our world, it may be time to balance things out and once again elevate the importance of simple acts of charity.

With these thoughts in mind, I suggest that you consider for yourself which strain of significant generosity—charity or philanthropy—is most appealing to you. Both are needed, and most people naturally will gravitate toward one or the other. Some of us want to serve on committees and make plans and evaluate budgets. Others want to play songs for shut-ins or coach sports teams or spend time with homeless children. Whatever seems most interesting and compelling to you, start doing it and be generous!

● ● ●

Generosity is universal. Each and every person in the world has the ability to be kind and charitable. Expressions of kindness or charity will differ based on individual circumstances, but helping people is an opportunity available to all of us every day.

At the same time, most of us also have some capacity to be philanthropic. There are large-scale problems we can help solve by applying our time, talent, or treasure in some way. The imperative for each of us is to act—to find out what generous acts of service we can do and then to do them.

CHAPTER 5

Generosity: Generous Attitudes + Generous Actions

AS NOTED AT THE OUTSET of this book, generosity requires considerate attitude + caring action. What are the elements of each that help produce the conditions needed for WISEgenerosity?

To have a *considerate attitude*, it helps to be positive toward others, to react generously to others, and to live hopefully in the present.

As far as *caring actions*, we benefit from aligning attitude and effort, focusing on generous inputs and outputs, and considering proximities, perspectives, and priorities.

In turn, these approaches help us in seeking service: applying our attitude and actions purposefully and productively for our own benefit and for the benefit of those around us.

GENEROUS ATTITUDES

Generous Attitude Part 1: Be Positive Toward Others

Kim Bearden is one of the most infectiously generous people I've ever met. Her positive energy and dedication are changing the lives of thousands of children and those around them while inspiring a movement in American education.

We'll explore the "exponential" impact of giving in chapter 25, but Kim's story provides a preview for now.

Kim's memoir, *Crash Course: The Life Lessons My Students Taught Me,* could be a textbook on generosity.[58] At every opportunity, she lifts up others, gives other people credit, and reveals the personal setbacks and challenges she's had that make her story so inspiring.

Kim is the cofounder, executive director, and language arts teacher at Ron Clark Academy (RCA) in Atlanta.[59] (The fact that Kim helped start and has dedicated her life to a school named after her work partner is itself a testament to her generosity.) Kim and Ron met in 2000 when Disney honored both of them as national Teachers of the Year. Ron had a vision for a new kind of school, and the two of them dreamed and labored to make their dream a reality. A gleaming RCA opened on the site of a formerly decrepit industrial facility in September 2007.

RCA is a unique institution. It educates middle school students from fourth through eighth grades. In addition, it is designed as a model for other educators.

Kim, Ron, and their colleagues apply highly engaged and child-focused methods to teaching students who largely come from trying environments. Adding to the unique aspects of the school, RCA deliberately places pupils with a full range of abilities, from gifted to challenged, in the same classroom. Each class has thirty students, similar to a typical public school. Overcoming individual and collective difficulties, the children thrive.

The school invites thousands of educators from across the country to visit each year in order to learn how they can replicate RCA's success in their own communities. I visited RCA in both the spring and the fall of 2014. While I was there, Kim demonstrated to me how a positive attitude is an essential quality of generosity.

The first thing you feel when arriving at the Ron Clark Academy is an amazingly positive energy. When I walked into the school for my initial visit, a group of students was waiting in the lobby for an activity to begin. Without prompting, they leapt up *en masse* and rushed over to greet me. I was surprised and delighted by this warm welcome.

Surrounded by the students, I shook hands with child after child as they introduced themselves by name and looked me squarely in the eye with beaming smiles. I felt like a hero returning home, even in a place I'd never been before. I also was amazed by the spontaneity of the greeting. Visitors are routine at RCA, and I was not an expected or special guest to them. Nonetheless, they set a tone with their attitude, which was infectious and made me feel great.

That initial impression was reinforced over and over again. Each classroom was dynamic, each student was focused, and there was a sense of shared purpose and passion in the building that one couldn't help but absorb. Kids were as quick to jump on their desks as to sit behind them. The entire visit, it was hard to stop smiling.

A telling example of the school's commitment to positivity is a rite of passage (literally) encouraged for all visitors. RCA is a two-story facility. As one would expect, there is a main staircase upon which people can move up and down from level to level. There also is a slide—an enclosed blue twisty slide right in the center of the place. It seems an apt metaphor. The heart of RCA is enthusiasm. Why walk when you can slide? Naturally, I accepted the invitation to become "slide certified."

While there is a lot of fun happening at RCA, the school is not a crazy free-for-all. There is a strong sense of discipline, order, and respect involved as well. Kim told me that the school strives for a balance between strictness and love, which is a key to their success.

Assuming the Best Is Generous

Kim explained RCA's approach in generous terms, describing how they "assume the best" in their students. High expectations are a key aspect of the RCA method. Most of the students are from backgrounds where, statistically, their chances of educational success are low.

In *Crash Course*, Kim writes:

When we set high expectations for others, we show that we believe in them. Setting low expectations tells a child that you believe they can't perform; they cannot achieve at a high level. And unfortunately, many of our schools are plagued by cultures of low expectations. We have somehow convinced ourselves that students who have challenges should have things cut in half or made easier for them; however, the world won't cut things in half or expect less. We should not expect less from these children; we should just teach them differently. If we can teach children, especially those who struggle, to have a strong work ethic, then we are better preparing them to succeed in whatever they choose to do in life.[60]

Believing in students, connecting with them practically and emotionally, and being willing to do the extra work required to nurture their success is generous. RCA teaches that "you get back what you give" in terms of commitment. Kim lives that motto, and the whole environment of the school is designed to create a virtuous cycle of engagement among teachers and students and everyone else involved in the institution.

One more example from RCA will help to illustrate the point about the importance of having a generous attitude when supporting others.

"Jacket Ceremony" at Ron Clark Academy, Atlanta, GA (Photo Courtesy of Kim Bearden, RCA)

I asked Kim how they created an environment with such a strong and positive culture. That is a challenge in all parts of society, let alone in a middle school.

To answer, she shared a photo of an important event at RCA:

What is the emotion you see in this picture? Joy? Excitement? Celebration? It is a great snapshot of an individual being honored and a community rejoicing in the recognition.

Here is the context. School benefactors purchase "letter" jackets annually for each member of the fifth grade class. The jackets are not given out immediately, however. They must be earned. The criteria are exemplary work ethic, character, enthusiasm, and discipline. The standards for earning a jacket are high, and every member of the RCA staff—from the founders to the custodian—must endorse each candidate before they achieve the milestone.

Kim then called my attention to the students in the front left portion of the crowd. These were fellow fifth graders, several of whom had been working hard but had not yet earned their own jacket. There is nothing in the world they wanted more than to be where their fellow student was at that moment. Even so, she noted their happiness. They were not jealous or put out in any way by their classmate's success. Instead, they chose to lift up their classmate, even as they had to wait on their own turn to be lifted up and celebrated.

Kim and her students taught me something important: WISEgenerosity requires having a positive, considerate attitude toward others regardless of our own situation.

Generous Attitude Part 2: React Generously to Others

Many aspects of life involve reacting to others. We can think about those reactions in two ways. First, the circumstances affecting the other person may be good or bad. Second, our reaction to those circumstances may be positive or negative—generous or ungenerous. Here's an illustration of how this works:

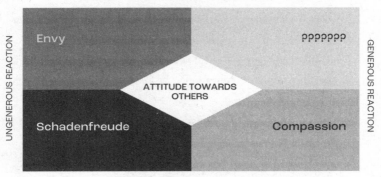

SOMETHING GOOD HAPPENED TO THE OTHER PERSON

UNGENEROUS REACTION · Envy · ?????? · GENEROUS REACTION

ATTITUDE TOWARDS OTHERS

Schadenfreude · Compassion

SOMETHING BAD HAPPENED TO THE OTHER PERSON

Generous or Ungenerous Reactions to Others

- Envy is reacting ungenerously to good happening to someone else.
- *Schadenfreude* (German for "harm-joy") is reacting ungenerously to bad happening to someone else.
- Compassion (meaning "shared suffering") is reacting generously to bad happening to someone else.
- There is no English word for reacting generously to something good happening to someone else. (I ask you, dear reader, what should this word be? Your suggestions are welcome to hello@wisegenerosity.com)

While there might not yet be such a word in English for reacting generously to good happening to someone else, there *is* such a word in Sanskrit: *mudita*. It means, "delight in the happiness and good fortune of others."[61] Supporting others in both their good fortune (*mudita*) and in their times of difficulty (compassion) is generous.

Generous Attitude Part 3: Live Hopefully in the Present

One recent study suggested that we spend almost half of our time thinking about things other than what we are doing at that moment. Moreover, much of this "mind wandering" is of the unhappy variety.[62] Many of our thoughts tend to dwell on negative experiences from the past or potential negative outcomes in the future.

Spiritual and practical teachings from around the world counsel that it is wise to live in the present. We cannot change the past, and we do not know the future. The strongest influence in our lives comes in the here and now.

The *Bhagavad Gita*, an ancient and sacred Hindu text, has a section describing "The Eternal Duties of a Human Being." Lord Krishna teaches his pupil Arjuna that enlightenment comes through acting in the world: "One cannot remain without engaging in activity at any time, even for a moment; certainly all living entities are helplessly compelled to action by the qualities endowed by material nature."[63]

We have choices to make about what we do every minute of every day with our own special skills and capabilities. The best thing we can do in this life is to use our time and talents for the good of others and to do everything with kindness and compassion. Likewise, Lord Krishna advises Arjuna to take the *karma yoga*, or "path to action."[64] Doing so is to be engaged in the world with purpose and humility and in service to others.

Being focused on the present may be wise, but inevitably our thinking will drift to the past or to the future. One key to living generously in the here and now is to channel those thoughts productively and to anticipate a positive future as much as possible.

The French writer and aviator Antoine de Saint-Exupéry wrote in *The Wisdom of the Sands*, "Your task is not to foresee the future, but to enable it."[65] Ideally, whatever consciousness we do not apply productively to the present should be working toward a positive vision of the future.

Hope is that positive vision of the future. Channeling our thoughts toward potential future good can have a positive influence on our behavior.

Here is a framework for this concept that I have borrowed from a friend:[66]

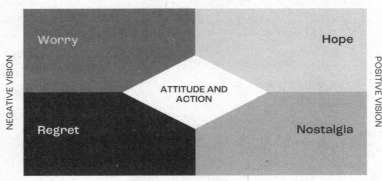

THOUGHTS OF THE FUTURE

NEGATIVE VISION

Worry

Hope

ATTITUDE AND ACTION

Regret

Nostalgia

POSITIVE VISION

THOUGHTS OF THE PAST

Generously Engaging the Past and the Future

- Regret is a negative vision of the past.
- Worry is a negative vision of the future.
- Nostalgia is a positive vision of the past.
- Hope is a positive vision of the future.

All four of these mindsets affect how we act. Worry can produce action, but it tends to be defensive and self-directed. Regret can be positive or negative: good regret motivates positive change, and bad regret paralyzes and prevents progress.[67] Dwelling on the negative past can take over our present and our future. Similarly, nostalgia is pleasant but can interfere with moving forward toward new goals. Only hope steers us toward positive change. As a result, it is the most powerful and positive foundation for action among these mindsets.

Generosity is best driven by a positive vision of the future. Generous people imagine a tomorrow that is better than today or yesterday and dedicate themselves to taking action that will help them realize that hope.

GENEROUS ACTIONS

Sharing in the joys or sufferings of others is generous. Living hopefully is generous. Looking to produce a positive future is generous. All of these attitudes are signs of a generous spirit. In and of itself, however, a generous attitude is unfulfilling. It needs to be combined with generous actions in order to truly make a difference.

Generous Actions Part 1: Aligning Attitude and Effort

Our motivations drive our interactions with each other. Likewise, our attitude drives our actions. So it makes sense that a generous attitude stimulates generous actions.

The world operates according to a set of established scientific rules. Newtonian physics offers some of the most basic, including the third law of motion: for every action, there is an equal and opposite reaction.

Human life is not so predictable. When it comes to attitude and actions, a major challenge we face is that our experiences can be greatly at odds with our expectations. We may treat someone well, only to have them treat us badly in return. We may try our best, only to fall short of a prized goal. Our aspirations and our experiences do not necessarily intersect.

So how do we translate generous attitudes into generous actions? First, we need to have perspective on the nature of our actions.

My children doubtless are tired of me repeating a particular mantra to them over and over again: *attitude and effort*. I believe the two things any of us most fully can control are our approach to circumstances (attitude)—good or bad—and the amount of work we are willing to do (effort). If my daughter and son take a positive approach to both, that is all my wife and I can ask. They and we should feel content with whatever results.

This approach presents a challenge in our achievement-oriented society. Too often, people are fixated on outcomes. They aspire to get into a certain college, find a certain kind of job, live in a certain neighborhood, or make a certain amount of money. Even immaterial goals can be outcome-driven. Some religious people see life as a test with heaven as the prize.

Generous Actions Part 2: Focusing on Inputs over Outputs

There is a major problem with an output-driven approach to life: we don't control much of what produces the outcomes we seek. Whatever our framework for understanding our place in the world, we know that fate, divine will, or other external factors all play a major role.

One of the more provocative books I've read deals with this theme. *Fooled by Randomness: The Hidden Role of Chance in Life and in the Markets* was written by investment trader/philosopher Nassim Nicholas Taleb. In the book, Taleb suggests that much of life is the product of randomness. He argues that uncertainty makes us uncomfortable, but is far more prevalent than we are willing to admit. He also suggests that we tend to see patterns where there are none and to credit success or failure to personal, rather than environmental, factors.

Taleb offers the story of two neighbors as an example. Both individuals live prosperous lives in an affluent neighborhood. To the outside world, they seem very similar. Looking a little closer, though, Taleb notes that one neighbor is a lottery winner and the other is a dentist. If the lottery winner had life to live a million times, the chances of ending up in their current situation were miniscule. On the other hand, the dentist walked a well-defined path. While there were things that could have come along to derail their good outcome, the probabilities were high that they would end up affluent.[68] The superficial output of each life seems equivalent, but the inputs were vastly different in terms of effort expended and probability of success.

With these thoughts in mind, it seems to me that we are wise to live in a way that prioritizes inputs over outputs. In other words, we should do our best with the things that we can control, like attitude and effort, in regard to determining our circumstances. After that, we should be thankful when things go well and have understanding when they do not.

Which one of the following two examples most resembles your life?

1. You have a vision of how you want to live. However, this vision rarely conforms to how you actually live. You strive and often fail. You get frustrated and sometimes depressed. As hard as you try, things rarely go the way you want them to. Brief moments of happiness are all too soon followed by disappointment. The people in your life are burdens as much as they are blessings. You feel like you are living a cycle of ups and downs that seems to repeat and repeat.

2. You take success or failure in stride. You are grateful when things go well, but you also are understanding when they do not. You strive for the best but don't view success as an end in and of itself. The people in your life aren't perfect, but you appreciate them for who they are. You approach adversity with both realism and hope. You are content.

Approach #1 prioritizes *outputs*. You may follow the rules and try to do the right things, but you are uninspired and unfulfilled. When things are good, you feel good. When things are bad, you feel bad. Along the way, there is inevitable and repeated stress and failure.

Approach #2 prioritizes *inputs*. You recognize your limitations. You dedicate yourself to serving others as well as yourself. You are humble and grounded. You appreciate small wins, and you celebrate big victories. You have the ability to accept defeat, knowing that you did all you could to succeed and that other—possibly better—opportunities likely await you.

Being focused on outputs is more natural; it is often how the world teaches us to view life. But being focused on inputs is more generous; it is concerned first about the connections between our actions and others, and it doesn't place more value than it should on things we can't control.

Let me explain this idea with an analogy: Our life is like a vessel. We fill it each day with the things around us. There are faucets that provide the inputs, and there is a spigot from which flow the outputs.

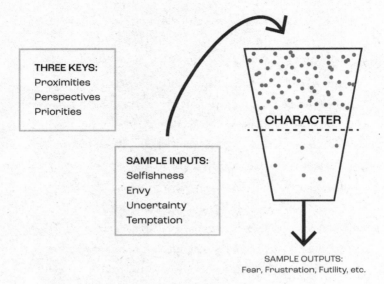

THREE KEYS:
Proximities
Perspectives
Priorities

SAMPLE INPUTS:
Selfishness
Envy
Uncertainty
Temptation

CHARACTER

SAMPLE OUTPUTS:
Fear, Frustration, Futility, etc.

Ungenerous Inputs

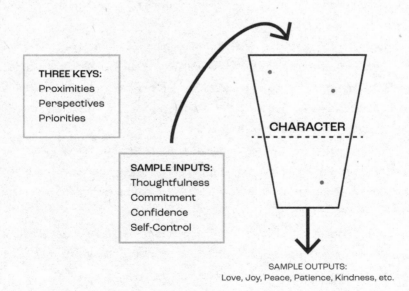

THREE KEYS:
Proximities
Perspectives
Priorities

SAMPLE INPUTS:
Thoughtfulness
Commitment
Confidence
Self-Control

CHARACTER

SAMPLE OUTPUTS:
Love, Joy, Peace, Patience, Kindness, etc.

Generous Inputs

The inputs are the key. We can make them generous or ungenerous. Generous inputs lead more to positive outputs. Ungenerous inputs lead more to negative outputs.

In the first diagram, the ungenerous faucet is polluted with negative inputs like selfishness, envy, uncertainty, and temptation. Our character may try to filter out these harmful forces, but our ability to do so is limited. The bad inputs pass through to produce bad outputs like fear, frustration, and futility.

In contrast, the generous faucet is cleaner. It contains positive inputs like thoughtfulness, commitment, confidence, and self-control. While there will always be some contaminants in life, our character has much less work to do if we use the generous faucet. We then are much more likely to enjoy positive outputs, like love, joy, and peace.

Generous Actions Part 3: Considering Proximities, Perspectives, and Priorities

A reasonable question at this point is: How do we cultivate positive inputs?

As with other generosity behaviors, conscious effort is needed. We need to steer deliberately toward more positive inputs in our lives. Here are three ways in which we can do so:

- **Proximities:** What do we surround ourselves with? We largely are at the mercy of our inputs. Are the people and places we see each day conducive to living well according to our goals? If not, do we need to make changes?
- **Perspectives:** What is the focal point of our time and energy? Is it constructive or not?
- **Priorities:** How do we manage our relationships? Do we focus on self at the expense of others? Do we seek out opportunities to help those in need, especially those closest to us?

Generous inputs have a higher probability of producing generous outputs. Generous attitudes lead to generous actions, which in turn are more likely to produce good outcomes for all involved. Prioritizing inputs over outputs in life helps us to be generous.

Here's another analogy: Life is like a recipe. What ingredients are you putting into yours? You're not going to be healthy if all you consume are potato chips and ice cream—it doesn't matter how many vitamins you take. The motto of a fitness guru I know is, "You can't outtrain a bad diet."[69] Computer programmers have a similar rule: "Garbage in, garbage out."

WISEgenerosity Example of Generous Inputs and Outputs: I'll Take Fudge, Please

Recipes make me think of my good friends Betsy and David Glass. While it is sensible to build healthy habits, part of WISEgenerosity is knowing when to indulge in a delicious treat like an amazing pie from Darden's Delights.

Betsy and David have two beautiful daughters: Darden and Anna. Darden has Down syndrome and is one of the most radiant children I ever have met. As Betsy and David were thrown into the challenges and blessings of parenting a child with a disability, they began to learn about all the support that would be necessary and everything they would need to learn. They then came to realize that many other parents of kids with Down syndrome lacked the support essential to navigate all of the challenges involved, from identifying government programs to coordinating therapeutic interventions.

Recognizing that they and their peers needed help in raising special needs children, the Glasses applied the inputs of their generous attitude and action to support organizations like All About Developmental Disabilities (AADD) and GiGi's Playhouse (a national network of "achievement centers" focused on education and empowerment for people with Down syndrome). Their support for these causes also became personal in a unique way.

Betsy is an amazing baker. Having shared her skills with friends and family for years, she and David started Darden's Delights from scratch. "DD" is social entrepreneurship—a venture with a charitable driver. The Glasses sell pies—lots of them—all across the country. They believe in harnessing the power of business for the benefit of individuals with disabilities. With each pie purchased, a "slice" of the proceeds is used to support organizations that enhance the lives of children like Darden. The Glasses strive to demonstrate that belief, creativity, and consistency, combined with long hours and patience, can create opportunity and a welcome place in a supportive community for anyone, whatever their disability may be.

Betsy and David transformed the entire basement of their house into a pie-making factory, producing Darden's Dangerously Delicious Fudge Pie, Off the Chart Chocolate Chip Cookie Pie, Smack Yo' Lips Lemon Chess Pie, and other delicious favorites. (Full disclosure—I *love* Darden's Delights pies!) The "Dardenomics" explained on their website shows how Pies + Passion + Purpose lead to amazing benefits for all involved. (Check out www.dardensdelights. com—you will thank me.)

The Glasses say that Darden's Delights has become their third child. While it takes a great deal of effort and time, it is also extremely rewarding. They enjoy seeing the business grow, and the feedback they've received adds to their passion to develop it further. According to Betsy, "The effort embodies what we value and reflects the courage to be creative and to challenge the status quo. We are very grateful that Darden's Delights has flourished over the years."

David notes, "We also are thankful that most people, especially in the South, still have a sweet tooth."[70] The community they have nurtured near and far seems to identify strongly with their purpose.

It took Betsy and David fifteen years to grow a small idea into a large and meaningful business. Their abundance mentality recognizes that challenges and opportunities are inherently intertwined. Overall, their inputs of dedication and commitment have led to great outputs. Delicious pies bring happiness to celebrations large and small, while generating positive impact for very worthy causes. Darden's Delights reflects WISEgenerosity in every way.

Seeking Service

Let's explore one last thought here on the topic of generous attitudes and actions. Prioritizing others before ourselves is a common theme throughout this book. Think about the Glasses, who started Darden's Delights to share delicious treats with the world and, by doing so, have been able to support families in need. A primary expression of a generous life is to *serve*.

An active community volunteer I know shared a great acronym reflecting the process and benefits of engaging productively to support those in need:[71]

S	<u>S</u>ay "yes"	WILLINGNESS
E	<u>E</u>ncourage with love	KINDNESS
R	<u>R</u>ally a team	RELATIONSHIPS
V	<u>V</u>alue the gift of serving	GRATITUDE
E	<u>E</u>njoy the process	BENEFIT FROM GIVING

The first step in generous attitudes + generous actions is being willing to step forward and participate.

The second step in generous attitudes + generous actions is being kind and showing compassion for those in need.

The third step in generous attitudes + generous actions is connecting with other like-minded people in mutually reinforcing relationships.

The fourth step in generous attitudes + generous actions is being grateful for opportunities.

The fifth step in generous attitudes + generous actions is to receive the goodwill that comes from being positively involved in the situation and to cycle that enjoyment back into more WISEgenerosity.

How to Be Generous: Five Types of Generosity

There are five major types of generosity:

- Possessional Generosity
- Personal Generosity
- Social Generosity
- Emotional Generosity
- Relational Generosity

For most people, this also is a hierarchy of generosity according to difficulty and importance. Being generous with our possessions and our personal attributes and our social connections is important, but it's less challenging and less meaningful than being generous with our emotions and in our relationships.

CHAPTER 6

→

Possessional Generosity

IN THIS CHAPTER, we are considering "money" and "stuff"—our possessions.

Societies celebrate the thing they prize most. A warrior society prizes courage. A religious society prizes faith. As a materialist society, modern America prizes possessions...and we have lots of possessions.

Most of us know on some level that coveting money and stuff is not a good way to live. Wanting possessions can make us want more and more if we're not careful. We focus a great deal of our time and attention on accumulating belongings—and then maintaining them—at the expense of other, worthier pursuits.

All of this acquisitiveness happens despite the unavoidable fact that we are only temporary custodians of everything we own. Rev. Don Harp, my late pastor and a great source of down-to-earth wisdom, once noted in a sermon that, "There are no moving trucks in funeral possessions."

At the end of our lives, what do we really want to show for the time we were here?

Generosity and Stewardship

The opposite of *generous* is *miserly*—being hard-hearted and unwilling to share with others. A leading exemplar of miserly life comes from literature: Ebenezer Scrooge in Charles Dickens's *A Christmas Carol*.

The story is familiar. Money-loving Scrooge has spent his life indifferent or outright hostile to the welfare of others. Supernatural forces allow him to see his life in the past, present, and future and provide the opportunity for him to change course before a horrible fate consumes him. A new man at the end of the story, Scrooge celebrates a rebirth of his own on Christmas Day and becomes a model of compassion and charity. In the process, his perspective on life is transformed from miserable to content.

The words *miser* and *miserable* share the same root. As Scrooge's transformation suggests, money and stuff are not ends in and of themselves. Possessions are tools. They give us the freedom and flexibility to live—and hopefully to live well.

Like any tool, what we do with our possessions matters. A hammer is good when used for carpentry but bad if used for assault. Tools alone tend to be "value-neutral." That is, they can be used wisely or foolishly, depending on who wields them and how they are wielded.

Money is a special case. It is the "meta-tool"—the tool by which all other tools are acquired. It is no wonder that we are so focused on it.

All of this raises an important question: How should we treat our possessions? Some years ago, I was introduced to an answer to that question: through *stewardship*. It is difficult to achieve true stewardship of our possessions, but it is a worthwhile end to pursue.

Webster's Dictionary defines a *steward* as "a person who manages another's property or financial affairs."[72] This ancient concept appears in the Bible and in many other sources. In the days before instant communication, it wasn't possible for wealthy people to be everywhere they had business interests. It was necessary to delegate responsibility for their affairs to local managers who were empowered to act on their behalf. That person was a *steward*.

The key to this relationship was twofold: *power* and *purpose*. Stewards had the *power* to act on behalf of their masters, and their promises were legally binding for their employer. At the same time and in spite of any temptations to the contrary, they had to make decisions and take actions in the employer's best interest. They were required to behave with *purpose* as though they were the master and not the agent.

Now, back to the lack of moving trucks at funerals. We ultimately don't keep any of the possessions we have now. Under the model of stewardship, the things that we own are only in our care temporarily. Ultimately, they get passed along to others. The question then becomes, What kind of legacy are we leaving? Two more questions naturally follow: Is this legacy positive or negative? And who ultimately inherits the good or bad that flows out of our lives?

If we accept this notion of stewardship, for whom are we being stewards? Family? Friends? Work? Community? The world around us? Do we have other objectives, like fame or fortune, that drive our behavior? If so, we should ask how our possessions—and the results of what we do with them—will outlive us, ideally by serving other people.

Generosity Produces Contentment

If we want to have "made a difference" somehow with our lives, the way in which we treat our possessions matters. A related and generous question is, How can our money and stuff amplify the good and diminish the bad in life?

Tying these threads together, my mind returns to the character of Scrooge. We could strive to amass riches. Ultimately, however, such hoarding leaves us empty and is meaningless. On the other hand, sharing as Scrooge learned to do can produce vastly more happiness, enlightenment, and fulfillment than what we started with. Possessional Generosity can have a large impact on the world and on those around us.

At the high end of the possessions spectrum, David Rubenstein is one of the wealthiest people I interviewed for this project. Rubenstein cofounded the Carlyle Group, a private equity investment firm based in Washington, DC. According to *Forbes*, he was worth about $3.2 billion in April 2023.[73]

When asked if it was harder to make money or give it away, Rubenstein responded that it was harder to give it away. "Sometimes people get on the merry-go-round of making money and they don't know how to do anything other than that, so they just keep making money and don't actually spend the time to figure out how to give it away.... I think that as you get to sixty, seventy, and eighty years old and you have billions of dollars and you haven't figured out how to give it away or do something with it that's productive, that's probably not a good thing for society or for you."[74]

Rubenstein says that he prioritizes generosity over money, and he views giving as its own reward: "[L]ife has many different components to it, but if you have a life desire to actually feel fulfilled and make sure you justify your existence on the face of the earth, I think you'll find your experience will be better if you've done...things for other people."

Of course, it may be hard for most of us to relate to being responsible for vast sums of money. All the same, it is generally recognized that very wealthy people are not necessarily happier than the rest of us.

Research shows that having an adequate level of money initially makes one more content. Eventually, however, diminishing returns set in. After a while, more money tends to *reduce* happiness. Nobel Prize winners Daniel Kahneman and Angus Deaton concluded in their 2010 research that the optimal amount of income needed to produce emotional well-being in the US was $75,000 per year.[75] Other studies suggest that the cause and effect of wealth and happiness works both ways. Money may make you happier up to a point, but happy people also make more money than unhappy people.[76] To summarize, you are more likely to be comfortable if you are happy, but less likely to be happy if you are rich.

In that vein, one of the best books on this subject that I've come across is *If You're So Smart, Why Aren't You Happy?* The author, Raj Raghunathan, is a business professor at the University of Texas McCombs School of Business and a regular contributor to *Psychology Today*.

Raghunathan's book has a section titled "Why Materialism Lowers Happiness."[77] He suggests that we adapt to having possessions, and it then takes accumulating even more possessions to produce the same level of satisfaction we had previously. We also have unrealistic expectations that money and stuff lead to happiness. When they don't, it amplifies our discontent. For example, lottery winners are no happier as a group than nonwinners just two years after the winners' windfall.[78] Lastly, focusing on material items makes us more self-centered and less compassionate.

Confirming Raghunathan's conclusions, a major research study surveyed 12,000 first-year college students in 1976. Reconnecting with the same group in 1995, those who listed "making money" as a primary goal when they were young ended up being far less happy later in life.[79] The conclusion of the study was that "materialistic people are more likely to compromise on things that actually bring joy and happiness—things like hanging out with friends and family or contributing to society—in favor of money, power, and fame."[80]

Risks of Affluence

Social psychologists likewise have done experiments showing how success can change people for the worse. One notable example was a study using a rigged version of Monopoly.[81] Two people were set up to play the well-known game. Based on a coin flip, one was given huge advantages in money and mobility that all but ensured their victory. As the contest progressed, the advantaged person often began to behave arrogantly. As their expressions of entitlement rose, their empathy and compassion for the disadvantaged player declined. When asked about the game afterward, the advantaged person tended to credit their skillful play rather than their lopsided position as the reason for winning.

The same researchers pursued other studies to see how wealth and success related to altruism. One experiment looked at whether or not drivers stop for pedestrians who were waiting at crosswalks, based on how expensive the driver's car was. Drivers of the least expensive cars stopped the most, while drivers of the most expensive cars stopped the least.

In all of these experiments, the outcomes were similar. Status and resources were negatively correlated with generosity.

Generosity = Rx for Accumulation

The research conclusions were not all bad for the wealthy, however. When the higher-status subjects were prompted in some way to be attuned to the needs of others, they ended up being comparably generous to the rest of the subjects. Hearing a story about people in need prior to taking a giving test seemed to ground them back into empathy. The conclusion reached was that we all need to exercise our generosity muscles regularly or risk having them atrophy. Furthermore, those who have accumulated a large portion of possessions are at increased risk if they don't share them generously.

Here's an example that further helps make this point. I've spoken with many people who have visited countries where standards of living are much lower than they are in the United States. In some cases, the people visiting these countries were there specifically to help those in dire physical need who lacked even basic necessities like food, water, and shelter. One common observation of the people coming into the economically challenged country from a wealthier country is how generous their hosts were. The people in the host country had little in the way of possessions, but they were happy to share what they had. Moreover, they seemed rich in relationships, compassion, and meaningful connections. More than one person confessed to being jealous about the lives of these "impoverished" people compared to their own "prosperous" lives.

At a base level, Possessional Generosity is an antidote for many of the negative side effects of affluence. And we all are prosperous compared to at least one other person we know. Leveraging our resources on behalf of others and sharing what we have in terms of physical and virtual possessions, including money, resources, and belongings, is generous.

Possessions define many people's perceived potential for generosity. When they think of giving, they think first of contributing cash or assets to a cause or a situation. Unfortunately, this perception is limiting. If you feel that you don't have "surplus" possessions, you don't feel a capacity to give.

In my view, we all have excess possessions. Regardless of how young or old you are or how much money you have or don't have, you always can find a way to help others.

Even more importantly, we each have an absolute excess because someday our need for possessions will disappear entirely. Everything we have ultimately passes on to someone or something else. We *all* share in the end—whether we want to or not. It seems to me that intentional sharing, done while we are around to see the benefits of it, just makes sense.

CHAPTER 7

Personal Generosity

TIME AND TALENT ARE THE ESSENCE OF LIFE ITSELF. Sharing these resources with others is known as Personal Generosity. How we spend our limited time defines who we are. It is fundamentally generous to use our personal attributes and capabilities on behalf of others.

We all know people who "give of themselves" generously. Hopefully, we aspire to do so ourselves. This category of giving is as diverse and comprehensive as we are as human beings. I'm sure you can think of many examples of Personal Generosity from your own life—people who have helped you as well as times when you have lent a hand to others.

As in the case of Possessional Giving, however, I believe that we define Personal Generosity too narrowly. Yes, volunteering at a homeless shelter is generous. Mentoring underprivileged kids is generous. Taking a meal to a sick neighbor is generous. Sharing your notes with a classmate who is struggling is generous. There are infinite ways to share our time and talent on behalf of others. All of these acts are virtuous and good.

That said, Personal Generosity is more than just performing good deeds. It also means living in service to others in all that we do. With this thought in mind, I'd like to share examples from an area that might not come to mind when considering this topic: business.

Generous Workers

Commerce can be seen as a purely bottom-line endeavor. Money goes in and money comes out. If the output exceeds the input, we record a profit. More profit is better than less. However, reducing an enterprise to numbers on a page can crowd out space for generosity.

Beyond the bottom line, business remains a human-based activity, with investors, workers, and customers all deeply involved. Businesses succeed by adding value to people's lives. They generate products or services that meet a need of some kind. In that process, they connect people in different ways and provide opportunities for Personal Generosity.

For some of us, work is an obligation. We do it to earn money to fund the rest of our lives. The necessity of work can make it seem routine and even tedious. We've all met people who are miserable in their work.

At the same time, we've all encountered people who seem to love what they do. This is true in all vocational areas: custodians, accountants, cashiers, teachers, mechanics, customer service agents, executives, restaurant servers, entrepreneurs. So what is the difference between being contented or discontented at work?

Psychological research suggests that the ability to find meaning in work is what separates positive and negative job experiences. The key is to make work relational and not just functional. There are tasks involved in every job, and the tasks may not all be rewarding in themselves. Relating the tasks to a higher purpose and to positive benefits changes a worker's perspective. In addition, there is an important social aspect to work. Participation in a community with shared purposes drives satisfaction as well.[82]

One study of attitudes toward work looked at zookeepers. "Though more than eight in ten zookeepers have college degrees, their average annual income is less than $25,000. The typical job description involves scrubbing enclosures, scooping waste and spending time in the elements. There's little room for advancement and zookeepers tend not to be held in high regard."[83] Zookeeping involves hard labor, little money, and little prestige. Two words come to mind: elephant dung.

Yet the study found that "zookeepers are a passionate bunch. Many volunteer for months or even years until a paid position opens up."[84] Similarly, "Working as a zookeeper felt like a personal destiny to many of them. They even shared stories about how events led them to the zoo, as if by fate."[85]

The research on zookeepers showed that "people who feel called to their careers are likely to find their work deeply meaningful.... Their personal connection with the job makes even the most trivial tasks feel significant."[86] In addition to the work itself was the benefit of being connected to like-minded coworkers with a shared calling. "It's not just that you do the same work, but you're the same kind of people. It gives you a connection to a community."[87]

Jobs perceived as purposeful connect a worker positively with clients and coworkers. Negative work is the opposite: a worker feels isolated while their tasks appear meaningless and their relationships with colleagues are poor.

With this context in mind, Personal Generosity approaches work as an opportunity for positive service to a common cause or calling. It also celebrates connection to the other people involved in the process. A generous mindset at work produces a positive ripple effect that benefits everyone involved.

A friend of mine attended a remarkable funeral years ago. The deceased was a woman who had worked in middle management for a national corporation. The way in which her colleagues reacted to the loss of their friend and coworker was striking.

Her boss gave a eulogy and described this woman as the model employee: kind, unselfish, caring, dedicated, and loyal. The focus was not on her profitability but instead on her many contributions to the culture of the company. She had taken extra time to mentor others, she was always available to help when needed, and she had engaged with her coworkers in countless ways that were not part of her official job description. In other words, she was generous.

The woman was so beloved, the boss added, that hundreds of colleagues around the country whose lives she had touched were unable to attend her memorial service in person, but they still wanted to remember and honor her. These people set up a conference call to celebrate her life and to come together to mourn their loss.

This woman had a huge impact on those around her. Her boss appreci-ated her value as an exemplary employee. Her colleagues appreciated the time and effort she spent nurturing their relationships and careers. Her loved ones appreciated the respect and admiration she'd received in her professional life. For those of us employed by corporations, wouldn't it be marvelous to have personally generous people like this woman to work with and to work for?

Generous Competitors

One perception of business is that of ruthless competition. Sayings like, "It's a dog-eat-dog world" or, "You eat what you kill" suggest that commerce is a violent zero-sum game in which the only way to get ahead is at someone else's expense. Evil corporations bent on domination or destruction are stock villains in Hollywood scripts.

There certainly are examples of exploitative and harmful corporate prac-tices. In reality, however, most business is helpful by definition. In simplest terms, businesses produce what people want to purchase.

Likewise, businesses evolve in response to changing conditions and opportunities. Economists use the term "creative destruction" to show how this process unfolds.[88] Competition means that there is an incentive to make things better and cheaper. In 1948, an original Admiral seven-inch, black-and-white television set cost the modern equivalent of over $23,000.[89] Compare that cost and viewing experience to a flat-screen digital TV today.

Similarly, I originally typed this paragraph on my MacBook, using my iPad for references while tethered to the internet by my iPhone, which also was playing unlimited jazz music to help my creative impulses. This combination of technological benefits would have been science fiction not long ago. It took risk, hard work, and commitment to great products to make these advances happen. In turn, Apple has built a hugely successful company.

Business at its best is generous. It gives to the world much more than it takes from it.

Of course, individuals with a competitive advantage in a market can profit from it. Done appropriately when willing buyers and willing sellers agree on an exchange of value, good business produces returns and is the basic mechanism of commerce.

As noted before, however, business is a human endeavor, and profit is not the only motive for it. We may choose voluntarily to give away a competitive advantage in pursuit of a higher goal.

My friend Kristen Lewis is a successful attorney. Her specialty is working with families who have special-needs children. There are many practical and legal challenges in such situations, and Kristen helps to make sure that each family is able to maximize their opportunities to care for their loved one.

Kristen's specialty is rare. There are many more families who need help with the planning she provides than there are qualified experts to support them. Even though it undermines the exclusivity of her own knowledge, Kristen publishes articles and runs training programs to help other lawyers operate in this area. Her goal is to make sure that no disabled child or family suffers through lack of access to the legal guidance they need.

Kristen's commitment to the community she serves is an excellent example of Personal Generosity. She has chosen to look past her own career advancement in order to benefit others. There are others like Kristen in every profession who mentor, who volunteer with trade organizations to raise standards in their industries, and who dedicate themselves to supporting potential competitors for the greater good. In my experience, these people are the most respected and successful individuals in their fields.

Generous Risk-Takers

Business involves risk. Courage is needed to start any venture, launch any new product, or invest in any uncertain initiative. This kind of courage and generosity are related.

No sensible investor puts money to work without analyzing the market they plan to serve. Will people want to buy this new tool or resource? Will the new item add value to the lives of its purchasers? An enterprise that starts by considering the broad potential benefits to its prospective customers tends to produce the best outcomes. Likewise, the greatest business triumphs often come from a commitment to an unselfish benefit that grows into something much larger.

Mark Toro is a successful Atlanta real estate developer. He and his wife, Nancy, are passionately involved in helping the areas of the city that suffer most under the strains of systemic poverty. They give time, money, and other resources to address the needs of the most vulnerable members of their community.

Mark and I have served together for years on the board of a remarkable Atlanta nonprofit organization called City of Refuge (COR). I'll talk more about COR in chapter 25, but suffice it to say that Mark has been invaluable to the efforts of this organization. His willingness to leverage his network of relationships has produced architects and builders who have built a school, job training centers, and treatment facilities, along with helping to raise the money to pay for them. He and the companies he had led—his former company, North American Properties, and his current company, Toro Development Co.—are models of engaged community generosity.

I interviewed Mark and Nancy about their civic engagement and learned something vital in the process. The foundation for Mark's business success was an act of Personal Generosity.

During the financial crisis of 2008–2009 and the years that immediately followed, property developers were under tremendous strain. Many projects went bankrupt as the economy suffered and the financing needed to keep them going dried up.

Atlantic Station had been a flagship reclamation development in Atlanta. The site was a 138-acre "brownfield"—a polluted old steel mill site adjacent to the city's growing Midtown district. Conceived as a massive fifteen million square feet of offices, residences, and shops, the huge area zoned as mixed-use development opened in 2005 and prompted the US Postal Service to give it its own ZIP code.[90]

Atlantic Station had a string of misfortunes and missteps that led it to the verge of bankruptcy as the Great Recession took hold. Mark watched this downfall from the outside and described how the likely failure of the project literally kept him up at night. He and Nancy had moved to Atlanta early in their marriage and had raised their family in the area. If Atlantic Station went under, it would create a huge void in the center of the city they loved—one that would have years of negative consequences for the community.

Others in the industry thought that Atlantic Station was without hope. In fact, Mark even consulted with a mentor who advised him to stay away from the development. It would destroy his career if he failed at trying to save it, and failure seemed all but certain.

However, Mark couldn't let the idea go. He saw a need and felt that he had to fill it. He was willing to dedicate his time and talent to the effort, risking the potential destruction of his own reputation and personal success. Motivated in large part by his commitment to Atlanta, he saw opportunity where others did not. He then overcame great obstacles to raise the money, and he purchased the property in 2010.

Skipping to the end of the story, Mark and his colleagues acted generously—and won. Atlantic Station recovered and now is a vibrant part of a growing Atlanta. Mark sold a large part of the property to another investor in 2015. The main retail space alone was valued at $200 million, up from the $80 million paid when Mark had made his original purchase five years earlier.[91] More than doubling his investment then became fuel for new developments as well as for his and Nancy's other community interests.

Personal Generosity—modeled by dedicating himself to a cause larger than a real estate deal alone—was a major factor in Mark's success. As in many aspects of business, real risk was involved. There was no assurance of success, and a bad outcome would have caused major damage. This is a good example of the effort and courage needed to practice WISEgenerosity.

Generous Career Choices

In monetary terms, David Swensen may have been one of the most personally generous people in America before he passed away in 2021. A select few people like David Rubenstein become billionaires and then rededicate their wealth to causes they care about. Swensen, on the other hand, forewent the opportunity to become a billionaire and instead dedicated himself to the success of the nonprofit institution where he worked.

Swensen was the Chief Investment Officer at Yale University, where he received a PhD in economics in 1980. He was hired from a job on Wall Street in 1985 at age thirty-one to manage the university's then approximately $1 billion endowment. Using a revolutionary and highly disciplined approach to investing (known now as the Yale Endowment Model), Swensen increased the size of that endowment to $42.3 billion as of June 30, 2021, in the year he died.[92] Along the way, Yale has been able to spend billions of additional dollars on campus improvements, faculty salaries, and scholarships.[93]

Trying to put his work into perspective, Yale had a party to honor Swensen for his twentieth anniversary on the job. The university displayed a series of charts showing the contributions of the largest benefactors in school history. These were titans whose names adorn the major buildings on campus. Here was the comparison:[94]

Comparative Value of Historic Financial Contributions to Yale University (2005 Dollars)

Edward Stephen Harkness:	$128 million
John William Sterling:	$151 million
William Sperry Beinecke:	$263 million
Paul Mellon:	$379 million
David Swensen:	**$7.8 billion**[95]

As impressive as this comparison is, these numbers are now many years old. The gap between Swensen and the others would be much larger today as the results of Swensen's work continue to compound.

Swensen did not seek the limelight. By all accounts, he enjoyed his life at Yale. He taught classes. He was active in community activities. He was well respected by his peers. He published books. He also was well compensated by normal standards. At more than $4.5 million per year, he was the university's highest paid employee.[96] He chose a life that suited him well.

Even so, one time when he spoke to alumni in New York, a businessman asked him only half-jokingly, "What's wrong with you?"[97] He was aware that Swensen could make a vast fortune doing similar work elsewhere, such as managing a hedge fund.

A hedge fund is a catchall category that includes a wide variety of different investments. Hedge funds are used by institutions and very wealthy individuals to try to get good returns relative to the risk assumed. Top managers in the field oversee billions of dollars and typically charge 2 percent of assets under management and 20 percent of high-water-mark profits for their efforts. These managers can get very rich themselves.

Yale calculated that Swensen added $26.6 billion compared to the average endowment over his first thirty years on the job.[98] That is a staggering sum. Looking back at Swensen's tenure at Yale and imagining that he had received 20 percent of this value added, he would have made $5.3 billion for himself.[99] Likewise, if he had left Yale at some point to run his own fund, he would have drawn billions in assets and produced huge wealth. Yet that wasn't his goal.

Swensen described at one point how he had ended up in his position: "I realized that my heart wasn't in Wall Street. My heart was in the world of education, and at Yale in particular. So I came up here, amazed that I was responsible, as Chief Investment Officer, for this portfolio."[100] This observation captures the roots of Personal Generosity well: self-awareness, humility, and dedication to others alongside yourself.

Now, I am not suggesting that well-paid investment managers are doing something wrong. Their efforts contribute to the financial health of their clients and to society as a whole. If there is demand for their services, clients can decide for themselves how much they are willing to pay. Likewise, many successful investors are philanthropic and share their wealth. Nonetheless, Swensen's

Personal Generosity was remarkable, and the Yale community is billions of dollars better off because of it.

• • •

In sum, Personal Generosity is being willing to share time, talent, power, and influence. It also involves effort, self-sacrifice, and letting go of your own agenda for the sake of others. Business is just one area where such giving can thrive. Similar benefits are available in every area of life. The question all of us should answer is, Am I being a generous steward of my time and of my talent?

CHAPTER 8

---→

Social Generosity

SOCIAL GENEROSITY CONSISTS OF ACTIONS that sacrifice the self in ways large and small for the sake of others in a community. Examples of Social Generosity include manners, hospitality, civic duty, and civility. Social Generosity often engages both Possessional and Personal Generosity.

Social Generosity currently is being subjected to many crosscurrents. Expectations of and awareness about how we relate to other people at all levels is changing. Technology is disrupting traditional means of connection and communication. Traditional values and customs are under pressure. Norms of "appropriate" and "acceptable" behavior are in flux. At the same time, a generational shift is underway as a cycle of individualism gives way to a stronger sense of community obligations.

With these forces in mind, WISEgenerosity offers the potential to guide us toward positive outcomes in our relationships with each other across all of society.

Manners

In today's highly distracted and seemingly self-absorbed age, manners often seem like an afterthought as we rush from place to place. Who has the time to observe polite formalities? Indeed, some argue against manners altogether as outdated, elitist, and stifling to individual freedom and expression.

Still, all societies have rules to help their members interact productively with one another. They range from elaborate rituals in monarchies of old to understanding that IT'S NOT OK TO SHOUT WHEN SENDING SOMEONE AN EMAIL.

My considerate Southern wife rightly criticizes my lapses in proper manners. She is trying to teach our children how to be better behaved than I am.

Toward this end, our daughter, Ellie, and our son, Reed, each attended an etiquette class when they were ten. The purpose as stated by the teacher was, "simple consideration of other people." There were three main points:[101]

1. Always follow the Golden Rule.
2. Always do your best.
3. Always choose to do the right thing.

It's hard to object to these standards. The needs of others should inform and guide our own behavior. Why should we pay attention to manners? A number of reasons come to mind:

- **Social skills:** Manners are lubrication for smoothly interacting with others.
- **Avoiding and resolving conflict:** Polite and respectful treatment is disarming and keeps problems from starting or escalating.
- **Outward appearance:** Manners provide impressions to others of who we are.
- **Inward progress:** Being considerate develops our own character in positive ways.

The founder of New College, Oxford—my graduate school home—thought this topic so important that he made "Manners Maketh Man" his personal motto.[102] How we treat others and behave toward them reflects strongly on who we are.

At their core, manners are an extension of the Golden Rule—we try to treat others as we ourselves want to be treated. The foundation of manners is consideration for others and courtesy toward their needs. Done well, manners are generous.

Hospitality

Hospitality is social sharing, involving others in our personal space and activities. In so doing, we recognize other people as important and valuable. Hospitality is generous.

Think of how great it feels to receive an invitation from a favorite friend to a fun party or event. There is an affirming sense of inclusion and intimacy. There also is appreciation and anticipation. Such personal connections—lived out in sharing time together—reinforce relationships and help make life satisfying.

Looking back on the origins of human behavior, hospitality is a core value in nomadic cultures.[103] In spite of living in difficult conditions, nomads sacrifice valuable resources to welcome others into their group. Guests are honored, and it is considered disgraceful for a nomad to treat strangers poorly. Even at the most basic level of living, there is something essential about hospitality.

One of my favorite personal travel stories is a tale of hospitality. Several friends and I embarked on a month-long driving tour of Europe just after I completed my master's degree in England. One of our first stops was the Festival of San Fermín in Pamplona—the famous annual running of the bulls. The Spanish know how to celebrate, and we were physically spent after two days and nights of revelry.

A friend had recommended a beach town in Portugal where we could relax and recover for a few days. Having started late for the drive across the Iberian Peninsula, it was dark by the time we approached the Atlantic Coast. Moreover, we were lost. (Stick with me, kids. This was in the days before smartphones and GPS.)

On a one-and-a-half-lane road, with our map turned inside out and upside down, we happened across a small village of twelve or so houses. One set of windows was brightly lit with a sign indicating that the building was a café. Determined to find our destination, I entered in search of directions.

It turned out that the proprietor, Senhor Major, had been a fisherman in France at one point. Since he didn't know English and I didn't know Portuguese, we communicated in mutually broken French. I attempted to explain where we were going. He kept shaking his head and saying we did not want to go there. After futilely trying to explain that we did, I finally got the message. He was insisting that we stay with him. Exhausted and in no condition to argue, our party went inside for a long-overdue dinner.

As we entered the café, I looked at the shelves lined with bottles behind the bar and attempted a lame joke in my poor French: *"Avez-vous des boissons?"* ("Do you have drinks?") Oddly, our host seemed confused and said, *"Non."* I chalked this up to the language barrier, and we moved on to a welcome dinner of roasted chicken and french fries that appeared like magic. We were then shuttled, half-asleep, to the house next door, where we all collapsed.

It was embarrassingly late—almost noon—when the four of us awoke the next morning. It was the first real sleep we'd had in days, but our hosts didn't know that. We sheepishly filed over next door to apologize and to offer thanks for the shelter and the meal. The proprietor wasn't there, but his wife said he would be back soon.

Not long after, Senhor Major returned with a beaming smile and a string of fish he'd just caught. *"Les poissons!"* he said happily. After a moment, I realized what had happened. When we'd arrived the night before, he had thought I'd had asked for fish (*poissons*) instead of drinks (*boissons*). Not able to oblige my request at the moment, he'd managed to find some at the next opportunity.

These were not just any fish. In our confused wandering the night before, we had landed in a time traveler's fishing village nestled in the dunes of the Portuguese coast. A short path led to an otherwise empty beach on which two traditional fishing boats launched into the surf each morning, returning later with harvests of sardines. Senhor Major had gone out on a boat that morning with his neighbors in order to produce the meal he thought I had requested.

A fish I knew only from the canned variety synonymous with tight spaces, these Portuguese sardines were beautiful and delicious. Senhor Major grilled them whole over a charcoal fire in his garden. With fresh bread, a salad of tomatoes, cucumbers, and onions, and local wine, this remains one of the most memorable meals I ever have eaten.

Senhor and Senhora Major became our fast friends, and we felt like their adopted children. A niece of theirs, who had spent time in Canada, appeared and was able to translate for us, greatly enhancing our conversation. My friends and I rested on the beach, played cards with the family in the evenings, and stayed several days longer than we'd planned.

It was amazing hospitality on every level. We figured out quickly that the Majors had given us their own house to stay in that first night when we'd arrived as weary travelers, and they insisted that we remain in it. Every time we tried to pay for anything, Senhor Major refused our offer.[104]

When we finally tore ourselves away, we drove to the original seaside town we'd been trying to find and discovered it was a forgettable tourist spot. It certainly was nothing compared to the experience of our accidental detour to the tiny village and the chance encounter with the special people there. These new friends we'd met were so different from us, but their generous hospitality had led to great joy and connection.

In contrast to my very intimate and personal experience in Portugal is the modern-day hospitality industry. Online searches reveal hundreds of entries related to running a hotel or restaurant that give advice on how to create engaging and memorable interactions with paying guests.

Such experiences are pleasant enough, but they also can feel contrived. Modern life has amplified the breadth and volume of social contact while reducing the depth and meaning of it.

Hospitality industry seems like an oxymoron to me. Businesses are trying to manufacture a personal connection that is relational at its essence. It may feel nice to get a room upgrade or a warm towel at dinner, but the emotions being stimulated fade quickly if they aren't based on real, interpersonal connections. True hospitality happens person-to-person, and it is most certainly generous.

Sociability—Friends and Family

Sociability connects manners and hospitality. *Sociable* is defined as "willing-ness to talk and engage in activities with other people." In this vein, the *Wall Street Journal* created controversy in 2017 when it published an article written by Elizabeth Bernstein entitled, "You're Not Busy, You're Just Rude."[105] Giving an example of how she was stung by a friend's rebuff after she made an effort to get together with her, Bernstein said that when people say they are unavailable in relationships, it is perceived as, "I am too busy for you. You don't matter enough to me."

The solution offered in the article was no longer to view "busy" as a virtue and to refrain from taking on so much activity that family and friends are crowded out. As an author of a study from Columbia, Georgetown, and Harvard Universities about the perception of busyness put it, "At the end of your life, do you want your tombstone to say: 'He was busy'?"[106]

Nonsense, said a rebuttal three days later in *Harper's Bazaar*.[107] "The [*Journal*] article suggests that 'busyness' is a brag, and that those who set hard restric-tions on their time are rude and inconsiderate. This is bull[*&$#]—anyone who thinks this way should be cut out of your schedule immediately. There is nothing worse than a 'friend' who feels entitled to your time." The disagreeing author said that she used to find relationships overwhelming:

> For years I sacrificed my own mental and physical wellbeing in service of other people's needs. I gave everything I had to every friendship and it was never enough. There were always more birthday parties, readings, dinners, drinks, bachelorette parties, and housewarmings to attend. There was always someone who wanted my time, or felt like hanging out or catching up, and I had no ability to say no.

The author then changed her approach: "Prioritizing my schedule and keeping busy with the things that are important to me has been key to my mental health." If a friend replies to an invitation with specific calendar demands, the author suggests, "Don't take it personally. They're probably just busy, and that's okay."

Clearly, there is a tension here between two conflicting personal needs. Both women want connections with loved ones. Both also want to be able to manage their time without being overwhelmed and feeling guilty. One takes a disciplined approach to scheduling in order to control her time. The other tries to cut back on activity in order to prioritize personal interactions.

Mediating remotely, it does seem that both women value relationships and are struggling with how to manage them. They are not alone. Such tensions are a real challenge today. All the same, relationships are central to life and require effort and hospitality to maintain. It is socially generous to invite others into our lives in meaningful and even sacrificial ways.

Sociability—Strangers

This struggle of prioritization and self-preservation makes me think of Bob Goff. Bob is a "Christian writer" in the way that full-on Fourth of July fireworks are a "lights display with noise features." The description does not do him justice.

Bob's book *Love Does* is an inspired attempt to share his radical, no-holds-barred efforts to make the world around him better by emulating the at-any-cost commitment to humanity he sees in the biblical gospel message. One of the best stories in the book is about sociability.

Bob is a successful attorney who lives on the water in San Diego, where strangers walk along a public path by his yard. Many are couples who stroll by hand in hand. Some wave to Bob and his wife when they're sitting on their back porch. They wave back. All very normal. Then lovestruck Ryan came along.[108]

Ryan motioned Bob down to the path from his porch one day. Awkwardly but with determination, he announced to Bob that he was in love. Moreover, he and his girlfriend walked regularly on the path by Bob's house. Ryan wanted to ask her to marry him in Bob's yard overlooking their favorite spot and asked Bob if it would be okay. He asked the right guy. Bob said, "Sure!"

Things progressed from there. Smitten and seemingly invulnerable to any sense of social decorum or boundaries, Ryan returned repeatedly with new and bigger ideas. How about dinner on the porch? Could he have twenty friends there to serve the meal and share the evening? Could they put speakers out for a slow dance before Ryan popped the question? Yes, yes, and yes, said Bob.

Finally, Ryan really lost it. He asked if Bob had a boat and if he and his girlfriend could end the evening on the water as Ryan proposed. In Bob's own telling: "Ryan was out of control. He had no idea what an outrageous thing he was asking. But you see, to Ryan, I wasn't a total stranger—no one was. To him, the whole world was full of coconspirators when it came to winning over his love."[109] Bob did have a boat, berthed in the marina across the way. And Bob was all in at this point.

On the big night, Ryan's girlfriend was repeatedly surprised by the events of the evening. She kept asking, "What are we doing?" as barriers of normal behavior fell aside and she and her beau moved farther and farther into Bob's personal space.

Finally on the boat, Ryan had fifty friends on the shore spelling out, "Will you marry me?" in candles as he got down on one knee. Bob had one last surprise of his own. He had convinced the local coast guard to rendezvous with his own boat at an appointed place and time. Given the signal that the newly minted fiancée had said yes, a fireboat let loose with all of its cannons and framed the scene with jets of water. Sorry to all other aspiring grooms. What a proposal!

Bob Goff was a willing catalyst for an extraordinary moment in the lives of people he didn't even know. That is incredible Social Generosity.

Why would Bob do this? What would possess him to expend great time and effort this way? He tells us:

Ryan's love was audacious. It was whimsical. It was strategic. Most of all, it was contagious. Watching Ryan lose himself in love reminded me that being "engaged" isn't just an event that happens when a guy gets on one knee and puts a ring on his true love's finger. Being engaged is a way of doing life, a way of living and loving. It's about going to extremes and expressing the bright hope that life offers us, a hope that makes us brave and expels darkness with light. That's what I want my life to be all about—full of abandon, whimsy, and in love. I want to be engaged to life and with life."[110]

Social Generosity is about being engaged positively in the lives of other people, even those outside of our immediate circle of family and close friends. Bob's extraordinary sociability and hospitality touched the lives of everyone involved, including himself.

The story didn't end there. After *Love Does* was published, others have been emboldened by the book to ask Bob about using his yard for proposals and even weddings. Bob and his (clearly saintly) wife have agreed whenever possible.

You may have decided that Bob is kind but over-the-top. If so, you're right—and he's even more so than you think. On the last page of *Love Does*, Bob gives his cellphone number with the following invitation: "I've found that the people in my life who have actually been the most influential have also been the ones who were the most available. If you ever want to talk about any of the ideas in this book that ping you, my phone number is..."[111]

On second thought, it's only fair to Bob that you get your own copy of the book to access the number. It's on page 224.

Love Does has sold hundreds of thousands of copies since its release in 2012.[112] That is a lot of "friends" who can (and have, according to Bob) called at any time of day or night.

Being available and sharing with others is sociable, and sociability is generous.

Civic Duty

My father, grandfather, and great-grandfather were all volunteer firefighters. About 85 percent of fire departments in America are all or mostly volunteer.[113] These types of fire departments provide service to one-third of the US population. In small towns across the country, if your house catches on fire, it likely will be a neighbor who risks his or her own life to save you, your family, and your home.

Volunteerism is one of the key aspects of American life. Many essential services and resources are provided by or augmented through volunteers. Historically, civic engagement has been identified as a primary differentiator between America and other countries.

Troublingly, volunteerism in the US has been declining for years. Government statistics show that only 25 percent of Americans volunteered at least once in 2015.[114] The number is higher for women than men (28 percent versus 22 percent). Thirty-five- to fifty-four-year-olds in midlife and mid-career were most likely to volunteer (29 percent), and young adults from twenty to twenty-four years old were least likely (18 percent). Ironically, working people were more likely to volunteer (27 percent) than people who were not employed (23 percent) or not in the labor force (21 percent). These last two data points remind me of the old saying, "If you want to get something done, ask a busy person."

While not a volunteer activity, jury duty is another example of civic engagement. A bedrock principle of our legal system enshrined in the US Constitution is that everyone accused of a crime has a right to trial by an "impartial jury."[115] This is a cornerstone of equal justice for all.

While not flawless, we enjoy the direct and indirect benefits of a generally humane legal system. Increasingly, however, most people consider jury duty to be a nuisance. According to data compiled from courts nationwide, about 32 million people are summoned for jury duty each year.[116] Of those summoned, only 8 million actually report. At least 3 million of the 24 million not appearing just don't show up—and don't provide any excuse for their absence.

I confess that I myself have complained the few times I've been called for jury duty. It can be a major sacrifice. While most people summoned do not serve and service most likely is short if you *are* called, an unusually long and involved trial can last for months. In essence, being on a jury is a sacrifice for the sake of our society, like other forms of civic duty. I will try to have a better attitude if I am called again.

We all have time; it is a question of how we prioritize and allocate it. The more people who volunteer and engage with others, the better off we all are. Civic duty is generous.

Civility

Civility means politeness in action or expression. The root is the Latin word *civilitas* or "courtesy."[117] It relates to the word "civilized," meaning "having an advanced or humane culture, society, etc." or "polite, well-bred, refined."[118] Civility addresses how we engage with our neighbors and others in our communities.

Civility is the form of manners, hospitality, and sociability for politics. It is where civic duty and Personal Generosity intersect. For a democratic system to function, there needs to be confidence in the system, tolerance for honest disagreements, and respect for other opinions. If civility is the input, compromise is the output. The goal of the political process is not to be "right," but to produce the best outcome for society.

How do you respond to these statements about civility? Perhaps with a wistful shaking of the head? My description of civility may seem a far cry from what passes for process in politics these days. Civility is under great stress.

On the one hand, our country has been torn apart by serious disagreements since its founding. There has been plenty of nasty name-calling and bruising behavior all along.

On the other hand, technology is making it easier and easier for us to filter out opinions we don't already accept. We don't just disagree on policies; we can't even agree on the facts behind them. This undermines any common ground we might share and polarizes opinions.

One commentator concerned about such matters defined the situation as follows: "Some of the most difficult and seemingly intractable political problems of our time—growing polarization, the loss of faith in governing institutions, the breakdown of family and community, the decline of civic participation, and the concentration of poverty and addiction in particular rural and urban enclaves—either arise from, or are exacerbated by, the loss of personal relationships and connections, and our growing alienation from each other."[119]

This quote is from Cherie Harder, president of the Trinity Forum in Washington, DC. Cherie and her colleagues have initiated "community conversations" to encourage civility in America by reengaging people with one another across political and cultural divides.

Here in Atlanta, the Trinity Forum sponsored a remarkable evening in February 2017. The panelists were a well-known conservative—David Brooks of the *New York Times*—and a dedicated liberal—former Morehouse College president and current Emory University professor Robert Franklin. In front of an audience of more than four-hundred people that cut across age, ethnic backgrounds, and political persuasions, the two gentlemen engaged in a heartfelt and humorous conversation about respect, constructive community engagement, and civility. (See this endnote for a link to the video.[120])

Afterwards, Trinity Forum convened multiple small-group discussions in order to bring fellow citizens from across Atlanta together to discuss substantive matters of mutual interest. I participated in these conversations and found them to be of great value. It was heartening to be in a room full of strangers gathered in a hospitable home to talk about serious matters without rancor and to search together for common values and perspectives.

Civility is of great importance for America going forward. I hope to address the topic at greater length another time. For now, suffice it to say that civil and constructive engagement with those who differ politically from us is generous.

WISEgenerosity Example of Social Generosity: The Civil Rights Movement

Social Generosity involves concern for relationships and community along with self-sacrifice in our personal actions to seek a greater good. We have a remarkable example of Social Generosity in relatively recent American history: the Civil Rights Movement of the 1950s and 1960s.

I am a born and raised Northeasterner living in the South. Having moved from Washington, DC, to Atlanta as pre-condition of our marriage, I later was informed by my wife, Courtenay, that I had graduated from "Yankee" to "reformed Northerner." I was pleased but then realized there was no room for further advancement. While I never will be considered Southern, twenty-five years later, I love my community and am happy to be living where we do.

Reflecting on my adopted home, I confess that I was largely ignorant of the full story of civil rights. It's an era of American history that was too recent to be covered in detail when I was in school. Aside from basic awareness of the time line and the key figures involved, I didn't know much about this period.

I confess that the more I learn, the harder it is to reconcile my country and its noble ideals with the ugly reality of oppression, hatred, and systemic violence endured by African Americans. The scars of this history are not confined to the South, and they still are visible in mistrust and misunderstanding among Blacks and whites alike. The ideas behind WISEgenerosity helped me better appreciate the powerful force of Social Generosity at work in the lives of Dr. Martin Luther King Jr. and other civil rights leaders.

Dr. King is a remarkable figure in American and world history. In the era of deeply rooted Jim Crow segregation, he combined a patriotic vision of America—as the place it was meant to be and not the place it was—with a determination grounded in faith that the prize of freedom was worth any sacrifice. His positive commitment to nonviolent change navigated between the entrenched forces of resistance to Black equality and the simmering frustration of a population that had been denied dignity and opportunity for generations.

The 1950s and 1960s were decades of great contrasts. Norman Vincent Peale was a Presbyterian minister in New York living during this time who reflected a "can-do" American spirit that was widespread in the post–World War II era. His book *The Power of Positive Thinking* (1952) described one tone of the era. It was a time of prosperity and optimism for many, and the book sold millions of copies.[121] Still, all was not well. Communism was on the rise worldwide, causing great insecurity and growing division about how to respond to it. Closer to home, the bitter legacy of institutionalized racism left over from

America's "original sin" of slavery and the upheaval of the Civil War threatened to boil over into widespread social strife.

Against the backdrop of these events, Dr. King provided a moral compass. On November 17, 1957, he delivered a sermon to the Dexter Avenue Baptist Church in Montgomery, Alabama, where he was the pastor. Rosa Parks had been arrested in the same city two years earlier for refusing to leave the "Whites Only" section of a public bus. Alabama overall was firmly segregationist and home to an active Ku Klux Klan and other groups willing to use fierce intimidation and gruesome violence to support Jim Crow practices.

Dr. King's sermon topic was "Loving Your Enemies," based on Jesus's admonition to his disciples to do so in the famous Sermon on the Mount from the Gospel of Matthew.[122] Dr. King's sermon is incredible, and I implore you to read and absorb it in full or, even better, to listen to the recording of it, which posterity graciously provided for us.[123]

Regarding the personal aspect of the great civil rights struggle, which was gaining momentum, Dr. King said:

> Another way that you love your enemy is this: When the opportunity presents itself for you to defeat your enemy, that is the time which you must not do it. There will come a time, in many instances, when the person who hates you most, the person who has misused you most, the person who has gossiped about you most, the person who has spread false rumors about you most, there will come a time when you will have an opportunity to defeat that person. It might be in terms of a recommendation for a job; it might be in terms of helping that person to make some move in life. That's the time you must do it. That is the meaning of love. In the final analysis, love is not this sentimental something that we talk about. It's not merely an emotional something. Love is creative, understanding goodwill for all men. It is the refusal to defeat any individual. When you rise to the level of love, of its great beauty and power, you seek only to defeat evil systems. Individuals who happen to be caught up in that system, you love, but you seek to defeat the system.

Thankfully for America, teachings grounded in nonviolent change were the foundation of the Civil Rights Movement. It is sobering to imagine what might have happened if voices other than these had prevailed in the struggle for equality.

Police Dog and Protestor, Birmingham 1963 [Image from AP]

Fire Hose and Protestors, Birmingham 1963 [Image from AP]

After 1957, there were many civil rights challenges yet to come. One major milestone was a sequence of events that took place in Birmingham in 1963, where local authorities responded to peaceful protests with brutal violence. Images of

African Americans being assaulted by police dogs and fire hoses shocked the nation and helped lead to a growing realization that change was needed.

Again, Dr. King provided invaluable moral leadership. Having been jailed for an "illegal" protest, he responded to published criticism from a group of leading white clergyman in the city. Their "Call for Unity" criticized the Black protests against systemic discrimination in Birmingham facilities and stores as "unwise and untimely" and appealed to "law and order and common sense."[124] Outraged by their obtuseness and lack of willingness to recognize legitimate demands for justice, Dr. King penned a masterpiece, "Letter from Birmingham Jail." Again, I recommend strongly that you read it.[125]

The tone of the letter is wonderfully generous. Dr. King is writing from jail where he is being disrespected and mistreated. Nonetheless, his tone is cordial and diplomatic. The salutation is to "My Dear Fellow Clergymen." He answers their criticisms and concerns calmly at first, using logic and rhetoric. He marshals an impressive array of authorities that his audience should respect, including the apostle Paul, Thomas Aquinas, Socrates, Abraham Lincoln, and Thomas Jefferson. As the letter goes on, though, Dr. King's frustration bubbles to the surface, and he allows the righteous anger of Old Testament prophets to surface. His closing paragraph then elevates to the heavens:

> I hope that this letter finds you strong in the faith. I also hope that circumstances will soon make it possible for me to meet each of you, not as an integrationist or a civil-rights leader but as a fellow clergyman and a Christian brother. Let us all hope that the dark clouds of racial prejudice will soon pass away and the deep fog of misunderstanding will be lifted from our fear-drenched communities, and in some not too distant tomorrow the radiant stars of love and brotherhood will shine over our great nation with all their scintillating beauty.

It is hard to imagine a more gracious or powerful appeal. In the months after it was written, mainstream media outlets throughout the country drew attention to and shared the words of Dr. King's letter. Millions of people had an opportunity to learn the morality of peaceful civil disobedience from this "son, grandson, and great-grandson of preachers."

Dr. King and his colleagues braved great danger and made many personal sacrifices in service to the cause of civil rights. There were numerous death threats and assassination attempts over the years along with grim jokes in their meetings about who would preach at each other's funerals.[126]

Dr. King was assassinated in Memphis, Tennessee, on April 4, 1968. The night before he was killed, his last speech ended prophetically:

> Like anybody, I would like to live a long life. Longevity has its place. But I'm not concerned about that now. I just want to do God's will. And He's allowed me to go up to the mountain. And I've looked over. And I've seen the Promised Land. I may not get there with you. But I want you to know tonight, that we, as a people, will get to the promised land! And so I'm happy, tonight. I'm not worried about anything. I'm not fearing any man. Mine eyes have seen the glory of the coming of the Lord.[127]

Recognizing the value and dignity of our fellow citizens is generous. Fighting injustice with determined character and grace is generous. While the legacy of segregation continues to exact a heavy cost in our own day, the Civil Rights Movement provides a history of positive change and Social Generosity for which we all can be thankful and from which we all can draw inspiration.

CHAPTER 9

Emotional Generosity

THE THREE PRIOR TYPES OF GENEROSITY WE'VE TALKED ABOUT—Possessional Generosity, Personal Generosity, and Social Generosity—are familiar. Giving money, sharing time and talent, and engaging with others in our communities are familiar aspects of life. They likely are what you always have considered to be "generous."

Our next two generosity types are more personal. Emotional Generosity and Relational Generosity are at the core of every positive connection we have. They are the means by which we are enriched or diminished in the most intimate and important ways. They are the factors that determine whether we are going to be elevated or denigrated by those around us. They also are the means by which we provide support for or inflict pain upon others. In sum, they are essential elements of our lives.

Defining Emotions: The Human Condition

There is an age-old distinction between our "heads" and our "hearts"— between reason and emotion. Each of us is wired differently in this way. Some are more naturally analytic and logical, while others are more naturally intuitive and emotional. In this age of science and technology, our society has the tendency to elevate reason. We want to be in control, and our brains seem easier to manage than our feelings.

These are not unique observations. Here are two famous writers on the subject:

"Life is a comedy to those who think, a tragedy to those who feel."[128]

—Jean Racine

"One ought to hold on to one's heart; for if one lets it go, one soon loses control of the head too."

—Friedrich Nietzsche

Part of the world is desperate for the relative clarity of logic and reason. Entire academic disciplines attempt to reduce unpredictable human behavior to neat formulas and equations. (Yes, I'm talking to you, Economics.)

It is tempting to suppress the messy and seek the clean. But is that real or authentic or true? Isn't our human experience immersed in emotion? There are millions of poems and songs about love; there are very few about science. In the words of two more voices from the past:

"But feelings can't be ignored, no matter how unjust or ungrateful they seem."

—Anne Frank, *The Diary of a Young Girl*

"My bounty is as boundless as the sea, my love as deep; the more I give to thee the more I have, for both are infinite."

—Juliet, *Romeo and Juliet*, Act II, Scene 2

British sage G. K. Chesterton made a marvelous observation along these lines. He wrote:

The real trouble with this world of ours is not that it is an unreasonable world, nor even that it is a reasonable one. The commonest kind of trouble is that it is nearly reasonable, but not quite. Life is not an illogicality; yet it is a trap for logicians. It looks just a little more mathematical and regular than it is; its exactitude is obvious, but its inexactitude is hidden; its wildness lies in wait.

I give one coarse instance of what I mean. Suppose some mathematical creature from the moon were to reckon up the human body; he would at once see that the essential thing about it was that it was duplicate. A man is two men, he on the right exactly resembling him on the left. Having noted that there was an arm on the right and one on the left, a leg on the right and one on the left, he might go further and still find on each side the same number of fingers, the same number of toes, twin eyes, twin ears, twin nostrils, and even twin lobes of the brain. At last he would take it as a law; and then, where he found a heart on one side, would deduce that there was another heart on the other. And just then, where he most felt he was right, he would be wrong.[129]

"Its wildness lies in wait..." That is one of my favorite observations. It is further interesting that the example chosen—the heart, which is the perceived seat of our emotions—is the irregularity in the body that would trap the logician.

"Wildness" is an apt word to describe our emotions. Racine and Nietzsche were wary of feelings because they are hard to control. Feelings can be great forces for good, or they can do terrible damage to those around us. Of all our attributes, emotions would seem to be an area where generosity is most needed.

Exploring Emotions

If we agree that we are emotional creatures, how do we better understand emotions and use them productively for ourselves and for the benefit of those around us? For understanding, let's turn to psychology. One well-established framework offers eight primary emotions: anticipation, surprise, joy, sadness, trust, disgust, fear, and anger.[130] We can understand any state of mind by evaluating and blending these core elements.

In turn, science teaches that emotions are hardwired into our physical being:

Emotions can be overpowering, but they are also the driving force of life.
It was long thought that emotion and thought were separate processes.
Brain science has begun to realise [sic] that the brain is not an organ of
thought, but that it is a feeling organ that thinks. A tiny almond shaped
structure deep in the brain, the Amygdala, is the first to respond to
an emotional event. It triggers a series of reactions within the brain's
emotional core and sends signals throughout the body that change body
posture, facial expression, heart-rate, breathing and awareness.[131]

Using these understandings and the idea of emotional interconnectivity,
I'd like to further categorize the eight primary emotions into two groups
of my own:

- **Righteous Emotions:**   Anger, Disgust, Fear, Sadness
- **Relating Emotions:**   Trust, Anticipation, Surprise, Joy

Righteous Emotions are more basic and defensive, while Relating
Emotions are more considerate and connective. Righteous Emotions are more
reflexive, while Relating Emotions are more thoughtful.

Righteous Emotions link to our sense of justice. They are produced when
we perceive that something has not worked out the way in which it should.
Righteous Emotions occur generally when something seems "wrong."

In contrast, Relating Emotions are tied to our sense of well-being. They
involve expectations and connections. They tend to be more personal. Relating
Emotions are oriented around things going "right."

Moreover:

- Righteous Emotions tend to be more reactive.
  - ▸ For these four (anger, disgust, fear, sadness), experience often
    produces feeling.
  - ▸ Emotion drives responsive action.
- Relating Emotions tend to be more proactive.
  - ▸ For these four (trust, anticipation, surprise, joy), feeling often is
    produced by experience.

▸ Action produces and drives emotion.

If I am angry or disgusted or afraid or upset, it is not in a vacuum. I am reacting to circumstances that have violated my expectations in some way. These feelings then prompt behavior. I can fight or flee or stare or sob, depending on how I react.

In contrast, if I am trusting or expectant or positively surprised or joyful, my behavior affects my circumstances. Confidence inspires more confidence. Expecting good results positively changes behavior. Putting a positive spin on an unexpected event orients us toward better potential outcomes. Joy is infectious.

Let's look now at how generosity and our emotions intersect.

Generous Emotions

Our emotions are the "heart" of who we are as human beings. When positive, they can wonderfully enhance our lives. When negative, they can damage us and those around us.

We've established that generosity is not natural. It requires effort and overcomes entropic forces in the world that tend to lead toward negative rather than positive outcomes.

Likewise, when it comes to the eight primary emotions, there is a "natural" approach and a "generous" approach to each. The natural approach is more likely to skew negatively in terms of our own health and welfare and that of the people around us. In contrast, the generous approach more often helps build relationships and produces better outcomes for all involved.

RIGHTEOUS	Natural Approach	Generous Approach
Anger	Lash out / Attack Lose control / Seek revenge	Pause / Calm down Be gracious / Forgive
Disgust	Recoil / Judge Reject / Feel superior	Sympathize / Support Understand / Accept

RIGHTEOUS	Natural Approach	Generous Approach
Fear	Protect / Escape Worry / Mistrust	Hope / Believe Release control / Trust
Sadness	Withdraw into self / Isolate Self-pity / Lose hope	Reach out for solace / Connect Comfort others / Look forward
RELATING	Natural Approach	Generous Approach
Trust	Be skeptical / "Trust, but verify"	Rely on promises
Anticipation	Guard against disappointment	Be open to success
Surprise	Negative reflex / "Other shoe to drop"	Positive reflex / View as opportunity
Joy	See as fleeting / Take it for granted	Expect it to return / Share it

I am not suggesting that natural emotions necessarily are wrong. We have emotions for a reason, and our natural responses in many cases stem from reflexes designed to protect us. This is particularly true for the Righteous Emotions. It is right to be angry at injustice. It is right to be disgusted by evil. It is right to be afraid of genuine danger. It is right to be sad when facing a serious loss. Righteous Emotions motivate actions based on our own needs and the needs of others.

If natural emotions are good, however, their usefulness tends to be short-lived. They can be corrosive if allowed to linger. A sensible fear that propels us out of a situation becomes paralyzing if it lingers too long. Prudent caution about trusting a new person becomes damaging if we never allow for confidence in anyone.

Similarly, Righteous Emotions can be dangerous if left unchecked. This is true particularly when we are motivated by selfish desires. If we are feeling a strong negative emotion, it is wise to ask ourselves why. Is there a larger reason, or are we just upset about not getting our way?

Relational Generosity is built on considering others along with ourselves. Generous emotions are others-focused and tend to prevent relational damage while providing support for others facing difficulties. Forgiveness, sympathy, hope, and comfort are prized and require effort to deliver.

The natural reaction to the Relating Emotions tends to dilute them. Society teaches us to be skeptical and cynical. We don't want to be exposed. It can seem easier to shield ourselves from trust, anticipation, surprise, and joy than to face potential disappointment. The generous expression of the Relating Emotions involves risk and hope.

Sometimes, Emotional Generosity means not acting on our negative feelings toward others. If someone cuts you off in traffic, do you express anger and risk escalating the situation, or do you let it go? Most of the time, you are better off letting it go. Doing so requires a sacrifice. You are giving up your righteous indignation at the other person's bad behavior, and you don't get to have the satisfaction of cussing them out (even if just to yourself). On the other hand, who benefits from your anger? No one. The other driver probably doesn't know or care that you are upset. Meanwhile, you waste precious time and energy, and your anger has no lasting benefits.

Other times, Emotional Generosity means acting positively toward others with no certain reward. There is sacrifice here as well. If you trust someone, you are making yourself vulnerable by opening up to them. They may prove to be unworthy of your trust. If you share a favorite possession with a friend and they ruin it, your trust was violated and you've paid a price beyond just the cost of the item and the inability to use it again. Your willingness to positively express a Relating Emotion leads not to happiness for you but instead to an unwelcome Righteous Emotion like anger or sadness.

Here are some additional observations:

- Righteous Emotions are about justice, and we all want justice—unless we are the offender.

- Relating Emotions are about love, and we all want love—unless it seems too costly to provide or receive.
- Accessibility and vulnerability are essential: we risk exposing ourselves to pain by being emotionally generous, but the opposite is to live walled off and isolated from others.
- It takes self-awareness to tell the difference between natural and generous emotions and to express ourselves accordingly.
- It takes self-discipline to harness our emotions productively and to use them generously.

WISEgenerosity Example of Emotional Generosity: An Emotional First Responder

When defining a behavior or attribute, looking to powerful examples helps us to understand the trait. A fascinating group of generous people are who we can call "emotional first responders." These are counselors and chaplains and others who are on the front lines of dealing with the most difficult experiences in life.

Like other first responders, emotional heroes engage in situations that others run away from. Most people try to avoid pain and suffering. I confess that I am a conflict-avoider by nature. I naturally am uncomfortable around situations that are difficult and try to avoid them when possible. For emotional first responders, however, seeing someone else's life on fire causes them to run into the flames rather than away from them.

Jessica Ethridge Chicken is an emotional first responder. I have known Jessica and her family for years. She is soft-spoken, engaging, and kind. She grew up in a household actively focused on community service, and from an early age, she spent time around people facing serious life challenges related to poverty and other difficult circumstances.

When she and I spoke about emotional generosity in 2017, Jessica was newly married, building a life and a career. Motivated to have a vocation in which she could help others, she went to graduate school at Princeton Theological Seminary, where she studied to be a chaplain supporting people in crisis.

Jessica's externship was at a state-run psychiatric hospital in New Jersey. The focus in this hospital is on long-term care, and patients often reside there for decades. Working at the hospital, Jessica witnessed particular kinds of grief related to loss of freedom, opportunity, family, and home. Intending to work there for one year, she requested to stay for two. As she put it, she discovered that "there is a suffering so deep all you can be is there to bear witness to it."[132] Her goal in life became reminding people that they are not alone but are cared for and valued as they are.

Returning home after the externship, Jessica started a residency at Children's Healthcare of Atlanta. There, she came into contact with a very different kind of intense grief: parents trying to cope with the illness or loss of a child. As a parent myself, such situations are the literal stuff of nightmares.

At Children's, Jessica discovered her passion for serving people in medical crises. She came into contact daily with families from all different backgrounds, circumstances, and spiritual traditions. In each case, she vowed to find a way to journey alongside the family and to support them.

During this time, a beloved cousin of Jessica's was stricken with a brain tumor and died. It was a horrible experience for Jessica and her family. While she and her other cousins took time off of work and school to sit around the clock with the patient and each other, she felt numb by the end. Her professional skills offered no immunity from the suffering. In fact, Jessica confesses that she would have been a bad counselee herself at that time.

The day after her cousin died, Jessica was on duty at the children's hospital, sitting with a family facing the awful decision of whether or not to withdraw life support for their child with cancer. Jessica recalled this situation with the self-awareness that there was "nothing I can do or say in that moment to take away the pain."

Jessica now works at a critical and palliative care center in Athens, Georgia, where the diagnoses are substantially life-altering or terminal, and the patients and families are coping with a whirlwind of practical and emotional challenges. Jessica appreciates that she has a gift for seeing grace in moments of pain. She uses that gift to offer support and encouragement to people who are in desperate need of it. "No one should have to take such a journey alone," she says.

Jessica is thoughtful and considerate. Her experiences, along with her schooling in thanatology (the study of grief and death), have provided her with great emotional wisdom. Like most generous people, she also is modest and not entirely comfortable talking about herself. She views it as a privilege to connect with people in their most intimate and vulnerable moments, saying at one point, "Maybe it's not me that's being generous. Maybe it's them for letting me into these sacred spaces."

When I asked Jessica how people respond to her offers of support, she told me that "relief" is their most common reaction. They welcome someone who is willing to listen, to distract them by playing cards, or to pray with them. According to Jessica, the key is "meeting people where they are." She doesn't deliver the bad news, but she does hold hands with those who receive it. She does patients' nails to help them feel attractive and attended to. She cries quietly while others weep and helps to validate their emotions.

At the same time, she certainly isn't there to "solve" anything. Some people will tell her to "get out" if they are not ready or willing to have anyone else in their space at that point of crisis. Even then, the key is to not abandon anyone. Jessica lets them know that she will be down the hall, and then she waits. Ninety percent of the time, they will come to her later. She then will do what they ask, from practical actions like calling a funeral home to just sitting quietly with them.

Jessica defines herself as "emotionally intuitive." Not all of us have her ability, but we can all work to become more emotionally intuitive. Emotional Generosity is comprised of what I call the three C's, which are useful tools that help us to give emotionally to others: confidence, calibration, and care. Here's a deeper explanation of the three C's, using Jessica's work and experiences as an example.

- **Confidence**—feeling comfortable with emotions and helping others do the same
    - ‣ Being able to know and accept your own and others' feelings.

- Recognizing that emotions are natural and acceptable.
    - Jessica is critical of social norms that teach us to suppress emotions.
    - Her goal is to create a "safe space" where people can feel whatever they feel, particularly the Righteous Emotions like fear, sadness, and anger that arise during the difficult times she witnesses routinely.
- **Calibration**—reacting well to signals and cues from others
    - This includes being able to adjust our emotions appropriately to match others' emotions.
    - It causes tension to respond to a mild emotion with a dramatic one, and it causes frustration to respond to a dramatic emotion with a mild one.
        - Jessica says that she often needs to take a deep breath and gather herself in order to respond in the best way possible to whatever the situation dictates.
- **Care**—being committed to the people around us
    - Jessica is present for her patients and their families in their time of distress.
    - She offers support in whatever way she is able to.
        - She believes that she is there to deliver comfort and peace, whether the people she serves are able to experience those feelings at that moment or not.
        - Jessica intensely lives the three highest motivations for giving: empathy, gratitude, and love.

Jessica observed that self-awareness, commitment, and practice have made her better and better at Emotional Generosity. When asked how she would guide others to be more emotionally generous, she gave some excellent advice:

1. Have emotional outlets—everyone needs guidance and support.
    a. We need to better understand ourselves and our own emotions.

    b. Ideally, we all should have a counselor, mentor, or friend with whom we safely share concerns.

    c. Correspondingly, it is generous to be such a resource for others.

2. Be vulnerable—be willing to share fears, anxieties, hopes, and insecurities.

    a. Communication is a key to Emotional Generosity.

    b. When facing conflict, be able to identify your own drivers: "I'm upset and anxious right now because I'm feeling insecure about…"

3. Be sensitive and engaged—ask questions to overcome suppressed emotions.

    a. Observe signals: "I feel that you are upset, is that right?"

    b. Validate emotions: "I understand."

    c. Then, kindly explore: "Why are you feeling that way?"

Jessica is a true emotional first responder. She also provides a marvelous window on how we can all cultivate Emotional Generosity in our own lives.[133]

Lessons from Emotional Generosity

Jessica helped me to see two important things about Emotional Generosity.

First, like all other forms of generosity, it is not about us. Being focused on others and not herself is what enables Jessica to serve so effectively.

Second, the closer we are to the people involved, the harder it is to be emotionally generous. In spite of her training and experience, Jessica was not better equipped to handle her cousin dying prematurely than anyone else in her family. Likewise, she observed that it is easier to be an emotional hero for strangers at work than it is for our families and friends at home. In other words, there is a paradox of distance when it comes to our emotions. It is easier in many ways to be engaged with emotions that are far away than ones that are close.

Everyone in my family teases me for crying easily. I tear up for little or no reason at all: watching a TV show, seeing a dramatic sporting event, witnessing a moving testimonial at a charitable fundraiser, or sitting in an audience when someone is being memorialized or celebrated. In fact, my children make a game out of looking over whenever anything sentimental comes up to see, "Is Daddy crying?" I can appreciate that this behavior seems silly, because many of these are things to which I am not strongly attached. My expressed emotions are out of proportion with the situations involved.

Perhaps my own heartstrings are taut. I sometimes wonder if that is why I avoid conflict. A close friend suggested wisely that I "value harmony" in life.[134] Sometimes, being emotionally connected to things I care deeply about is more intense than I can handle.

One step toward becoming emotionally generous is to focus on kindness, but it's not always easy to know what to do. How should we offer emotional support to people in need? What is the best way to approach a loved one in pain? How do we say or do the right things?

Ron Greer is a wise friend, a spiritual counselor, and the author of several excellent books connected to Emotional Generosity, including *The Path of Compassion: Living with Heart, Soul, and Mind.* In this book, he gives guidance on how best to approach someone suffering heartache:[135]

- If you don't know them well, send them a card.
- If you know them moderately well, take them anything from your favorite bakery.
- If you know them well, stop by to see them and give them a hug.
- If you know them really well, pull up a chair, ask them how they are doing, and plan to stay awhile.

In ways large and small, Emotional Generosity is an important foundation for living a connected, positive life. This realization is a good segue into exploring our highest level of generosity: Relational Generosity.

CHAPTER 10

Relational Generosity

WE ARE RELATIONAL CREATURES. Our human existence revolves around other people: our families, friends, colleagues, neighbors, and others in our world. Relationships are the foundation of life. We spend most of our time engaged in them, and most of the lasting happiness or suffering we experience comes about because of them.

The best relationships are a source of love, encouragement, and resilience. The worst relationships are disturbing, disabling, and destructive.

A friend of mine had a brother-in-law who was a juvenile corrections officer. For years, this man counted down the days to retirement due to the difficulty of his work, including multiple instances of being violently assaulted. Starting out as a counselor with the noble aim of rehabilitating and restoring young men convicted of crimes, he soon discovered that nearly all of the inmates had been physically or sexually abused early in life by people close to them. When others who were supposed to have nurtured and cared for them did the opposite, the result was brokenness and brutality.

Connecting back to the prior chapter on Emotional Generosity, Dr. Guy Winch is a licensed psychologist and author. In a post for *Psychology Today*, he describes "5 Ways Emotional Pain is Worse Than Physical Pain."[136]

Dr. Winch concludes that emotional pain is much more damaging to self-esteem and long-term mental health than physical pain. "Physical pain has to be quite extreme to affect our personalities and damage our mental health...but even single episodes of emotional pain can damage our emotional health. For example...a single painful rejection can lead to years of avoidance and loneliness, bullying in middle school can make us shy and introverted as adults, and a critical boss can damage our self-esteem for years to come."[137]

In contrast, each of us has the capacity through Relational Generosity to build personal connections that are positive and meaningful, especially with the people we are closest to. The closer we are, the more meaningful the impact. That said, and echoing our earlier emotional paradox of distance, the closer we are to someone, the more difficult it can be to behave generously when our own self-interest is at stake.

Exploring Relationships

Thousands of pop songs steer us toward a common conclusion: love is our relational aspiration. *Billboard Magazine* publishes a list of "Top 50 Love Songs of All Time."[138] Here are a few representative selections:

- From the 1960s: "I Can't Stop Loving You" by Ray Charles
- From the 1970s: "Love Will Keep Us Together" by Captain & Tennille
- From the 1980s: "Endless Love" by Diana Ross and Lionel Richie
- From the 1990s: "I Will Always Love You" by Whitney Houston
- From the 2000s: "Crazy in Love" by Beyoncé featuring Jay-Z
- From the 2010s: "We Found Love" by Rihanna featuring Calvin Harris

Of course, these are just the tip of the iceberg. Any music library is filled with songs about love. Love also dominates many bookshelves and movie collections. In chapter 11 we will identify love as the highest and best motivation for generosity. We all seek love.

One of the foundational books I've read on relationships is *The Four Loves* by British author C. S. Lewis.[139] Lewis is famous for his Christian commentaries like *Mere Christianity* and *The Screwtape Letters* and for his fables like the Chronicles of Narnia series. At Oxford University, he was a scholar whose academic work focused on understanding love in European literature dating back to Medieval times.[140]

Lewis posits that there are two types of love: "Need-love" and "Gift-love."

Need-love is inwardly focused. We *need* care, attention, and love from others. Need-love is "natural." It fills a void and reflects scarcity and incompleteness in our lives. A frightened child fleeing into a parent's arms is an example of this. Need-love risks becoming selfish if it crowds out concern for others. At its best, it is comforting. At its worst, it is a force driving behavior that is damaging to others for our own sake.

Gift-love is outwardly focused. We *give* care, attention, and love to others. Gift-love is "generous." It involves abundance, sharing, caring, and sacrifice. The best and most nurturing impulses of parents for their children are Gift-love. This type of love tends to be positive in its expression. At best, it is pure and selfless.

Both Need-love and Gift-love are present in most relationships. We need others and, in turn, are needed by them. The ways in which we manage these sometimes competing forces is the key to how each relationship develops.

Lewis offers four expressions of relational love.

Affection is "warm comfortableness...satisfaction in being together."[141] It is "the humblest ... of loves ... in which our experience seems to differ least from that of the animals."[142] Examples include affection for grandparents and grandchildren, pets, old friends, and habitual places. Affection prizes comfort and familiarity and can mix with the other loves. Threats to affection include change, selfishness, and jealousy. According to Lewis, "Affection is responsible for nine-tenths of whatever solid and durable happiness there is in our natural lives."[143]

Friendship is "pleasure in cooperation . . . mutual love and understanding."[144] It also is "the least *natural* of loves; the least instinctive, organic, biological or necessary.... [W]e can live and breed without friendship."[145] Yet, good friendships are satisfying and durable. Friendship begins as companionship and grows when two or more people find passions they have in common. We can go years without seeing a dear friend, only to pick up

immediately where we left off when we see them again. Once such bonds
of friendship have been built, they tend to last. Midway through life, I find
myself treasuring more than ever relationships built earlier and welcoming
every opportunity I have to spend time with these people who have been a
part of my life for such a long time.[146]

Romance—or "Eros"—is "that state which we call 'being in love.'"[147] This
includes both sentimental and sexual love. Romance usually begins as a "delightful
pre-occupation with the beloved."[148] According to Lewis, many people mistake the
fundamental nature of romantic love. "Eros does not aim at happiness."[149] We would
rather be unhappy with our lover than seek happiness elsewhere. Passion is the sign
of romantic love. At its best, it is heavenly. At its worst, it is demonic. Over time, the
"businesslike intimacy of married life" guards against misguided passion. So does "the
Affection in which Eros is almost invariably clothed."[150] A healthy romantic relationship involves elements of all four loves.

Sacrifice ("Charity" in Lewis's version) "desires what is simply best for the
beloved."[151] The word choice is connected to the apostle Paul's famous observation from the New Testament (often used at weddings): "And now abideth faith,
hope, charity, these three; but the greatest of these is charity."[152] Modern trans-
lations change "charity" to "love." The root word in both cases is Greek: *agape*.
The Greeks had several different words for love, and this one essentially was
the same as the Gift-love to which we already referred. Based on his Christian
faith, Lewis equated this type of love with God. "In God there is no hunger that
needs to be fulfilled, only plenteousness that desires to give."[153] Sacrifice does
not replace the other loves; they ideally are combined with it in order to become
more powerful and complete.

When it comes to love, there is a danger in loving too much, but there
is more danger in loving too little. Natural emotions like anger, disgust, fear,
and sadness can interfere with our willingness and ability to love. We must be
willing to take risks in order to have relationships. Love can lead to bliss, but
it also can lead to stress, disappointment, and loss. According to Lewis, "To
love at all is to be vulnerable. Love anything, and your heart will certainly be
wrung and possibly be broken.... The alternative to tragedy, or at least to the

risk of tragedy, is damnation. The only place outside of Heaven where you can be perfectly safe from all the dangers and perturbations of love is Hell."[154]

Relational Interactions

Relationships take time and effort. We can't truly know anyone without sharing experiences with them. The sum of those accumulated experiences and our mutual reactions to them form each relationship.

If we love or even "like" someone, there is ongoing interaction with them. We might imagine that each of us has a reservoir of feelings regarding that other person. These may be negative as well as positive. For a nemesis, the reservoir is deep with bad experiences or expectations, while the reservoir for a friend or loved one generally is full of good ones.

This is not a unique observation. In fact, there is a similar idea even in the cut-and-dried world of accounting. "Goodwill" is a concept used to reflect the fact that the value of a company includes intangible as well as tangible assets.[155] Along with the value of its patents and facilities and receivables, analysts consider its reputation, brand name, customer and employee loyalty, and other nonfinancial factors when calculating its value. This makes sense—people are more likely to do business with a company they think well of than one they do not.

In a similar way, our behavior toward each other affects our relationships action by action. When we are kind and supportive, we nurture our connections. When we are selfish or stupid, we weaken them.

Relational Generosity = Rx for the Unlovable in Us

It is vital that we practice generosity in our relationships. Doing so is greatly to our benefit and the benefit of those around us. Treating others well makes it more likely that they will act well. Being kind to others increases the likelihood that others will be kind to us. The accumulated impact of our generosity or lack thereof will affect the quality of our relationships now and in the future.

More, stronger, and healthier relationships make for a better life. This involves us giving to others as well as needing. It also involves them giving to us.

If we are honest, generosity in relationships is not only something we do for others, it is something they do for us as well. Returning to C. S. Lewis:

> There is something in each of us that cannot be naturally loved. It is no one's fault if they do not so love it. Only the lovable can be naturally loved. You might as well ask people to like the taste of rotten bread or the sound of a mechanical drill. We can be forgiven, and pitied, and loved in spite of it, with Charity; no other way. All who have good parents, wives, husbands, or children, may be sure that at some times—and perhaps at all times in respect of some one particular trait or habit—they are receiving Charity.[156]

Pride is my own biggest barrier to generous relationships. One of the main takeaways I've had from studying giving is the realization of how my own self-centeredness is the root of nearly all of my struggles with other people and with myself. The easiest first step toward overcoming pride is practicing generosity toward other people.

Foundation of Relational Generosity: Seeking the Best in Others

When I began to explore this topic, I found some fascinating research about relationships. Several studies in particular looked at behavior that supported strong marriages. An intimate and successful lifetime partnership navigating through inevitable ups and downs is a good place to start in evaluating what makes relationships work. How do people committed to a life together overcome all the inevitable challenges involved?

Here was one primary conclusion:

"Find the most generous explanation for each other's behavior and believe it."[157]

Interestingly, this quote came not in a "how-to" guide for couples but in a book about business leadership. The author viewed the point as so important that he used it as an example of how "One Controlling Insight" can be transformational to relationships and success. The book by Marcus Buckingham is called *The One Thing You Need to Know*, and the rule is to be as generous to people as you possibly can.

Buckingham points out that, when we are in love with someone, we start out with "positive illusions." In successful relationships, "these positive illusions weave their strength into the fabric of the relationship, until they actually become the relationship."[158] Seeing the best in each other is a key to sustaining love.

In contrast, "knowing" the other person—who they really are, good and bad—neither helps nor harms the relationship. It is not awareness but instead generous behavior that drives success.

The Power of Kindness in Relationships

Kindness may be the most direct and powerful tool of generosity in relationships. In chapter 4, we learned about how author Shaunti Feldhahn describes kindness as a "superpower."[159] More specifically, she writes: "Why does such a simple tool, *being kind*, bring such dramatic results to restore, build, or improve any relationship we care about? Because it improves how we feel about another person, and it ultimately makes us *want* to be kind."[160]

Feldhahn connects kindness with generosity in relationships:

A crucial part of kindness involves putting others first and focusing on them—not on yourself—in acts of generosity Whether we are being generous to someone with whom we have a difficult relationship, a person we are close to, an arm's-length colleague at work, or a stranger at the grocery store, simple acts of generosity matter.[161]

As we are seeing repeatedly, generous behavior is not only beneficial for receivers but for givers as well. Addressing the related question of what helps us to thrive in life:

> [A]bove all that is one greater factor: *whether we thrive depends far more on how we choose to treat others than on how we ourselves are treated*. In fact, when handled well, that one factor often leads to those other things that light us up. When handled poorly, it often leads to misery.
>
>   The path to our happy place starts with one choice: whether or not to be kind. Especially when we really don't want to be.[162]

Feldhahn believes that kindness has three components: thought, word, and action. Her challenge for us is to direct specific, dedicated kindness toward another person for thirty days. Importantly, the other person should not know that they are receiving the benefit of our kindness. This is about how *we* behave, not how *they* behave. Here are the three corresponding steps:[163]

1. **Nix the Negatives:** Say and—as much as possible—think nothing negative about the person, either to them or about them.
2. **Practice Praise:** Every day, find one positive thing about them that you can sincerely praise or affirm.
3. **Carry Out Kindness:** Every day, do a small act of kindness or generosity for your person.

That's it. It seems so easy, but such a simple effort can have dramatic effects. Feldhahn's work is based on analyzing thousands of people who actually put her principles into action. What she discovered is that 74 percent of people believed that the object of their kindness improved as an individual during the thirty days.[164] If we change for the better—even if the other person is unaware— they likely will change for the better as well. More impressively, 89 percent of people who committed to practicing focused kindness toward a specific person in their life saw the relationship improve over one month.[165] The benefits were reciprocal and significant. Most impressive of all, 95 percent of the participants became more aware of how their behavior affected their person—good or bad.[166] This awareness in turn created the opportunity for long-term positive growth in themselves and in the relationship.

Feldhahn believes that kindness can change the world one relationship at a time. I agree. If we are looking for opportunities to serve, there may be no easier or more accessible place to begin. And the effects are large and lasting: "Thankfully, if you *do* repeat kindness, a new habit is easily built because the rewards are so great. Most people prefer a life marked by kindness. So build a habit. Then build a lifestyle."[167]

A "kindness lifestyle" involves loving others as we love ourselves. This is the generous life to which I hope we all aspire.

Believing Is Seeing in Relationships

The world teaches that "seeing is believing." In relationships, "believing is seeing." If we train ourselves to think of the people we love as lovable, they will seem lovable to us. Even more importantly, chances are they actually will be more lovable. Psychologists confirm that people tend to behave based on expectations. If we are seen as and expected to be good and faithful and loving, we are much more likely to actually behave that way.

Self-help guru Wayne Dyer provided a similar observation: "Change the way you look at things, and the things you look at change."[168] I see two meanings in this statement. First, you influence your perception—how you see what you see—with a generous or ungenerous attitude. Second, a more generous attitude also changes what you look at in the first place and makes you focus on the positive and not on the negative in people and in circumstances.

Generosity inspires reciprocity. In order to live and love to the fullest, we must employ Relational Generosity.

In relationships, it is vital to give others the benefit of the doubt. We should look for the good in the other person's behavior *even if we imagine it*. Employing *sympathy* and *empathy* reduces our natural self-centeredness. If someone is mean to us, then we should imagine the most benign reasons why. We should put ourselves in their shoes. We should not use their offense as an opportunity to retaliate (even if it would feel good in the moment to do so). *In sum, it is best to be relationally generous.*

This is not to say that we should be fools in suffering abuse at the hands of others. It just means that we always should "love the sinner" even if we "hate the sin." If we need to distance ourselves from someone, we should forgive them and try to understand their bad behavior in the most generous terms possible. The effort of will required to behave in this way—and it does take effort—helps to reduce resentment and reinforce kindness.

The only thing I remember from my Introduction to Psychology course in college is an otherwise small concept that has stuck in my mind for all these years: Fundamental Attribution Error.[169] This principle is a fancy way of saying what your grandmother may have taught you: "Don't judge a book by its cover." We all have the tendency to observe behavior and to generalize other people based on what we see, particularly when what we see is negative. For instance, we assume that a person who cuts in front of us while we are waiting in a long line must be selfish and mean-spirited.

Strikingly, we tend to do exactly the opposite where we ourselves are concerned. We readily find excuses for our own bad behavior. "Well, yes, I shouldn't have reacted with that outburst, but you should have heard what she said about... " Beyond being natural rationalizers, this happens in part because we attach context to our own mistakes and tend not to give the same benefit to others.

Rob Fletcher is one of my closest friends and is a coach and counselor for successful leaders. He teaches the same lesson a different way, noting that we hold ourselves accountable based on "intent" while we hold others accountable based on "impact."[170] Relational Generosity allows others at least the same latitude we give ourselves.

A powerful example of how this tendency affects people came from a panel discussion I heard in 2016 on "returning citizen reentry"—the many challenges that former prisoners have in reintegrating into society after their sentence has been served. One of the speakers was Frank Fernandez, who was then with the

Arthur M. Blank Foundation (and now is with the Community Foundation for Greater Atlanta). He made a point that hit home: "Imagine being judged and treated for life based on the worst thing you've ever done." That should be a sobering thought for all of us.

Relational Conclusion

Fred Rogers was known to a generation of children (including me) for his PBS TV show *Mister Rogers' Neighborhood*. He also was a Presbyterian minister who believed in teaching morality simply and directly. He reportedly carried a quote in his wallet that said, "Frankly, there isn't anyone you couldn't learn to love once you heard their story."[171] That is an excellent description of Relational Generosity.

In a similar vein, there is a wonderful expression of generosity from the Bible's book of Proverbs: "Some give freely, yet grow all the richer; others withhold what is due, and only suffer want. A generous person will be enriched, and one who gives water will get water."[172]

If we apply this teaching to relationships, what does it tell us? What impoverishes when we withhold it selfishly but enriches when we give it freely? Love.

Love is the goal of our relationships. Love builds on generosity. And Relational Generosity is based on a simple principle: find the best in the other person and believe it. That leads us back where we were earlier. The important question to ask in any situation and at any time is, "What does love require of me?" The answer is always *generosity*.

● ● ●

Living Generously: My Reflections

We've covered a lot of ground in section 1. Essentially, these pages have presented WISEgenerosity as an answer to two questions: "*Why* should we give?" and "*How* should we give?" In turn, these queries underlie the even more basic questions posed at the start of the book: "Why are we here?" and "What do we do about it?" To me, a generous approach to life allows us to address these existential considerations more quickly and completely than any other attitude we can have or actions we can undertake.

In my own life, generosity has become a calling and a focal point. It is a frame of reference to which I turn when considering decisions from the small ("Do I let this person who just cut in front of two dozen cars stuck in traffic merge ahead of me?") to the significant ("Does pursuing this project require major life changes?").

I confess that spending ten years on this journey has given me tunnel vision to some degree. You likely are familiar with the expression, "If you're a hammer, then everything is a nail." I confess that I've become a "generosity hammer"—I see opportunities for or the failed potential of generous behavior everywhere I look.

Overall, this generosity focus has been a blessing. Thinking more carefully and consistently about giving to those around me and to the world at large has helped to answer my why and has given me more happiness, enlightenment, and fulfillment. Specifically, a new perspective on my work life emerged based on WISEgenerosity. I feel called by what I now term the four A's: to be an *advisor*, to be an *advocate*, to be an *ambassador*, and to be an *author*. These elements have become part of my *how*.

In this vein, as an *advisor*, my wealth management practice now is focused even more on "Optimal Giving"—realizing the full potential of charity and philanthropy by working with donors, nonprofits, and other advisors to maximize the benefits of giving for everyone involved. This work extends out from my own clients to supporting other professionals as an *advocate* by sharing WISEgenerosity resources and the techniques behind them. The goal is to promote more meaningful and productive conversations about financial and asset giving as widely as possible. I likewise hope to join a chorus of voices offering positive and purposeful approaches to living and giving by being an *ambassador* who speaks to audiences of all types about this topic. Lastly, I hope to continue to write and to be an *author* of material that promotes giving as essential to a life well-lived. WISEgenerosity has had a similar impact in my faith life, in my personal relationships, and in my focus on my community service.

Of course, you have your own unique circumstances. How does an understanding of your purpose help to inform your decisions, both small and large? How does considering your opportunities for kindness, charity, and philanthropy as we've defined them steer you toward meaningful and effective engagement with others? How can your own possessions, personal abilities, social connections, emotional assets, and relationships benefit from the caring and considerate perspective that WISEgenerosity provides?

Now may be a good opportunity to pause and reflect on these questions. When you are ready, we are going to shift next toward exploring a new set of questions: What should we give? When should we give? And where should we give?

Giving Wisely— The Path to a Productive Life

What You Should Give: Drivers, Motivators, Personality, and Direction

The basic "what" of giving is our time, talent, and treasure. These resources are the stuff of how we engage generously with others.

Underlying these elements are the drivers that produce our giving, the motivations that promote our giving, and the personality elements that present our giving and relate it to the people around us. We also will consider how wisely focused generosity can overcome generosity resistance.

---→

CHAPTER 11

Generosity Drivers and Motivators

WE ARE DRIVEN BY IMPULSES AND INCENTIVES. What we do results from the underlying forces at work in our decisions and from the rewards and benefits we expect to receive from our actions. Accordingly, let's consider how our behavioral drivers and motivations relate to generosity.

Drivers of Giving: Heart, Head, and Habit

There are three underlying *drivers* or prompts for generosity: heart giving, head giving, and habit giving.

Heart giving is generosity aligned with sentimental connections and emotional decisions. We are drawn to a situation or a story and feel compelled to engage in some way. Americans·can be relied upon to give in response to a disaster or tragedy. Seeing others suffer makes us want to do something, and so we get out our wallets or serve personally however we can. In our W.I.S.E. model, heart giving is Inspired.

Head giving is generosity aligned with intellectual interests and analytical decisions. If we want to have a lasting impact on a situation, we will consider carefully how best to do so. We will engage with experts, research different options, and evaluate the best partners and people who will help us get the work done. In the W.I.S.E. model, head giving is Well-grounded.

Habit giving *is sustained and transformative generosity combining head and heart.* For generosity to realize its full potential, it must have both emotional and intellectual foundations.

WISEgenerosity is based on more than just a passing emotional whim. It also has more depth and richness than a sterile flowchart. Ultimately, habit produces sustainable giving and is the proper goal for relationships between donors and the nonprofits they support.

All that said, we can summarize:

- Heart-driven generosity determines *whether* you will give.
- Head-driven generosity determines *how much* you will give.
- Habit-driven generosity determines whether you will *keep* giving.

Which of these drivers is strongest in your life? Which might you need to develop further? Considering these answers will help you better understand what type of giving will be most productive for you and those around you. The same factors also help illuminate your motivations for giving.

The Four C's of Generous Motivation: Compulsion, Connection, Conviction, Compassion

Why do we give? What causes us to push back against selfish impulses and instead to turn our focus outward? Where does the impulse come from to look for ways to make a positive impact on others' lives rather than caring only about our own?

Different people will be motivated by different factors in being generous.[173] As a student of generosity, I've observed that there are four categories of reasons why people give: *compulsion, connection, conviction,* and *compassion.* I list these in order of least altruistic to most: the more altruistic the gift, the more likely it is to be effective and meaningful for both the giver and the receiver. Of course, there may be (and often is) more than one motivation for making a gift, but I believe we can find the root of our impulse to give in at least one of these four reasons.

Let's run through these Four C's of Generous Motivation in detail. The type of charitable or philanthropic generosity used in these examples is a common one: a monetary gift to a nonprofit or civic organization. Similar factors apply to other examples of giving in our lives. There is a lot to say here, so I'll try to keep it brief by breaking everything down into bullet points.

Motivation #1: Compulsion
- Compulsion can be expressed through *Law*.
  - Legal-based giving redirects assets otherwise obligated to a government or other authority.
  - Fulfillment is control-directed—we may make the gift because we like giving better than paying taxes (the alternate destination for our mandatory social resources).
    - There are only five things we can do with money: save it, share it with loved ones, spend it, give it away, or use it to pay taxes.
    - Through the tax system, the government effectively designates portions of our money for society—we can describe this as "Community Capital."
    - We are obliged to give up possession of this money, but we are often able to decide between taxes and nonprofit giving.
- Compulsion can be expressed through *Peer Pressure*.
  - Peer-motivated giving happens when someone asks us for help. Often, it is harder to say no than to give something.
  - Fulfillment is socially directed—we give because of a personal connection.
    - This kind of giving is a favor, and we do it because someone asks us to.
    - We then are likely to ask for a similar favor in return.
    - Such *quid pro quo* giving is common, especially within social circles.
- Compulsion can be expressed through *Ego*.

- ► Ego-driven giving is a means to achieve status, recognition, and respect.
- ► Fulfillment is self-directed—we want to be affiliated with and celebrated for our support.
  - o Names of large donors are on and in every university building and nonprofit hospital campus.
  - o Sometimes, what could be seen as ego is more an interest in stimulating others to give (see "Example" under the category for Motivation #3: Conviction).
  - o There also can be negative ego—plenty of giving is done anonymously.

Motivation #2: Connection

- • Connection can be expressed through **Obligation**.
  - ► Obligatory giving derives from responsibility based on an ethical or social code.
  - ► Fulfillment is morally directed—adhering to certain standards can require us to be generous.
    - o The major world religions all support giving as a core value.
    - o Other moral traditions support giving as well.
    - o In this framework, we give because "it is the right thing to do."
- • Connection can be expressed through **Investment**.
  - ► Investment-focused givers seek a substantial return on their giving.
  - ► Resources applied to a problem or opportunity will help achieve a desired goal.
  - ► Fulfillment is practically directed—the motivation for this giving are "bottom-line" oriented.
    - o In this sense, philanthropy becomes like other investments.
    - o There is an expectation of certain results.
    - o There will be some form of quantification to measure results.

- Connection can be expressed through *Admiration*.
  - ▸ Giving due to admiration results when the leaders of and/or participants in a cause are worthy and compelling.
  - ▸ Fulfillment is respectfully directed—we want to support compelling people accomplishing noble goals.
    - ○ Our connection to the cause may be less important than our belief in the leaders.
    - ○ We have confidence in good outcomes based on the people involved.
    - ○ We like to be associated with others who are worthy and successful.

Motivation #3: Conviction

- Conviction can be expressed through *Example*.
  - ▸ Giving done by example wants to demonstrate "good behavior" for others.
  - ▸ Fulfillment is family- or community-directed—we provide a model for teaching others.
    - ○ Elders in a church or temple lead by example.
    - ○ Leaders in a city or town guide the way toward collective goals.
    - ○ Parents and grandparents model generous behavior for their families.
- Conviction can be expressed through *Experience*.
  - ▸ Experiential giving connects personally to a need, often because of challenges faced by a loved one.
  - ▸ Fulfillment is cause-directed—we feel compelled to help others overcome whatever obstacle we or those close to us have experienced.
    - ○ We contribute to a scholarship fund after a friend received an award from it.

- o A family losing a member to a disease rallies support in the effort to find a cure.
- o Parents whose child was healed at a local hospital volunteer for and donate to that organization.
- • Conviction can be expressed through *Outcomes*.
  - ▸ Outcome-focused giving desires to make a positive difference in a situation or environment.
  - ▸ Fulfillment is results-directed—there is an emotional connection as well as a practical one.
    - o An outcome focus can be a combination of investment and experience.
    - o We want to see results, and we are committed to the effort due to a personal connection.
    - o This type of giving can be focused and intense.

Motivation #4: Compassion
- • Compassion can be expressed through *Empathy*.
  - ▸ Empathetic giving imagines being in another person's situation and wants to help them.
  - ▸ Fulfillment is emotionally directed—we feel connected to whomever we are helping.
    - o One example is a wave of gifts resulting from a publicized tragedy or disaster.
    - o There is a feeling of urgency to the appeal.
    - o This type of giving can be powerful but short-lived.
- • Compassion can be expressed through *Gratitude*.
  - ▸ Grateful giving is based on appreciation for the means and opportunity to do so.
  - ▸ Fulfillment is others-directed—we want people to experience something good that we have experienced.
    - o We give money to a school we attended in order to support future generations of students.

- We value the opportunities we have enjoyed and want to support others in the same pursuits.
- We appreciate our advantages in life and want to help those who have fewer opportunities.
- Compassion can be expressed through **Love**.
  - Loving, sacrificial giving is based on wanting the best for the recipient.
  - Fulfillment is a complimentary cycle of other- and self-directed—this is when we truly feel that it is "better to give than to receive."
    - The person being helped receives the maximum benefit due to our emotional and practical commitment to the gift.
    - We in turn receive a special sense of positive reinforcement and energy.
    - Love giving is the way in which we most experience the paradox of generousity—multiplying our resources through giving them.

Generosity Awareness

One way in which this information may be useful is to make us more self-aware. If we are getting involved in generosity, it is good to know why. Doing so will help us manage the level of commitment we are willing to make. Hopefully, we also aspire to be more generous. If our giving tends to be stimulated by obligation, investment, or admiration, we can consider how to work toward giving stimulated by empathy, gratitude, and love.

We can also use awareness of generosity motivations to help us become more attuned to others. I was the development director for a national nonprofit earlier in my career. Understanding why people were interested in supporting the organization I worked for was a critical part of deciding how to approach them effectively with a gift request. This knowledge is not just of interest to professional fundraisers; we all need support in many forms. Appreciating the nature of the relationships we have with other people and why they may be interested in helping us is crucial to appreciating their motivations of generosity toward us and ours toward them.

At the start of this section, I proposed that some reasons for giving lead to higher levels of effectiveness and meaning. If we contribute to a cause or provide a benefit because we were pressured or because it satisfies our own ego, it still may have a meaningful impact on those to whom it is directed; however, that impact probably will be less than if it had been carefully selected and presented. In like manner, we are not going to get much out of the gift ourselves beyond superficial satisfaction or a passing feeling of pride.

On the other hand, if we are strongly connected to the object and purpose of the gift, it is more likely that what we give will have the positive impact we desire. Moreover, the strong connection we feel to the gift and to the recipient will provide us with greater satisfaction and pleasure.

WISEgenerosity Example: Compelling Drivers and Motivations for Giving Can Come from Anywhere and Anyone

One theme of this book is that generosity is an opportunity available to everyone in any circumstance and in any stage of life. Oseola McCarty is a marvelous example of how the drivers of and motivations for giving we just considered come to life.

The New York Times picked up Miss McCarty's story in 1995, shortly after news of her extraordinary gift was made public.[174] She was a washerwoman in Hattiesburg, Mississippi, who had spent a lifetime taking in bundles of dirty clothes and making them "clean and neat for parties she never attended, weddings to which she was never invited, graduations she never saw."[175]

Miss McCarty left school herself in the sixth grade to go to work because her grandmother became sick and needed help. Miss McCarty never married and never had children. Family faded away from her life, and she lived by herself for years and years. She focused on her faith and her work, and she was thankful for both. Her only expressed regret was not having attended school herself.

Through hard work and very simple living, she took her income over the years—small bills and coins—and saved and saved. Those humble seeds grew into a sturdy sum—more than $150,000. As she got older, Miss McCarty faced the question of what to do with the money she so diligently had accumulated.

Since I serve as a professional advisor who helps people make financial decisions, another favorite part of Miss McCarty's story for me is her meeting with Paul Laughlin. Identified by the *Wall Street Journal* as a "small-town banker,"[176] Mr. Laughlin found himself in an unusual client meeting with Miss McCarty, then a frail eighty-seven-year-old bank customer.

She needed to decide what to do with her surprisingly substantial assets. Inspired by the situation, Mr. Laughlin produced ten dimes, each representing 10 percent of her money. Asked how she would divide up the coins, Miss McCarty put one dime aside for her church and one each for three cousins. That left the remaining six for the University of Southern Mississippi.

USM is a focal point of life in Hattiesburg. Most of Miss McCarty's washing clients over the years had been staff members and students. She had been surrounded by them throughout her career and appreciated the energy of college life and the opportunity a college degree gave people. She also personally experienced the barriers that made it difficult for some young people to attend.

Aligning these interests, Miss McCarty set up a fund supporting African American students from southern Mississippi, for whom the opportunity to attend USM would otherwise not be possible. Inspired by her example, the community raised additional money. As of 2023, more than $630,000 worth of scholarships had been awarded to 130 students.[177]

The trajectory of the recipients changed for the better as they went on from success in college to having careers and families. "I am forever grateful," said one.[178] Another expressed that she wants to someday donate to the fund that did so much to help her. In the same vein, when University of Southern Mississippi alumni decide to make a legacy gift of their own, they are invited to join the McCarty Legacy Society. The logo is a tree with six branches and a dime at the end of each.

New York Times writer David Brooks made a thoughtful observation in his book *The Road to Character* about the difference between "resumé" virtues and "eulogy" virtues.[179] In a society sometimes obsessed with the former, Miss McCarty is a powerful reminder of the importance of the latter.

The *Times* revisited Miss McCarty's story with an obituary in 1999. After her death at the age of ninety-one, the "newspaper of record" for the nation paid tribute to a humble woman who embodied the virtues of hard work, thrift, and—yes—generosity.[180]

One great part of the story is that Miss McCarty was celebrated in her remaining lifetime for her kindness and commitment to others. She received the Presidential Citizen's Medal (America's second highest civilian award) from President Bill Clinton, was awarded an honorary doctorate from Harvard University, carried the Olympic torch in her hometown in 1996, and even threw the switch that dropped the ball in Times Square on New Year's Eve later that year. A woman who spent much of her life alone became famous in the end.

Horace Fleming, later the president of USM, was asked by a cynical out-of-town reporter if the whole story was true. "In a world in which people are suspicious of things too good to be true," he said, "Miss McCarty really was good and true."[181]

In her own words, "There's a lot of talk about self-esteem these days. It seems pretty basic to me. If you want to feel proud of yourself, you've got to do things you can be proud of. Feelings follow actions."[182]

The most telling quote of all was related by Aubrey Lucas, who was president of USM when Miss McCarty's gift was made. He described how, after attending a football game at which she was given a long ovation, a reporter asked why she wasn't spending the money on herself. She replied, "I am."[183]

Few people exemplify the positive drivers and motivations of giving as well as Oseola McCarty:

- *Heart Giving*: Miss McCarty turned a lifetime of hard work into an opportunity to help others seek dreams that she herself had not been able to pursue. She found happiness, enlightenment, and fulfillment in doing so.

- *Head Giving*: Miss McCarty gave to meet a need she saw in her community and which resonated strongly with her personally. She knew from experience the benefits that would come to others through education.
- *Habit Giving*: Miss McCarty harnessed her lifetime habits of hard work and saving into a meaningful giving opportunity. While the gift was made all at once, the effort that produced it was built over a lifetime.
- *Compulsion*: Prompted by a helpful advisor, Miss McCarty recognized that a legacy provision was needed for the money she had saved.
- *Connection*: All of Miss McCarty's giving was directed toward places and people that were meaningful in her life: her church, relatives, and the campus she long had served.
- *Conviction*: After years of dedicated physical labor, Miss McCarty wanted to make it possible for others from her community to have broader opportunities.
- *Compassion*: Miss McCarty was motivated by empathy, gratitude, and love.

Miss McCarty had an impact well beyond the students she helped to educate at USM, and her inspiration will resonate as long as her story is told. In just one example, Ted Turner credited Miss McCarty when he announced a $1 billion pledge to the United Nations in 1997.[184]

While Miss McCarty gave later in life, she did so while she still was able to enjoy the fruits of her giving. We've seen in this and other stories that WISEgenerosity produces a virtuous cycle of benefits for both giver and recipient. It is hard to find a more Well-grounded, Inspired, Satisfying, and Effective example than Oseola McCarty.

CHAPTER 12

Your Generosity Personality

WHAT SHOULD BE OUR FOCUS WHEN IT COMES TO GIVING? What kind of personal and civic engagement is going to be most rewarding and best harness our unique strengths and individual interests?

Personality and Giving: What Kind of Generosity Suits You Best?

Have you ever taken a personality test? It can be interesting to see how we fit into a structural framework of behavior and beliefs. Even if you haven't formally done such an assessment, you likely have a sense already of who you are and what you like.

Do you prefer being around and getting energy from other people (extroverted), or are you happiest in quieter situations (introverted)? Do you make decisions based on careful consideration of information (analytic), or do you trust your instincts and gut feelings (intuitive)? Are you more prone to cooperate or to challenge the status quo? Are you generally confident or careful?

If we carry over the concept of personality types to the ways in which people express generosity, we can say that there are four main types of givers:[185]

- Focused Givers
- Expressive Givers
- Considerate Givers

- Disciplined Givers

As in other areas of personality, we are not completely one or other. Each of us is a unique blend of traits. The more we understand those traits and direct our giving in a way that best suits our personalities, the more likely we are to be generous and the more effective that generosity will be.

Here's an example. Let's say you want to help others in the field of health-care and wellness. How do you decide what area to pursue? Based on the generosity types framework, you may decide along the following lines:

- **Focused:** Surgeons take action to address a specific problem.
- **Expressive:** Advocates educate and inspire better health choices.
- **Considerate:** General practitioner MDs and nurses use good "bedside manner" to engage with patients directly and to give comfort while treating them.
- **Disciplined:** Researchers find new methods for preventing and curing diseases.

A matrix illustrates this concept:

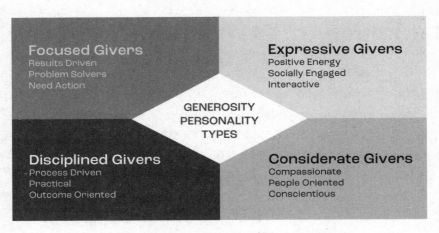

Focused Givers
Results Driven
Problem Solvers
Need Action

Expressive Givers
Positive Energy
Socially Engaged
Interactive

GENEROSITY
PERSONALITY
TYPES

Disciplined Givers
Process Driven
Practical
Outcome Oriented

Considerate Givers
Compassionate
People Oriented
Conscientious

Generosity Personality Types

On the WISEgenerosity webpage, there is a Generosity Personality Types profiling tool:

You may want to pause here, take the assessment yourself, and also imagine how people around you (family, friends, colleagues) would respond to the questions.

Where do your answers place you on the chart? Are you Considerate leaning toward Expressive? Focused leaning toward Disciplined? How about others you know?

In fairness, I'll share about myself. Having spent years working on this content and preparing to deliver it, it will not shock you to learn that my strongest trait is Expressive. My next two tendencies are toward Disciplined giving and Considerate giving, in that order. Interestingly, my #1 and #2 traits are opposites. Lastly, I have very little Focused energy. I clearly need help from others in making sure my efforts bear fruit (as the many people who have helped with this project can attest).

Once we have identified our traits toward giving, how do we harness and apply this knowledge?

Building on your purpose (chapter 2), you may pursue happiness, enlightenment, or fulfillment. Part of success comes from knowing your goals. The other part comes from knowing how to pursue them based on your unique personality and circumstances.

Let's reflect now on your passions, motivations, and interests. The goal is to assess and focus your generous abilities and inclinations so that you can give wisely and well.

As covered earlier in chapter 4, there are three primary ways in which we can be generous:

1. Kindness
2. Charity
3. Philanthropy

Looking at each again, how do they relate to purposes that best suit your personality traits as a giver?

- *Kindness*
  - ▸ Giving to those we already know
  - ▸ The goal is to aid, support, or nurture people in our immediate surroundings
  - ▸ Example: visiting a friend in the hospital; taking a meal to their family; running errands for them as they recover from an illness
- *Charity*
  - ▸ Giving to those we don't know
  - ▸ The goal is to provide sustenance, comfort, and hope to people in need outside of our immediate circle of relationships
  - ▸ Example: volunteering at a hospital and caring for patients there; providing money to cover the cost of care for those without the means to do so themselves
- *Philanthropy*
  - ▸ Giving to improve a situation or meet a need that affects a multitude of people
  - ▸ The goal is to address the root causes of a problem rather than the effects of the problem
  - ▸ Example: funding research into and action toward eradicating a disease

So, which of these ways of being generous is best?

Sorry, trick question. All are important, and each of us has the ability to contribute in each area. The question is, *which is most appealing to you?*

People Helpers are kindness givers. They are relationship-driven and attentive.

Neighbor Savers are charity givers. They engage directly with others in need and are concerned about improving lives with or without a personal connection.

Problem Solvers are philanthropy givers. They want to make significant improvements in the world and focus on big-picture needs and strategy more than on people.

These are not mutually exclusive pursuits. Some generous activities will overlap between categories. So much the better.

As we combine these purpose-driven elements together, a structure begins to take shape. We can develop a pattern for engaged generosity consistent with the different personality traits and giving elements. Here is such a framework:

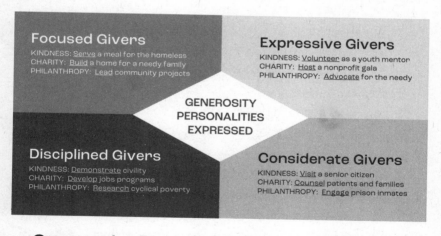

Generosity Personality Types Expressed

Each of the verbs underlined in the graphic reflects generosity suited to each type of giver:

- Focused givers *serve*, *build*, and *lead*.
- Expressive givers *volunteer*, *host*, and *advocate*.
- Considerate givers *visit*, *counsel*, and *engage*.
- Disciplined givers *demonstrate*, *develop*, and *research*.

Each of us may be called upon to do any one or all of these things, and it is good to stretch our boundaries and comfort zones. At the same time, it is beneficial to us and to others if we know where we are in terms of commitment to giving (kindness, charity, philanthropy) and the modes of giving that are likely to be most productive for us individually when giving and living.

In sum, here are the general traits for the four Generosity Personality Types:

- Focused Givers
  ‣ Results-centered, analytic
  ‣ Favor outward action and big-picture concepts
- Expressive Givers
  ‣ Socially centered, intuitive
  ‣ Favor making connections and big-picture concepts
- Considerate Givers
  ‣ People-centered, intuitive
  ‣ Favor personal contact and narrower focus
- Disciplined Givers
  ‣ Process-centered, analytic
  ‣ Favor detailed engagement and narrower focus

Understanding our personality traits and what kind of giving appeals to us helps focus our giving of time, talent, and treasure in directions that will be the most motivating and rewarding. Joined with an understanding of "Why" and "How," this awareness of "What" when it comes to giving is an important tool toward effective and meaningful generosity.

CHAPTER 13

WISEgenerosity Overcomes Generosity Resistance

YOU MAY HAVE THOUGHT ALREADY AT SOME POINT IN READING THIS BOOK, *If generosity is so marvelous, why isn't it practiced everywhere and all the time?* This is an excellent question. A lengthier explanation will need to wait until another time, but for now, here are three common excuses that keep people from being more generous:

1. My effort is not needed—*importance.*
2. Someone else is already doing it—*redundance.*
3. It doesn't make a difference—*effectiveness.*

WISEgenerosity is intended to reduce or remove these barriers to giving.

Addressing Importance: Your Giving Matters

One of my motivations for creating WISEgenerosity is to dispel the mistaken notion that financial giving is only for the ultra-rich or even the semi-rich. Many of us might say, "Of course people with money should give lots of their income and assets away. What else are they going to do with it all? But I don't have that kind of money."

As it happens, Bill Gates got his inspiration for the idea of a billionaires' "Giving Pledge" (a commitment on the part of many of the wealthiest Americans to give away at least half of their fortunes) not from other megarich people but from highly generous people who are much more like the rest of us. One was a group called Bolder Giving, which celebrated and encouraged everyday folks who give large percentages of their time and money to others.[186] This group was one of the first three recipients of money from the Gates Foundation as part of the "Giving Pledge" and was cited as a source of inspiration for the entire concept.[187]

Likewise, WISEgenerosity believes that everyone can be uncommonly generous. In the Christian Bible, Jesus makes such an example of generosity as follows:

He [Jesus] looked up and saw rich people putting their gifts into the [temple] treasury; he also saw a poor widow put in two small copper coins. He said, "Truly I tell you, this poor widow has put in more than all of them; for all of them have contributed out of their abundance, but she out of her poverty has put in all she had to live on."[188]

We noted earlier in chapter 3 that an abundant mindset is an essential part of WISEgenerosity. The wealthier donors to the temple had plenty of money to spare, but the poor widow felt compelled to share the little she had out of a giving spirit that transcended her circumstances. Elsewhere, Jesus describes the rewards for such generosity:

Do not store up for yourselves treasures on earth, where moth and rust consume and where thieves break in and steal; but store up for yourselves treasures in heaven, where neither moth nor rust consumes and where thieves do not break in and steal. For where your treasure is, there your heart will be also.[189]

Of course, opportunities for generosity include much more than money. As we explored in chapters 6–10, giving is Possessional, Personal, Social, Emotional, and Relational.

We will take nothing we currently possess with us after this life. The only lasting impact we make on the world is in the way our attitude and actions affect the lives of others. This legacy—generated by generosity toward those around us—is the "treasure" to which Jesus refers. We are what we give.

Addressing Redundance: No One Else Can Give What You Can Give

One novel that made a strong impression on me years ago was *A Prayer for Owen Meany* by John Irving. (The movie *Simon Birch* is based loosely on the same story.) Owen Meany is an unnaturally small boy who never physically grows up. He speaks in a strikingly high voice that draws attention in any setting. He is uncommonly smart and mature. He also lives most of his life with the strong conviction that he has been placed in the world by God to do something very specific: he will die on a certain date and save others in the process. He even dreams about the circumstances, although the visions are fragmented and hard for him to understand.

I first read this book during my college years, and it is not for everyone. The setting primarily is the tumultuous 1960s, intersecting with the social upheaval of the Vietnam era in the US, and the plot is uplifting at times and profane at others. Amid great personal drama and constant shifts back and forth in time, the story moves relentlessly toward the fulfillment of Owen's dream.

Spoiler alert: Owen's premonitions are correct. Without revealing the exact ending, it turns out that all the elements of his being—his intelligence and natural calm, his tiny physical stature, and his penetrating voice—are essential to saving the lives of others at the cost of his own. Even the childhood game other kids made of tossing him back and forth like a human beanbag is essential to fulfilling this calling.

A Prayer for Owen Meany is narrated by Owen's best friend from the small New Hampshire town where they grew up. Having been present at Owen's death, John Wheelwright can't escape the loss of his friend, the ways in which their lives intertwined, or the sense that there was a shared destiny that transcended them both. The last lines of the book are:

> When we held Owen Meany above our heads, when we passed him back and forth—so effortlessly—we believed that Owen weighed nothing at all. We did not realize that there were forces beyond our play. Now I know they were the forces that contributed to our illusion of Owen's weightlessness; they were the forces we didn't have the faith to feel, they were the forces we failed to believe in—and they were also lifting up Owen Meany, taking him out of our hands.
> Oh God—please give him back! I shall keep asking You.[190]

When the opportunity came after years of preparation, Owen was able to perform an act of self-sacrifice that only he was capable of. No one else could have been the hero that he was meant to be. Moreover, Owen Meany fully demonstrated the determined attitude of service and willingness to act that underlies all good giving.

Every interaction we have with every person is an opportunity to lift them up in some way special to the situation. We may not be called to give up our lives today, but we can sacrifice our self-centeredness, our indignance, our frustration, our self-righteousness, and our pride for the sake of others. These are the daily acts of personal kindness, charity, and philanthropy that matter in life.

My interpretation of and inspiration from *Owen Meany* is that each of us finds ourselves constantly in places and with people where our abilities and inclinations present unique opportunities. In ways large and small, WISEgenerosity means always looking for ways in which we can serve and support others.

Addressing Effectiveness: Your Giving Makes a Difference

There is a fable about giving told by the late University of Pennsylvania professor, essayist, philosopher, and literary naturalist Loren Eiseley that reads:

Once, on ancient Earth, there was a human boy walking along a beach. There had just been a storm, and starfish had been scattered along the sands. The boy knew the fish would die, so he began to fling the fish to the sea. But every time he threw a starfish, another would wash ashore. An old Earth man happened along and saw what the child was doing. He called out, "Boy, what are you doing?" "Saving the starfish!" replied the boy. "But your attempts are useless, child! Every time you save one, another one returns, often the same one! You can't save them all, so why bother trying? Why does it matter, anyway?" called the old man. The boy thought about this for a while, a starfish in his hand; he answered, "Well, it matters to this one." And then he flung the starfish into the welcoming sea.[191]

It is easy to look around at the magnitude of problems in the world and feel overwhelmed. Even the difficulties in your immediate surroundings can seem insurmountable at times. WISEgenerosity recognizes challenges but identifies opportunities and steers us toward solutions, one starfish at a time.

WISEgenerosity Example: Overcoming Generosity Resistance at Home (and with Home)

One family who lives in Atlanta is an example of extraordinary generosity coming from "ordinary" circumstances. By their own description, the Salwens were a "fairly typical" upper-middle-class family of married professionals and growing kids focused on "the standard American life—school, work, and youth sports."[192]

At age fourteen, their daughter Hannah was struck one day by the plight of a homeless man, comparing her own comfortable circumstances to his challenging ones. Inspired by Hannah's determination to do something bold for the benefit of others, the family of four "launched an audacious family project. We decided to sell our 6,500-square-foot landmark home, move to a nondescript house that was half as big, and donate half of the sales price to help alleviate poverty in one of the neediest corners of the planet."[193]

Hannah and her dad, Kevin, wrote of their adventures, struggles, anxieties, and triumphs in a uniquely moving book, *The Power of Half*. The results of the Salwens' actions were significant, and not just for the Ghanaian beneficiaries of their financial resources. The family itself grew closer, stronger, more trusting in each other, better able to communicate, more purpose-driven, and more capable of coping with challenges.

This was not an easy commitment to keep in the end. The financial crisis of 2008–2009 came along during the process, and Kevin's start-up company closed. The family had moved to their new smaller house, but the larger original house that was funding both the giving project and the new home failed to sell. When the time came to make good on their funding pledge, money was scarce. Faced with a decision to keep their promise or to keep their financial cushion, the Salwens dipped into their savings and college funds in order to send the money overseas.

True to life, the book raises questions as well as provides answers. The family and the individuals in it wrestle with tough decisions and varied perceptions—both internal and external. In the end, they conclude the following:

> [W]e had always called our adventure "the family project," because first and foremost it was about our family. It was enlightened self-interest. The Secret Sauce to family togetherness was being out in the community for others, regardless of how *community* was defined—the neighborhood, the city, the world.
>
> Friends and others who asked us about the whys, wheres, and hows of our project always focused on the magnitude and experience: the big house, the big donation, or the trip to Africa. They never appreciated the transformational energy of the process—the worksheets, the debates, the critical power-sharing votes. They never saw the internal workings of a family eager to stand up for something collectively, to

stop accumulating, to get off the treadmill, to unify around a single purpose.[194]

Thinking back to the paradox of giving, the Selwens ended up receiving benefits they prized far above what they gave away. They found a purpose that justified all the sacrifices made on its behalf.

Interestingly, the power of the gift was more in the day-to-day change it made in their family dynamics than it was in the headline results of the gift itself. They found a meaningful and effective "Why" that transformed their lives and untold others.

Referencing the three excuses keeping people from being more generous:

1. *Addressing Importance*. The Selwens' effort was meaningful and effective. It also enabled their family to overcome significant challenges through the generous purposes and practices that brought them together.

2. *Addressing Redundance*. No one else was doing what the family undertook—and their giving required uncommon courage, discipline, and sacrifice.

3. *Addressing Effectiveness*. Their attitude and actions didn't just benefit the faraway recipients of their financial support but also provided an inspiring example for their friends, their neighbors, and everyone who read their book and heard their story.

In sum, WISEgenerosity overcomes resistance to giving and provides a better life in the process for everyone involved.

When You Should Give: Evaluating W.I.S.E. Giving

From strife in our nation to conflict across the globe, evidence of ungenerosity seems everywhere. Deficiency, difficulty, and division are all around us. In such an atmosphere, a focused commitment to caring for and sharing with others may seem ineffective or even naïve. Does generosity really matter? Is it even dangerous to be generous?

If you've made it this far, you must be attracted to or at least curious about the benefits of generosity to a life well-lived. Even so, part of you may be wondering how such a positive outlook on life holds up when history and our own experience include myriad examples of harmful and sometimes devastating behavior by people toward other people.

This section explores the psychological foundations of generosity as a way to understand how it is essential to human flourishing. We then will offer a tool that can be used to "test" if gifts will be Well-grounded, Inspired, Satisfying, and Effective. First, we will examine giving that does not fulfill its positive potential in the most difficult circumstances and what to do about it.

CHAPTER 14

Understanding "Bad" Giving— and How to Prevent It

PHILOSOPHER AND ECONOMIST ADAM SMITH WROTE in *Theory of Moral Sentiments* that: "proper benevolence is the most graceful and agreeable of all of the affections." [195] In other words, *if done wisely and well—in the right way and for the right reasons—we can't be too generous.*

Ah, but that is a potential stumbling block. Is all giving done the right way and for the right reasons? We know that the answer is no.

While meaningful and effective giving are the goals of WISEgenerosity, we have to acknowledge that giving isn't always as good as it could be. At times, it even can be harmful. *Toxic giving hurts.*

Returning to the list from chapter 11 of reasons why people give, we recall that there is a hierarchy of motivations. Giving out of obligation or social pressure is less likely to produce a good outcome than giving due to empathy, gratitude, or love.

There also are two parties to generosity: the giver and the receiver. Both are involved in producing optimal results. Fear that others will take advantage of or misuse our gifts can be a barrier to giving in the first place.

These difficulties especially are true when we are trying to help someone in desperate poverty grappling with a set of difficult, interwoven needs. I believe this challenge is the most important one facing our country and our world. The gap between "haves" and "have-nots" is large and growing in many places. It is right and good to want to remove barriers to opportunity and to provide the means for others to succeed. But when and how are such efforts best pursued?

How Do We Ensure That Our Giving Is Good (Meaning)?

There are two books I recommend on this topic: *Toxic Charity* by Robert Lupton and *When Helping Hurts* by Steve Corbett and Brian Fikkert. The authors are Christians who minister to the most vulnerable and needy members of our society and our world. They are dedicated servants who demonstrate a generous attitude combined with generous actions.

Through their work, the authors have seen well-intentioned people inflict damage on others while wanting to do the opposite. To their dismay, these authors themselves also have done so. Their perspective challenges conventional wisdom and offers us a starting point to address our question of how to avoid unintentional damage in our desire to help others.[196]

For example, *When Helping Hurts* addresses a disconnect about poverty early on in the book. After years of disappointing and even damaging efforts of its own to support basic human needs around the globe, the World Bank commissioned an extensive effort to document the concerns of poor people. Published in 2000, *Voices of the Poor: Can Anyone Hear Us?* is a three-volume collection of comments.[197]

Corbett and Fikkert point out that the definitions and priorities between the interviewees and a typical North American are profound:

Poor people typically talk in terms of shame, inferiority, powerlessness, humiliation, fear, hopelessness, depression, social isolation, and voicelessness. North American audiences tend to emphasize a lack of material things such as food, money, clean water, medicine, housing, etc.[198]

[T]his mismatch between many outsiders' perceptions of poverty and the perceptions of poor people themselves can have devastating consequences for poverty alleviation efforts.[199]

Likewise, people attempting to help the poor often fail to recognize the kind of support required for the situation: Relief, Rehabilitation, or Development.[200] The authors give victims of a tsunami as an example. Relief is responding to the immediate need with "urgent and temporary"[201] supplies and support. Rehabilitation "begins as soon as the bleeding stops; it seeks to restore people and their communities to the positive elements of their pre-crisis conditions."[202] Development, in turn, is a relational, empowering process that enables the people and community to thrive over the long-term. It is "not done *to* people or *for* people but *with* people."[203]

If our neighbor's barn just burned down and we show up with new seeds and livestock, we are not being helpful. Our neighbors need Relief, and they are not able to use these donated items yet. Likewise, if we come by with a casserole and a well-meaning pat on the back as they are going through the laborious process of rebuilding, that is not very useful either. They are in the process of Rehabilitating and would welcome us helping them. Finally, as they turn to Development, a real commitment to their recovery would involve taking time away from our own planting and harvesting to assist them in getting back on their feet. Aligning our support with their needs is a critical part of being generous.

Here are three takeaways from *When Helping Hurts*:

First, *avoid paternalism*. "Do not do things for people that they can do for themselves."[204] We will explore this further in a moment when we consider the book *Toxic Charity*.

Second, *engage the people being served*. Vast amounts of time and money have been wasted on projects that sounded good in conference rooms but were hugely out of alignment with what the recipients wanted or needed. Corbett and Fikkert suggest that we get participation from those being helped as far along this continuum as possible in each case: Coercion, Compliance, Consultation, Cooperation, Co-Learning, and Community Initiated.[205] Essentially, the more central the beneficiaries are to every stage of support, from planning to implementation, the better the outcomes will be.

Third, *focus first on assets, not needs*. Start with the question, "What is right with you?"[206] This positive approach leads with abundance, not scarcity. I participated in a strategic planning process at my church years ago. The nationally known consultant brought in to support the effort started by asking everyone to assess programs and resources across twelve dimensions.[207] When analyzing the results, we were not allowed to speak in terms of "weaknesses," but only in terms of "strengths" and "potential strengths." That idea has stayed with me ever since.

How Do We Ensure That Our Giving Does Good (Impact)?

In his book *Toxic Charity*, author Bob Lupton is blunt. After four decades working in inner-city Atlanta and beyond, he opens his book with the following broadside: "In the United States, there's a growing scandal that we both refuse to see and actively perpetuate. What Americans avoid facing is that while we are very generous in charitable giving, much of that money is either wasted or actually harms the people it is targeted to help."[208]

Lupton believes that, while our motives are good, "we have neglected to conduct careful due diligence to determine emotional, economic, and cultural outcomes on the receiving end of our charity. Why do we miss this crucial aspect in evaluating our charitable work? Because, as compassionate people, we have been evaluating our charity by the rewards we receive from service, rather than the benefits received by the served."[209]

Tell us how you really feel, Bob!

Toxic Charity takes us on a tour of well-meaning but ineffective programs, large and small, and we see that short-term volunteerism actually has the potential to do more harm than good. The book concludes that leaving common sense and business acumen aside during charitable efforts generally will lead to failure.

Lupton offers wisdom gleaned from years of experience. He knows that building relationships matters even more than meeting immediate needs.

Addressing real issues involves investments of time and effort at a grassroots level. Anything less is likely to be a top-down, superficial effort that encourages dependency more than it helps people. A whole chapter, "No Quick Fixes," emphasizes this point. Big problems in our society have built up over many years, and they will take many years to address.

Reinforcing the message of *When Helping Hurts*, Lupton offers the following "Oath for Compassionate Service:"[210]

- Never do for the poor what they have (or could have) the capacity to do for themselves.
- Limit one-way giving to emergency situations.
- Strive to empower the poor through employment, lending, and investing, using grants sparingly to reinforce achievements.
- Subordinate self-interests to the needs of those being served.
- Listen closely to those you seek to help, especially to what is not being said—unspoken feelings may contain essential clues to effective service.
- Above all, do no harm.

There also are a series of sensible directions on how to implement generous activities, like organizing a productive day of service in the community or deciding how individually to invest and volunteer.

Ultimately, the message of *Toxic Charity* rests on personal experience. Lupton points out that "those who have been devalued by society are unusually sensitive to the signals they receive from the dominant culture. Those in service work have the responsibility to listen to what those in need are saying and... also to what is not being said."[211]

Lupton recounts a conversation with one of his neighbors in the poor section of the city where he and his own family had lived for years. It is worth sharing at length:

"I hate it when volunteers come down here," Virgil muttered, just loud
   enough for me to hear. We were sitting on my front porch steps as a

white fourteen-passenger van crept past. We didn't need to read the lettering on the side to know that it was a church van—the smiling, light-skinned youth waving from the windows told us that. Virgil's reaction surprised me. A church group had invested $20,000 and eight weekends of labor to build his home. Another one had helped him purchase and install attractive landscaping. I assumed his response to volunteers would be positive.

Bewildered, I asked him why. "Do you know what it's like to have people look down on you like you're poor, like you need help?" he said. "I know they're just trying to be nice but, damn, they insult you and don't even know it! Like one lady mentioned to me and Tamara how clean our house was. I guess she thought it was a compliment. What she was really saying was, 'I'm surprised to see your house isn't infested with roaches and filled with trash like most black families.' A couple people told me how smart and well-behaved my kids were, surprised that they weren't dumb and rowdy like most inner-city black kids. I see through their words. I hear what they really think."

"But," he continued, "you have to keep smiling and act like you don't know what's going on. I really hate it!"

It had taken five years for Virgil to reach this level of candor with me, five years of being neighbors, raising our kids together, being in each other's homes. Had he been a less secure man, these highly personal feelings would likely have remained concealed in the closed domain of his and Tamara's private lives. Especially considering that I was one of his white benefactors. I was the one who orchestrated the construction of his home, mobilized church volunteers, raised the money. I knew Virgil was grateful to have a permanent home for his family—he expressed it many times.

What I didn't realize until this day on my front porch steps was the price he had paid to be a recipient of my charity, the damage it had inflicted on his manly pride. Nor would I ever have known had we not become neighbors and trusted friends.

Virgil's honesty and candor caused us to revise our ministry, prompting a marked change in our approach.[212]

Later on, Bob says to his readers that it "is far better to enter the neighborhood as a learner than an initiator."[213]

These are hard lessons to absorb. Bob's situation was as caring and compassionate as he thought he could make it. He dedicated himself to serving others. He moved his family to live alongside the people he wanted to support so that his work would be relational. His friend appreciated his efforts on one level but was disturbed and undermined by them on another. Giving wisely and well is not easy.

In the end, my conclusion is that individuals matter more than anything. We risk doing harm if we have any intention or agenda other than their success. Being completely focused on people in need is a key part of WISEgenerosity.

My Own Experience

My firsthand experience serving organizations fighting systemic poverty in inner-city Atlanta and elsewhere has reinforced the messages above.

First, any effort to help must rest on a solid foundation. One example is the Social Genome Project from the Brookings Institute in Washington, DC.[214] This think tank has spent years looking at ways in which we can remove barriers to success. Their work has produced the following key indicators for fighting poverty:

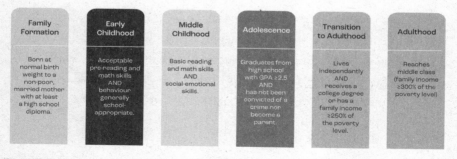

Social Genome Project "Success Sequence" (The Brookings Institute)

The organizations with which I work use this strategic framework as a blueprint to evaluate where and how to apply resources in service to those whom they serve. In financial terms, one goal is to support achieving middle class by middle age, with "middle class" defined by the Pew Research Center as "two-thirds to double the national median income."[215]

Second, the best plans only are as good as the people involved with them. Heroes of giving succeed in service because they are passionate about others. It is their personal dedication and commitment and that of their colleagues that lowers defensive barriers, creates meaningful engagement, and fosters individual dignity and progress.

We considered the differences between charity and philanthropy earlier in chapter 4. The word *charity* can have negative connotations, but I view it positively as delivering resources to individuals where and how they are needed. The key is a person-to-person connection.

Lastly, and along the lines of the World Bank report mentioned earlier, the needs of the poor go far beyond material goods. Charity providing personal, supportive connections is needed at least as much as systemic philanthropic efforts, which are not geared toward or capable of providing such individualized support. Moreover, success comes best from bottom-up processes led by the members of the communities involved and not by others, however well-meaning the outsiders may be.

What conclusions then have I drawn from my own experience? Being thoughtful, focused, and disciplined in our service to others is essential to WISEgenerosity. Making sure that we do so with humility and compassion and awareness is necessary as well. Focusing on the positive and starting with what is "right" and not with what is "wrong" is vital to success. Lastly, meaningful service and support address not just material needs but also focus on emotional and spiritual well-being. Like generosity itself, these elements of constructive engagement can apply to any area of our lives where there are challenges to overcome and opportunities to pursue.

WISEgenerosity Challenge Question

Now, it's time for a challenge. What is the generous response when a stranger approaches you on the street to ask for money?

Trick question. There is no clear-cut answer. Even seasoned social servants disagree. *Christianity Today* asked three veteran urban ministers for their opinions.[216]

- The first said to "give freely." It is not our place to judge those in need but to help them without question.
- The second said to give "only as a last resort." In his experience, very few panhandlers are impoverished. Most walk to their car and drive home after a day's work.
- The third said to "don't give in this way." Their opinion is that this type of giving encourages destructive behavior. If a short-term fix is needed, we should offer to buy the person a meal and listen to their story. "People almost always need love even more than money."[217]

All three agreed that ongoing support in a caring community was far better than handouts. Regardless of whether we give cash, it is generous to help people find whatever assistance they need.

This topic has come up repeatedly in conversations with people about WISEgenerosity. Many have expressed frustration in having helped a stranger who seemed to have a specific critical need, only to catch them later peddling the same story.

Others noted that some people don't really want help. One extended conversation and an offer of substantial but nonimmediate assistance ended with a panhandler brush-off. The person said disdainfully, "This is the life I like," and wasn't interested in changing.

Some expressed honestly that they give, but it's with a sense of guilt that they wouldn't miss the money and may not spend it any better than the person asking. One of the people interviewed in the *CT* article offered a similar story:

[C. S.] Lewis and a friend were walking down the road and came upon
a street person who reached out to them for help. While his friend kept
walking, Lewis stopped and proceeded to empty his wallet. When
they resumed their journey, his friend asked, "What are you doing
giving him your money like that? Don't you know he's just going to go
squander all that on ale?" Lewis paused and replied, "That's all I was
going to do with it."[218]

I confess that I have gone back and forth on this topic myself and have
taken all the actions listed above at one time or another. If you, too, are struggling to figure out your own generous response, you may want to revisit the
Generosity Personality Types material in chapter 12 and the profiling tool on
the www.wisegenerosity.com website to consider how your own disposition
connects to such a real-life question.

CHAPTER 15

Giving and Human Needs

THE HISTORY OF PSYCHOLOGY IS AN INTERESTING PARALLEL to the tension between recognizing the negativity in the world around us and still focusing on a generous approach toward life.

At its origins, traditional psychology focused on what was going "wrong" with people. It identified "weaknesses" in its subjects and attempted to address them. In contrast, the field of positive psychology developed to take the opposite approach. It identifies what is "right" in people's lives and aims to build on those strengths to promote flourishing.[219]

The contrast can be expressed in this diagram:[220]

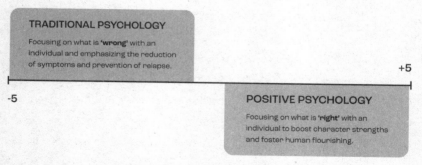

TRADITIONAL PSYCHOLOGY

Focusing on what is **'wrong'** with an individual and emphasizing the reduction of symptoms and prevention of relapse.

+5

-5

POSITIVE PSYCHOLOGY

Focusing on what is **'right'** with an individual to boost character strengths and foster human flourishing.

Traditional vs. Positive Psychology

In this -5 to +5 scale, traditional psychology seeks to move subjects from a negative state back to a neutral state. Positive psychology looks to move people from negative or neutral to a more positive place.

Positive Psychology and Generosity

Positive psychology makes sense to me. Imagine other areas of life. Would you learn to be a great baseball player by focusing on all the ways you could strike out? Would you become a great guitar player by learning all the notes not to play?

While many situations do require remedial support, doesn't it seem better to (when possible) focus on how to improve rather than being caught up in how to avoid making things worse? This approach parallels the direction to "focus first on assets, not needs" from *When Helping Hurts* in the previous chapter.

A general mindset along these lines can be summarized as follows:

Positive psychology focuses on the positive events and influences in life, including:
1. Positive experiences (like happiness, joy, inspiration, and love)
2. Positive states and traits (like gratitude, resilience, and compassion)
3. Positive institutions (applying positive principles within entire organizations and institutions)

As a field, positive psychology spends much of it time on topics like character strengths, optimism, life satisfaction, happiness, well-being, gratitude, compassion (as well as self-compassion), self-esteem and self-confidence, hope, and elevation.

These topics are studied in order to learn how to help people flourish and live their best lives.[221]

While WISEgenerosity is based on spiritual and philosophical principles independent of positive psychology, I imagine that you can see the similarities between them.

Along the same lines, a life focused on giving is based on a sense of optimism but also on a levelheaded view of reality. Being "positive" does not mean ignoring difficulties.

The definition of wisdom offered at the outset of his book is "values + experience." Our experiences can be good or bad—wisdom is about addressing what happens in our lives through the light of our core values and purpose.

Likewise, the definition of generosity offered earlier in chapter 1 is "considerate attitude + caring action." If applying our values toward our experience helps us to be wise, approaching situations with thoughtful concern for others and a deliberate desire to help them makes us generous. In turn, WISEgenerosity leads to the human flourishing that we all would like to see in ourselves and in those around us.

WISEgenerosity and Meeting Human Needs

Continuing on the subject of human flourishing, Abraham Maslow was one of the academics on whose work positive psychology is built.

Maslow was the son of Jewish immigrant parents who escaped violent upheaval in Russia and then absorbed the horrors of the Holocaust from the safety of the United States. Far from living in an "ivory tower" removed from reality, he was more than familiar with evil and the capacity for human depravity.

In 1943 and while World War II raged, Maslow published his now famous "hierarchy of needs" to try to explain the tension between "deficiency" and "growth" in human behavior. One of his key questions was: Why don't more people progress toward the best version of themselves? During a time when millions of people were dying in a more far-reaching conflict than humanity had ever before witnessed, Maslow asked a very basic question about human experience: What prevents individuals from thriving?

You likely have seen the framework Maslow devised to answer this question. The "hierarchy" typically is presented as a pyramid in which satisfying the need for physical and psychological essentials builds toward more elevated opportunities for individual fulfillment:[222]

Self-Actualization
Desire to become the most that one can be

Esteem
Self-respect, status, recognition, strength, freedom

Love and Belonging
Friendship, intimacy, family, sense of connection

Safety Needs
Personal security, employment, resources, health, property

Physiological Needs
Air, water, food, shelter, sleep, clothing, reproduction

Maslow's Hierarchy of Needs

At the top of the pyramid is our capacity to "self-actualize." Self-actualization needs "are the highest level in Maslow's hierarchy, and refer to the realization of a person's potential, self-fulfillment, seeking personal growth, and peak experiences."[223]

According to Maslow, there are a set of characteristics typical of people who are able to self-actualize. These include:[224]

- Truth (honesty and purity)
- Goodness (rightness and benevolence)
- Beauty (aliveness and richness)

- Wholeness (integration and interconnection)
- Dichotomy (accepting contradictions)
- Aliveness (spontaneous and full-functioning)
- Uniqueness (individual and idiosyncratic)
- Perfection (everything in its place)
- Necessity (things are what they are)
- Completion (fulfillment)
- Justice (fairness and impartiality)
- Order (lawfulness and rightness)
- Simplicity (stripping away excesses)
- Richness (complexity and totality)
- Effortlessness (lack of strain)
- Playfulness (sense of fun)
- Self-sufficiency (independence)

Looking at this list, two things strike me. First, most of these characteristics are relational. They largely exist based on how we connect with the world and the people around us. Second, all them serve the cause of generosity. Each behavior or tendency enables us in some way to live positively and to care for others. Essentially, I understand generosity to be the means by which Maslow's positive life outcomes take place.

Generosity Beyond "Self"

As it happens, the generosity framework we have been exploring and Maslow's hierarchy align. Here are how the five types of giving shared in chapters 6–10 match with the levels of Maslow's pyramid:

- Possessional giving feeds physical needs.
- Personal giving feeds security needs.
- Social giving feeds love/belonging needs.
- Emotional giving feeds esteem needs.
- Relational giving feeds self-actualization needs.

From an individual standpoint, the most fulfilling life is an inversion of Maslow's pyramid, with less of our time, talent, and treasure being spent at the physical end of the spectrum and more at the relational end. The goal is to use our social, emotional, and self-actualized well-being in support of others, which could be expressed graphically like this:

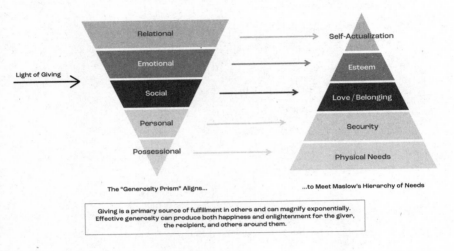

The "Generosity Prism" Aligns...   ...to Meet Maslow's Hierarchy of Needs

Giving is a primary source of fulfillment in others and can magnify exponentially. Effective generosity can produce both happiness and enlightenment for the giver, the recipient, and others around them.

This aligned generosity model is like a "generosity prism." The full-spectrum "light" of giving is split into separate elements. In turn, our considerate and caring efforts on behalf of others using these elements support progress upward in their hierarchy of needs.

I also love equating giving and light. In the Christian spiritual tradition, Jesus taught, "Let your light shine before others."[225] I believe that generosity was the essence of what he meant.

Generosity is light and love. It applies meaningful use for our possessions, it provides purpose for our personal abilities, it delivers the means by which our social interactions can elevate rather than depress, it nurtures the positive connections made possible by our emotions, and it is the driver for what is solid and sure in our relationships. The smallest amount of light can dispel a great deal of darkness.

Transcendent Giving

Looking again at the aligned pyramids of giving and needs, it seems true to me that the ratios of generosity to impact are inverted. A modest amount of possessional giving can go a long way toward meeting someone else's physical needs. On the other hand, it takes constant and dedicated use of relational giving to help those around us become self-actualized.

In that vein, the term *self-actualization* seems somewhat out of place. SELF-actualization sounds lonely. I imagine instead a generous interconnectedness through which each of our selves positively reinforces and in turn is positively reinforced by others. As the poet John Donne famously wrote:

> No man is an island entire of itself; every man
> is a piece of a continent, a part of the main;
> if a clod be washed away by the sea, Europe
> is the less, as well as if a promontory were, as
> well as any manner of thy friends or of thine
> own were; any man's death diminishes me,
> because I am involved in mankind.
> And therefore never send to know for whom
> the bell tolls; it tolls for thee.[226]

Maslow came to agree with this poetic perspective. In later years, he revised his hierarchy and added three additional elements: [227]

- Cognition—seeking knowledge and awareness
- Aesthetics—seeking beauty
- Transcendence—being motivated by values that go beyond the self

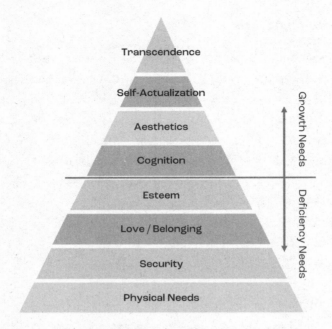

Maslow's Expanded Hierarchy of Needs

In its complete form, the hierarchy recognizes all the elements of WISEgenerosity. Helping others meet their needs provides the basis for giving that is purposeful and practical.

Maslow's hierarchy supports the belief that helping others must be wise in order for it to be meaningful. Using the Maslow framework, we have to meet the right set of initial needs before we can move on to any others. Misaligned giving is ineffective, or worse.

Along the same lines, it is W.I.S.E. to consider how any gift relates to the recipient in terms of Maslow's model. What are you trying to accomplish with the gift in terms of meeting one of these needs? In turn, is the gift being offered Well-grounded and Inspired? Does it have the potential to be Satisfying and Effective for everyone involved?

WISEgenerosity seeks to answer such questions.

WISEgenerosity Example: Harnessing Protection, Provision, Power, and Peace

Pastor Bruce Deel is a mentor and friend and the founder and CEO of City of Refuge in Atlanta. Bruce and his amazing wife, Rhonda, exemplify WISEgenerosity. I'll tell their story in more detail later in chapter 25. Meanwhile, something I learned from Bruce makes sense to share now.

Bruce lives out the W.I.S.E. giving elements as well as anyone I've ever known. Underlying his lifetime commitment to serving others is a deeply personal, purposeful, and practical faith.

Having been a minister most of his life, Bruce finds many occasions where he turns to prayer. Much of the time, he ends his petitions to God on behalf of himself and others with a request for the same four blessings: protection, provision, power, and peace. I love and have adopted this approach for myself.

Reflecting over time on what I call "Bruce's Four P's Prayer," I've come to appreciate that these elements align with and directly overcome the four D's that we all face in life: danger, deficiency, difficulty, and distraction. Moreover, the four P's connect with the types of generosity and human needs we've just explored.

WISEgenerosity Overcomes Danger, Deficiency, Difficulty, and Distraction

Danger appears in our lives in many forms—from illnesses, to accidents, to financial stresses, to professional challenges. Threats large and small risk disrupting or derailing our physical well-being and security. Protection is needed to overcome danger.

Deficiency—real and perceived—is a source of anxiety and a barrier to progress in life. We lack or feel as if we lack many things that keep us from living our best lives: money, time, relationships, and more. Provision is needed to overcome deficiency.

Difficulty is omnipresent in the world. Nothing worthwhile happens without the need for considerable effort, along with courage and determination to address obstacles. Power is needed to overcome difficulty.

Distraction is rampant in the world today. The tools and technologies that make our lives more convenient and productive also funnel our attention away from things that ultimately may be more important. The relentless buzzes and beeps and flashing lights around us make it harder to see the more significant sources of happiness, enlightenment, and fulfillment that do not actively call attention to themselves. Peace is needed to overcome distraction.

WISEgenerosity is a source of protection, provision, power, and peace, and, in turn, reinforces their strength and effectiveness. By helping others and receiving help in return, we are able to harness generous forces in order to overcome obstacles that prevent us from living the best life we can.

WISEgenerosity and Human Flourishing

The complete "Hierarchy of Needs" illustrates the point:

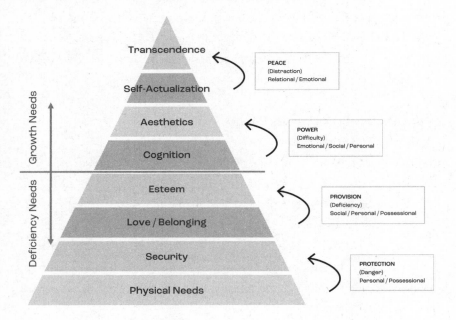

A WISEgenerosity Model for Human Flourishing

Let's go through the pyramid again from bottom to top with the new elements added.

Sharing our money and stuff (Possessional Giving) and time and talent (Personal Giving) provides *protection* to overcome danger faced by others in the form of physical needs and insecurity. When we are at risk, we can seek protection and support along the same lines.

For example, someone fighting cancer benefits directly from logistical assistance and potential financial support by their loved ones in order to get treatment. Their medical team in turn shares expertise and the ability to provide effective care. Those who donated money to the nonprofit hospital behind the process made the necessary underlying resources available. WISEgenerosity is evident from all involved.

When facing deficiency, Possessional, Personal, and Social Generosity all can deliver the *provision* needed. Lacking the essentials we need in life produces insecurity, undermines love/belonging, and negatively affects our internal and external esteem. Providing missing resources allows these needs to be met.

Imagine a child who lacks access to educational and career opportunities. Providing scholarship funds so they can attend a better school, offering time in counseling and mentorship, and making personal connections available so they can find ideal work are all ways to provide for this student.

Power is multiplied when others come alongside to assist us in overcoming obstacles. We all need emotional support, social engagement, and personal help to address challenges.

If you are struggling with an important project at your job, you need power from others to overcome the difficulties involved. Your family and colleagues with whom you are close can offer encouragement. Your department teammates can share guidance and support. Your boss can take extra time to work through whatever issues are involved. These generous efforts then enable you to succeed.

Peace desperately is needed everywhere today, as evidenced by the high levels of distress we see in individual lives and across communities. Compellingly, the desire for it in Bruce's original prayer means something much more special and significant than might be clear at first. "Peace" in the Bible refers to the Jewish term "shalom." Shalom is greater than "calm" or the absence of conflict. Shalom is a state of being in which each element of life finds its proper place. It means balance and wholeness.

This kind of peace truly addresses the myriad distractions we face in life. It also radiates out from individuals toward a more ideal society that provides balance and wholeness for others. Shalom is produced by emotional and relational generosity and enables the pursuit of knowledge (cognition) and beauty (aesthetics) that are high up the Maslow pyramid. Ultimately, generous forces meet our human needs and provide the potential for self-actualization and transcendence that we all want to experience.

At the start of this book, I offered the promise that giving done wisely and well is a transformational force and an essential virtue of a life well-lived. I hope now that the full potential of generosity to produce human flourishing is becoming more and more evident to you.

CHAPTER 16

Generosity Dimensions

GIVING INHERENTLY INVOLVES TWO PARTIES. Aligned with every giver is a receiver, and without a recipient, there can be no gift. Since we all are both givers and receivers in life, it is wise to be generous in giving and in getting gifts. By definition, generosity involves giving something away. The more valuable something is, the more meaningful is the act of sharing it. Yet, while giving is self-sacrificial, it also is mutually beneficial. We recognize that when we give, we also gain. This is the generosity paradox we considered earlier. In a similar vein, here is another way of thinking about giving.

Generous Exchanges

First, consider purely commercial exchanges. I can trade my own goods or services (my possessions or personal assets) for money. This is the nature of work. Then, I can trade my money for other people's goods or services. These interactions are based on reciprocity. In a proper market, both parties in the exchange come freely to an agreement based on their individual perception of the worth and utility of the items involved.

After a transaction, one party or the other may feel that they've received a "bargain" (paying less or receiving more than they expected). Bargains can happen negatively out of ignorance on one side—not knowing what something truly is worth. Bargains also can happen positively if there is a commitment on both sides to fairness and to delivering value. This can lead to a situation where both parties feel they came out ahead, and it is the optimal outcome of any business arrangement.

Even a two-way bargain is not a gift, however. It is part of a deal—an arrangement in which both sides are seeking a positive outcome primarily for themselves. Such natural self-interest underlies one core principle of commerce: *caveat emptor*, or "let the buyer beware."

In contrast, givers are not wary. In fact, they can be careless—even reckless—in shifting concern away from themselves and toward others. Likewise, generosity is not deliberately reciprocal. A well-meaning gift is provided without expectation of return. We are willing to give up something with no intent of getting anything back.

Nonetheless, we do receive benefits from our giving. Examples abound in literature, philosophy, and life experience. One of my favorite sayings in this vein often is attributed to the Chinese sage Confucius: "If you want happiness for a year, inherit a fortune. If you want happiness for a lifetime, help someone else."

Considering the nature of giving and receiving, generous exchanges often are not "in kind." We don't get like for like. We may give possessionally (belongings) and get back emotionally. We may give personally (time and talent) and get back relationally. In these cases, and in contrast to what we see in nature, the gravitational pull of generosity is upward. A gift of something less valuable (like a possession) can create or nurture something more valuable (like a relationship).

Even generosity that is like-for-like can have a magnified effect where $1 + 1 > 2$. If we are socially generous (including others positively in our lives), the effect tends to ripple outward. If we involve others in our own memorable and important moments, they are likely to do the same. Often, additional people become involved as well. The networked effect of such generous behavior can be dramatic, and we will explore the potential for such Exponential Generosity later in chapter 25.

For now, let's consider a tool that can be used to help evaluate the meaning and impact of WISEgenerosity for both giver and receiver.

Generosity Dimensions: A Tool for Evaluating W.I.S.E. Giving

Our physical world is three-dimensional. The size of an object is determined by its height, width, and depth. While generosity can't be reduced to a formula, we can imagine generosity occurring across three dimensions when it comes to its elements and outcomes. Givers and receivers each have three attributes—which I will call the three S's—that correspond to the effect of their involvement in a gift.

The three S's for givers are:
- Sincerity
- Sacrifice
- Significance

Sincerity is an input. In chapter 5, we considered the idea that we determine inputs—like attitude and effort—for our lives but that we often do not control outputs. We choose to be sincere or not with a gift we give (input) regardless of how the receiver responds (output). Sincerity derives from attitude. If we approach a gift with proper humility and commitment, we should feel good about it.

Sacrifice also is an input. We choose how much we are willing to offer another when we are giving. Larger gifts cost more in money, time, and commitment. Larger gifts also have the potential to be more meaningful than smaller gifts. Sacrifice derives from action. We must offer and then release a gift in order to complete it.

Significance is an output. The impact of a gift depends on circumstances and the attitude and actions of both giver and receiver.

The three S's for receivers are:
- Satisfaction

- Substance
- Significance

Satisfaction is an input. In receiving a gift, we control how we react: with appreciation and gratitude or not. Satisfaction is derived from attitude. As receivers, we decide whether or not to be engaged and responsive or entitled and dismissive. Perhaps a gift fulfills a physical need, like hunger being satisfied by a meal. Perhaps it fulfills an emotional need, like a longing for connection to another person being satisfied by an embrace.

Substance also is an input, and it mirrors Sacrifice. We can respond to a gift with an equal or even greater response, or we can be half-hearted and noncommittal. Substance derives from action. Our reaction as receivers determines what kind of results a gift produces.

As it is for givers, *Significance* for receivers is an output. Repeating the thought above, the impact of a gift depends on circumstances and the attitude and actions of both giver and receiver.

Based on this framework, we can chart the Generosity Dimensions for givers and receivers like this:

GIVER		
Attribute	*Orientation*	*Essence*
Sincerity	Input	Attitude
Sacrifice	Input	Action
Significance	Output	

RECEIVER		
Attribute	*Orientation*	*Essence*
Satisfaction	Input	Attitude
Substance	Input	Action
Significance	Output	

We also can map them out as follows:

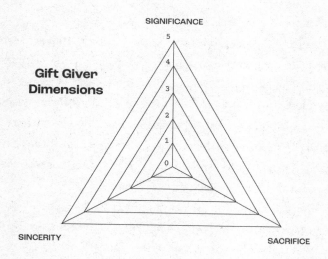

"Three S" Dimensions for Generosity: Giver

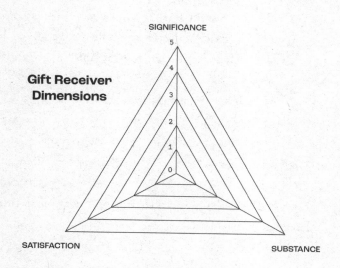

"Three S" Dimensions for Generosity: Receiver

In this system, each dimension is recorded on a 0–5 scale. The result is a pyramid reflecting the strength of the impact involved. A higher score in any dimension increases the volume of the resulting shape and illustrates a more powerful result for either the giver or the receiver.

It bears repeating that I am using these illustrations abstractly and not as a means to "measure" generosity. The graphics are not a geometric proof but rather visual depictions of the results that Generosity Dimensions have on the meaning and impact of gifts. Three dimensions of giving connect naturally to form a pyramid shape, as is shown in these examples.

The ultimate point is that a sincere, sacrificial, and significant gift received satisfyingly, substantially, and with similar significance is going to be more important than a gift lacking any or all of these dimensions.

Generosity Dimensions Illustrated

My teenage son, Reed, loves sports, delicious but unhealthy food, and amusement parks. We had the opportunity a few years ago to spend a wonderful father/son weekend in Kansas City, during which we ate world-famous BBQ or steak for every meal, rode roller coasters together until we were dizzy, and enjoyed the home opener of Patrick Mahomes (one of Reed's favorite players) and the Kansas City Chiefs at legendary Arrowhead Stadium.

I was very Sincere (5 out of 5) in my excitement to provide this experience for us to enjoy together. It was a significant Sacrifice (4 out of 5, based on our schedules and recreation budget) to leverage the time and money needed. The results were Significant (5 out of 5) father/son moments, which created memories for us both of us to treasure. When charted on the pyramid, these giver dimensions look as follows:

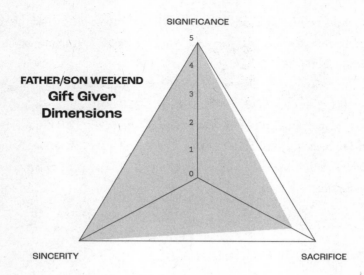

My son responded by being Satisfied (5 out of 5) in appreciation. My efforts were Substantial (5 out of 5) to him and positively reinforced our relationship. Likewise, he views the experience as Significant (4 out of 5) and still relishes our sharing it together. These receiver dimensions look as follows:

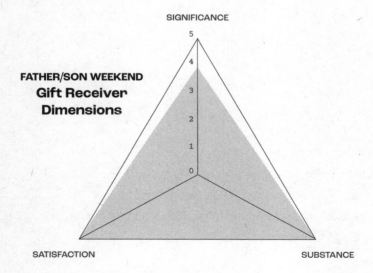

In each case, there was positive reciprocity. My son's generosity dimensions positively affected mine, and vice versa. We each came away from the experience happy and fulfilled.

Conversely, imagine a situation where someone unloaded some unwanted concert tickets on me to see [insert the name of a band you don't love here]. I wasn't excited about the show and only took the tickets out of obligation. I decided to make the best of the situation by bringing my college-age daughter, Ellie, along. Those giver dimensions might look as follows (Sincerity 1, Sacrifice 1, Significance 2):

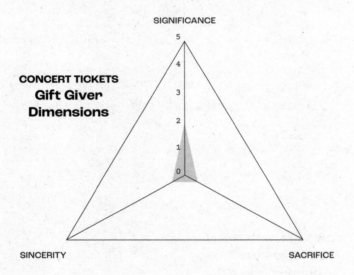

During the evening, Ellie's attention was not on the show. We clashed about her being buried in her electronic device, to our mutual annoyance. While it always is good to spend time together, in this case we would have been better off staying at home. Those receiver dimensions might look like this (Satisfaction 1, Substance 2, Significance 1):

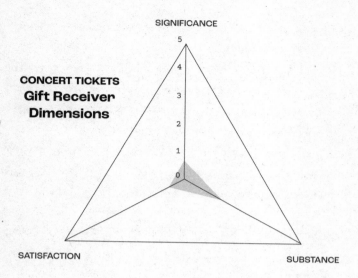

SIGNIFICANCE

CONCERT TICKETS
**Gift Receiver
Dimensions**

SATISFACTION   SUBSTANCE

Clearly, this would not be nearly as positive an outcome. (Sorry, Ellie! On the bright side, this less-than-fully generous misspent evening was pretend. I look forward to some real fun with you soon.)

Generosity Effects—Exponential

There is a further observation to be made from these examples: the exponential effect of WISEgenerosity. Giving expands farther and faster with each increase in the underlying components.

In the dimensional charts, each resulting 3-D shape is a pyramid with a triangular base. Considering the way in which stronger ratings in the dimensions affect the outcome of giving, we can use the resulting geometric relationships to analogize the impact of generosity.

If you love math, this may be the first part of the book that's captured your attention. If you aren't a math fan, please humor me. Either way, the calculations related to the following numbers are detailed in this endnote.[228]

In the father/son weekend example, the overall giver impact (the volume of that 5 × 4 × 5 3-D pyramid) is 16.6. The overall receiver impact (the volume of that 5 × 5 ×4 3-D pyramid) is 16.6. Adding the two together gives a total rating of 33.2.

As expected, the concert example was much less impressive. The giver impact (1 × 1 × 2) was only 0.33. The receiver impact (1 × 2 × 1) also came in at 0.33. The two together equaled a total rating of 0.66. This makes the weekend scenario fifty times more potent than the concert scenario.

Charting and graphing this model of dimensional giving may make the relationship even clearer. Here is what results from a progression where the giver and receiver dimensions all are 1, then 2, then 3, then 4, then 5:

Giver Dimensions	Receiver Dimensions	Total Impact Rating
1 x 1 x 1	1 x 1 x 1	0.33
2 x 2 x 2	2 x 2 x 2	2.67
3 x 3 x 3	3 x 3 x 3	9.00
4 x 4 x 4	4 x 4 x 4	21.33
5 x 5 x 5	5 x 5 x 5	41.67

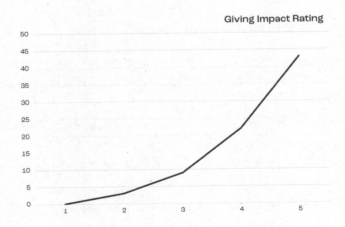

Giving Impact Rating

Exponential Impact of Generosity: Giving Dimensions

The steepening upward slope of this curve indicates an exponential rela-tionship. Each addition to the generosity dimensions multiplies the impact of the outcome. Again, this is an analogy, but I believe that it is indicative of reality: giving truly does offer potential outputs far greater than the inputs that go into it. Moreover, a little extra effort as a giver or receiver can produce outsized results for both.

One other observation about this model is the effect of a null input. A zero in any one (or more) of the giver or receiver elements results in a gift that literally doesn't leave the ground. The shape produced is either two- or one-dimensional. I recall from my experience as a student the devastating impact that a 0 percent grade on an assignment can have on an overall average. The same is true for giving. Lack of engagement in any dimension collapses the entire process.

Ultimately, this quantitative exercise illustrates a more fundamental qualitative point about WISEgenerosity. The *inputs* we bring to a gift (Sincerity and Sacrifice) largely determine the *outputs* produced for the receiver (Satisfaction and Substance). The Giving Dimensions tool helps us to see more clearly the potential meaning and impact of our giving. Ideally, my generous engagement with my children and with others serves to build the purposeful and practical connections that are fundamental to these relationships. If done well, these efforts are W.I.S.E.—Well-grounded, Inspired, Satisfying, and Effective.

CHAPTER 17

Wealth Success and Wealth Failure

ONE MOTIVATION FOR THIS ENTIRE PROJECT was a sense of frustration and missed opportunities in my professional experience from having seen families fail to achieve their best potential outcomes in terms of the things that mattered most to them.

Syd Walker is a consultant to wealthy families and a good friend with whom I have collaborated for years. He and I define "Wealth Success" as thriving relationships and productive resources sustained through generations.[229] Effective generosity is key in both areas.

Optimal Giving and Wealth Success

Successful families harness *internal generosity* in their relationships. They identify and support the individual needs of each family member. They treat each other with respect, care, compassion, and love.

Successful families harness *external generosity* with their resources. Looking outside of themselves, they invest to benefit their communities and donate thoughtfully to effective causes.

With that last point in mind, purposeful and practical charitable and philanthropic engagement is central to successful families. External generosity provides an opportunity for family members to align their individual values

and purposes. Meaningful and effective giving also engages younger generations and teaches that sharing time, talent, and treasure is essential to living a
good life.

Optimal Giving for affluent families in this context involves communication, coordination, and collaboration between the family, the nonprofit
organizations to which they are donating, and the professional advisors who
are supporting them. Facilitating such outcomes is the focus of my wealth
management practice, and it is a pleasure and privilege to have work that is so
personally and professionally rewarding.

WISEgenerosity Example: The Rockefellers vs. The Vanderbilts

We can contrast Wealth Success and Wealth Failure using an historical example.
According to *CNN Money* and adjusted for current dollars, John D. Rockefeller
and Cornelius Vanderbilt were the first and second wealthiest Americans ever.[230]
Their family trajectories were very different, however.

The Rockefellers generally were successful at maintaining their relationships and their resources through multiple generations. The Vanderbilts, in
contrast, suffered dramatic and rapid decline. Two concepts and their connection with WISEgenerosity help to explain these contrasting outcomes: Family
Capital and Financial Capital.

Family Capital is relationship-focused and is produced by people, values,
experiences, and social connections. These largely intangible qualities are
comprised of the family's talents and abilities, character, practical capabilities,
and community engagement.

Financial Capital is resource-focused and is made of actual and potential
assets. These more tangible elements consist of business interests, property,
and investments, along with the ability to generate more of the same through
continued productive efforts.

At the risk of oversimplifying one family's success and the other's failure, the Rockefellers were generous to each other and to others, while the Vanderbilts were not.[231]

Contrasting Approaches to Living

The Rockefellers had an internal culture (Family Capital) that generally was nurturing and positive. The older generations focused on developing their children into people who were able to function well personally and in society and to live up to the responsibilities that came with being so wealthy. John D. Rockefeller Jr. reflected later in his life, "I was always so afraid that money would spoil my children...and I wanted them to know its value and not waste it or throw it away on things that weren't worthwhile."[232]

In contrast, Cornelius Vanderbilt treated his children with contempt and sowed seeds of discord and disfunction in the process. As the son who had been tapped to take over the entire family fortune, William Vanderbilt endured constant berating and belittling by his father. Cornelius, "The Commodore," insisted on calling William "Billy," even though (or perhaps because) William hated it. That was in relatively good moments. The "choice collection of epithets he barked at his son whenever something went wrong" included barbs like "blatherskite" and "chucklehead."[233] It was an abusive relationship in many respects. In one episode, Cornelius told William to give up cigar smoking. William dutifully agreed to quit on the spot, and then the elder Vanderbilt blew his own smoke spitefully in his son's face.[234]

Both families were controversial and stirred much criticism of the business practices that produced their fortunes. Even so, the operations of the Rockefeller family (Financial Capital) were outwardly focused and concerned primarily with productively benefiting society. The operations of the Vanderbilt family, however, were inwardly focused and concerned primarily with their own enjoyment and prestige. Along these lines, both families produced impressive structures in New York City, but in remarkably different ways and with starkly different results.

Rockefeller Center in central Manhattan was the largest private building project of its time and was built in the 1930s during the height of the Great Depression.[235] Going ahead with such a monumental effort in such difficult conditions was modeling deliberate generosity. The Rockefellers wanted to demonstrate their belief in America and to put thousands of people to work when the national economy otherwise was in shambles. They took considerable risk by cashing out a large amount of their legacy Standard Oil stock (the root of the family fortune) at depressed prices to fund the effort.[236]

In the end, the returns on this project were impressive. By the time they sold a majority stake in the property in 1989, the Rockefellers had made a useful 5.42 percent compounded annual return on their capital. Moreover, the holdings produced generous quantities of rental income that helped to fund the family for two generations.[237] Containing offices, shops, restaurants, and entertainment hubs like Radio City Musical Hall and NBC Studios, the complex has been a centerpiece of work and fun in New York City for nearly a century and has been enjoyed by millions. The old saying "Doing well by doing good" certainly worked in this case!

In contrast, the Vanderbilts' signature real estate project in New York was an opulent mansion completed by Cornelius Vanderbilt II (the Commodore's oldest grandson) and his wife in 1893. The house was massive—built across an entire city block at Fifth Avenue between Fifty-seventh and Fifty-eighth Streets. Moreover, the driver behind constructing it was almost entirely selfish. "It was a common belief at the time that Alice Vanderbilt set out to dwarf her sister-in-law [Alva]'s Fifth Avenue chateau, and dwarf it she did."[238]

One of the family's many enormous mansions, the structure was "chilly and uncomfortable, built for social functions but not for living."[239] It also was a tremendous waste of money—underused and unwanted. The property was built for $6 million and eventually sold in 1926 for $7 million, only to be torn down so that the Bergdorf Goodman department store could be built on the land.[240] That is a negligible return of 0.47 percent per year. Even worse, the house demanded decades of expensive upkeep that consumed nearly all the income from Alice Vanderbilt's trust fund for an ultimately futile purpose.

Contrasting Approaches to Giving

Each family's approach to external giving could not have been more different.

Following the pattern of their Family and Financial Capital, the Rockefellers invested thoughtfully in projects meant to improve the country and the world on a scale consistent with their resources. The Rockefeller Foundation helped create modern philanthropy by remaking "personal charity into an organized, institutional enterprise modeled on corporate business practices."[241] The family also transformed the National Park System by donating land and infrastructure from Acadia in Maine to Yosemite in California and from the Virgin Islands to Hawaii.[242] They demonstrated significant motivations (connection, conviction, and compassion) and substantial effects (strong meaning and solid impact).

While later generations of Vanderbilts were generous in their communities, so much of the family fortune had been wasted by then on self-serving projects that there was much less left to share. The one significant gift made by Cornelius himself was $1 million to help found and endow what then became Vanderbilt University in Nashville.[243] The Commodore was convinced to make the donation by his younger second wife, who was close to the school's founder. The motivation was compulsion (domestic harmony and ego), and there seems to have been little meaning attached by Vanderbilt to the gift and little impact by it on him.

WISEgenerosity Produces Successful Families

The Rockefeller name lives on, and the family remains on lists of the wealthiest in America in spite of more than 150 years of having money diffused through an ever-larger family tree. While the Vanderbilt name also is prominent, its legacy largely is in the form of lingering monuments from its heyday. Cornelius died in 1877, and most of the family's money was gone within fifty years of his death.[244]

While you aren't likely to have the same resources or responsibilities that the Rockefellers or Vanderbilts once did, the forces that applied to them then still apply generally to families now. Being generous nurtures family prosperity through thriving relationships and useful resources. Not behaving generously breeds division and inevitable dissolution over time.

You might have heard the saying, "Shirtsleeves to shirtsleeves in three generations." This old adage refers to the commonplace failure of children or grandchildren to properly manage the wealth that was handed down to them by previous generations. This pattern is seen in humanity throughout its history: fortunes made quickly tend to crumble quickly. WISEgenerosity offers an antidote—families who are thoughtful and effective at giving among themselves and to their communities tend to succeed.

Where You Should Give: Proximity, Proportion, Production, Power, and (the) Present

"What should I give?" and "When should I give?" are central questions for WISEgenerosity. A considerate approach to giving accounts for your drivers, motivations, and personality. Thoughtfully avoiding attitudes and actions that can undermine successful giving is also essential. Having reflected on these elements, the next question is, "Where should I give?"

In this section, we'll explore the components of WISEgenerosity, beginning with the elements that make giving practical and productive. The better we apply our generosity, the more effective the results will be and the more we will be motivated to continue giving.

There are essential elements to giving well, and I call them the five P's: Proximity, Proportion, Production, Power, and the Present. Let's look at each.

CHAPTER 18

Proximity: Closer Is Better

IN WISEGENEROSITY, CLOSER IS BETTER.

The more connected we are to a person in need or to a cause or a community, the more effective our giving is likely to be. We will know more, understand more, and empathize more.

Proximity: Radiating Priorities

Purpose flows from the priorities in our lives that govern how we spend our time, our talent, and our treasure. We should apply that purpose to a radiating set of priorities, as illustrated by this diagram:

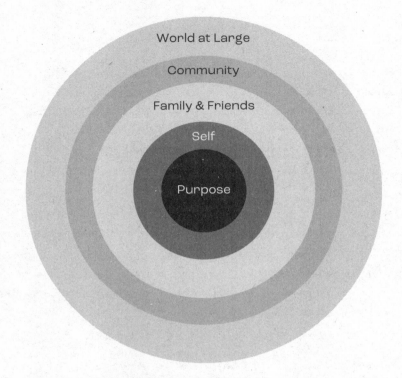

The Proximity Progression

First is self. It may seem counterintuitive to put ourselves closest to the center of priorities in a book about giving. Truly, though, if we aren't generous to ourselves, how can we sustain a healthy generosity toward others?

A wise client of mine would say this as his parting words at the end of every meeting: "Be kind to yourself." That conversation closing has stuck with me through the years. Are we as kind to ourselves as we should be? Not always.

In terms of Possessional Giving—that is, providing sufficient resources for our own security—are we working hard and saving for the future?

In terms of Personal Giving—our time and talent—are we committed to our own physical and mental well-being?

In terms of Social Giving—contributing positively to those around us— are we willing to engage for mutual benefit?

In terms of Emotional Giving—attending to our spiritual wellness—do we give ourselves the space and time needed for our internal health?

In terms of Relational Giving—allowing ourselves to grow with experience—are we willing to forgive and learn from our own mistakes, or do we beat ourselves up over them?

If we can't be kind to ourselves, we will end up being a burden and in need of support ourselves rather than being able to extend support to others. There is a reason why every airplane flight includes the instructions to, if necessary, put on your own oxygen mask first—even before helping your children. You are no good to others if you are distressed. Taking care of yourself is generous.

Second in the Proximity Progression diagram is family and friends. Where do we have the most impact? On the people closest to us. Where is our effort multiplied on behalf of others? Where it penetrates the deepest due to pathways that already are open. Where can we do the most damage with selfish, unkind behavior? Also to those closest to us. Am I doing everything I can to support and serve my wife and children, my family, my friends, my clients, my colleagues?

Several years ago, I tried to take advice from a friend about finding time for spiritual reflection in my life. For a period of weeks, I started every day in my room reading and meditating. It was positive and energizing. Sadly, however, the effects were limited. One morning, after a few minutes of quiet contemplation, I emerged from the peace of my bedroom to find that my wonderful wife and children were at odds about some minor aspect of family life. Before you could say "calm and considerate," I was in the middle of the melee, crossly admonishing and shooting arrows of opprobrium all around. How quickly my spiritual efforts evaporated.

The old adage, "Charity begins at home," came to mind both then and now.[245] Serving and being considerate to those we love is generous.

Third in the progression is community. Proximate giving is based on access and understanding. Are there people in need around me? Are there new neighbors I can welcome? Is there an elderly friend I can visit? Are there children without access to educational, recreational, or economic opportunities whom I can support? Will I dedicate time and expertise to people who can benefit from it? What problems are facing my community that I can help to solve? These can be the most satisfying generosity engagements we have.

I witnessed many great examples of generosity growing up. One was "Pop Pop" (my father's father). He was unassuming and principled, like many other members of the Greatest Generation. Whenever we went to visit our family in southern New Jersey, I saw examples of his deep connection to and commitment to his neighbors and friends. Pop Pop led the volunteer fire department and was mayor of the small town in which he lived. He volunteered many hours at local service organizations. In business, he and his brothers were wholesalers of fruit and vegetables to the hotels and restaurants of Atlantic City and the surrounding area. They had low margins and fierce competition. Pop Pop still provided the best products, best service, and best prices he could. He got up at 3:30 a.m. every weekday to be the first at work and to make sure all was ready for the day. When we visited, my brother Jon and I would go to "the Market" on Saturday mornings and climb around on the boxes of produce stacked to the ceiling of the warehouse while he checked on accounts. More than once, I found Pop Pop outside speaking with a ragged-looking person from the tough surrounding neighborhood. Kind words were accompanied by a subtle sharing of a bill or two from his wallet. In so many ways, he never called attention to himself and was an inspiring example of community generosity.

Fourth in the progression is the world at large. The rest of the planet is important, of course. Still, we need to recognize that our greatest impact on others is close at hand rather than far away. Systemic solutions to global problems start with each of us. The famous saying "be the change you want to see in the world"[246] exhorts us to consider proximity.

If you're concerned about the environment, where will you do the most good? You can be kind (picking up trash around you when you see it), be charitable (engaging in local efforts to conserve resources), and be philanthropic (supporting groups that have a meaningful long-term impact on environmental issues). In each case, involvement locally likely will be the most effective.

I have a hypothetical example in mind for this part. Some famous people get attention for giving. (Although, sadly, not many people worthy of admiration get famous purely *from* giving.) These already renowned personages may affiliate with a worthy cause. They may write a check and fly in for a photo op with some needy people. This causes a buzz in social media. It may even do some good in calling attention to a problem. But what if they go back home and are dreadful to their family, their employees, and everyone else around them? Would we think of them as truly generous? I don't think so. What happens close to home matters a lot more than what happens far away.

Let's look back at the center of the proximity diagram. The key decision of our lives is the purpose we place at the heart of this circle. If we want to make a difference in our lives and in the world around us, focusing closer to the center is better.

Please know I am not suggesting that we should apply generosity to distant problems only if we can be present in person. There are very real needs in every part of the world, and some of the largest are far removed from us physically. Giving in terms of proximity is not an all-or-nothing proposition. If necessary, we can use on-the-ground intermediaries who are connected to the issues involved and thus able to produce a potentially positive impact.

The point of proximity is that having a positive impact on any problem requires being connected to it. Proximity—practical, physical, organizational, virtual—to the object of your efforts makes generosity more effective, no matter who you are and how much of your time, talent, and treasure you plan to contribute.

There is a saying from Shantideva (an eighth-century Buddhist teacher) that has stuck with me ever since I read it: "Where would there be leather enough to cover the entire world? With just the leather of my sandals, it is as if the whole world were covered."[247]

Each of us tending to our own walk of life with kindness, charity, and philanthropy can change the world one relationship at a time. As we'll explore later, the exponential effect of that collective effort could be transformative. Making the world a better place is generous and starts with the lives around us.

CHAPTER 19

Proportion: Larger Is Better

IN WISEGENEROSITY, LARGER IS BETTER.

"Larger" in this sense relates both to scale and to attitude. Continuing a reference to Buddhism, there are three levels of giving presented by Buddha: miserly, kindly, and kingly.[248]

Miserly Giving

Discarding leftovers in which you are not interested.

Kindly Giving

Sharing what you would want yourself.

Kingly Giving

Providing even more and better than you would use yourself.

Proportional Giving in Buddhism

Here is a reframing of the same concepts using Western thinking:

Proportional Giving in Western Terms

Tin Giving could be expressed as "stooping to help others" when we're disposing of things we no longer need or sharing when it's not by choice.

Golden Giving relates directly to the "Golden Rule"—do to others as you would like them to do to you.

Diamond Giving means doing even more for others than you would do for yourself. This last concept is known as self-sacrificial *agape* love in Greek philosophy and in Christian theology. *Agape* giving is very much like the kingly giving suggested by Buddha.

Tin Giving is common. One might even point to some large and celebrated examples of giving as "Tin." I spoke with an observer of nonprofit fundraising who disparaged the giving practices of some major philanthropists as "waste management." He meant that the donors had far more money than they ever could spend and elected to give some of it away rather than burning it or dumping it in the ocean. Not being personally connected to their giving made it hollow and less powerful than it could be.

Still, Tin Giving can be effective in terms of helping people. Thinking in terms of W.I.S.E. giving, discarded possessions or time or talent given even unwillingly to a worthy cause still can be Effective. The missing part of the equation is Inspiration or Satisfaction on the part of the giver. Tin Giving is not

Well-Grounded, either. Any positive impact is a fortunate coincidence. Overall, the effects of Tin Giving are one-dimensional at best.

Golden Giving is common as well and more virtuous. Both the giver and the receiver share in the positive impact. As the Adam Smith quote in chapter 2 illustrated, there is something about our nature that feels good when we engage in helping others. If we see someone lacking something that we value and we share it with them, both sides benefit.

I enjoyed opportunities for this type of giving with my children when they were younger. Shopping with them for backpacks filled with supplies before school started or for presents to be shared with other kids at Christmas reminded us all that others don't have some of the blessings we might take for granted.

Using the W.I.S.E. giving model, Golden Giving has the potential to fulfill all the WISEgenerosity criteria. If done well, it is Well-grounded, Inspired, Satisfying, and Effective.

Diamond Giving is precious and rare. Like its namesake, it also is strong. Just as diamonds can cut almost anything, Diamond Giving can slice through the most difficult of circumstances.

City of Refuge in Atlanta, where I volunteer, has an affiliated House of Cherith program that helps restore the lives of women rescued from the modern slavery of sex trafficking. These women have experienced years of devastating treatment at the hands of others. Recovery begins when someone possessing uncommon compassion connects with one of these women and starts to chip away at the shell that has built up because of her suffering. Hours and weeks and months and years of relationship building eventually replace abuse with self-worth and despair with dignity. This is a slow process and requires love even more powerful than the dark forces that produced the trauma. Like a diamond produced from carbon, intense pressure, and time, the end result can be strong and radiant.

Diamond Giving amplifies WISEgenerosity. Not only are all the W.I.S.E. elements represented, but the Generosity Dimensions we considered in chapter 16 are reflected as well. Diamond Giving is magnified by the sincerity, sacrifice, and significance of the giver and by the satisfaction, substance, and significance enjoyed by the receiver.

Proportionality and Circumstances: The Lottery Question

Shifting gears, here is a challenging thought: Should our commitment to generosity be proportional to what we have? If we are well-provisioned in terms of possessions, personal capabilities, social opportunities, emotional capacity, or relational engagement, should our capacity affect how much we give?

It is unsettling to say so, but I think that the answer is yes. Jesus taught, "From everyone to whom much has been given, much will be required; and from the one to whom much has been entrusted, even more will be demanded."[249] By this Christian understanding, the more we have, the more we need to give.

Even outside of religion, the world is full of cautionary tales about what happens to people who have more money or freedom than they can handle. There seem to be natural limits on what we can and should use for our own personal benefit from the total resources we have at our disposal.

Along these lines, imagine what would happen if you won a huge jackpot in a state-sponsored lottery. If you had vast sums of money, compared to what you have now, what would you do with it all? Of course, you would enjoy it. But is that all? And does the amount you "won" affect what you do with the total sum?

One of my own small touchstones in exploring generosity has been to revisit this question. Georgians seem to love the lottery, and there are billboards promoting it all over Atlanta. I drive by them regularly, and the new generation of advertisements have huge digital signs showing the vast amounts of the latest and largest jackpots. My attention can't help but be drawn to them. When making my way through the daily grind of traffic and responsibilities, my mind wanders to what I would do with such huge amounts of money.

I confess that my first instinct always used to be selfish. I imagined what I could do and where I could go and what I could buy. (Beach house, anyone?) This came to trouble me, though. The exercise was fun at first, but it quickly left me feeling empty. Is that all I was? Is that all I cared about? Is that all I aspired to?

I've tried over time to train myself away from this natural reaction. Some quick lottery math is involved. If the prize is $400 million, factor half of that for the single-pay option and then half of that gone in taxes. That leaves about $100 million.[250] What then? What if I give away $10 million to worthy causes? That could do a lot of good. People would say I was generous. And I'd still have $90 million left.

For anyone who has belonged to a synagogue or church, the thought process above likely is familiar. Giving 10 percent of one's income to charity (particularly one's house of worship) is known as *tithing*. The principle comes directly from the Bible and was encoded into Jewish law and later into Christian practice.[251] For people of faith, the idea is that all provision—material and spiritual—is a blessing from God. In recognition and gratitude, the "first fruits" of what we receive should go to serve God and help others.

A key is that these are minimum thresholds. The faith teaching is that everyone should give at least this base amount. There is no upside limit, however. The more we have, the more we should give.

The lottery question points me in a similar direction. What would I do with $90 million? Really. It is common knowledge that lottery winnings can ruin your life. Personal temptations combined with those looking to take advantage of my sudden wealth easily could be toxic. Perhaps having less *would* be better, and we really shouldn't take on more than we can handle. But what is that amount? I don't know, honestly; however, I do know that it's a lot less than 90 percent.

Proportion and Wealth

It turns out that very wealthy people undergo a similar thought process. Warren Buffett famously said that he wants his children to have "enough money so that they would feel they can do anything, but not so much that they could do nothing."[252]

Whether we're in a league with Mr. Buffett or somewhere far down the wealth spectrum, if we want to practice generosity, we need to determine how much we should give from the resources available to us. We can approach the answer in much the same way that I do in my professional practice when I'm helping a client develop a personal financial plan.

Good financial planning is goals-based. A solid strategy looks to align the mission, vision, and values of a client with intended outcomes for their money and a set of tactics and tools that can be used to achieve the goals. This means building the financial plan from the bottom up.

First, we make sure that clients have enough money to take care of themselves: personal goals. Second, we explore how any money left after their lifetimes can be used for the benefit of those to whom they are closest: family goals. We also ask about causes and groups that are important to them: community goals. In a normal case for a generous couple with a healthy level of savings, most of the money available takes care of personal needs, heirs get the next largest share, and funds are then allocated for charity and good works.

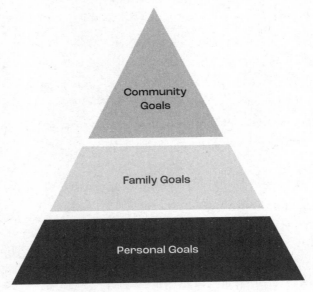

A "Normal" Progression for Using Wealth

However, the more money one has and the more committed one is to generosity, the more this calculation changes.

If there are ample resources to secure a comfortable lifestyle and/or a priority placed on financial giving, personal goals do not take up the majority of what is available. In such situations, the elder generation also tends to be concerned about not passing along too much to heirs for fear of undermining their self-sufficiency. Inheritance is planned so it can serve family goals, but within limits. That may leave much, if not most, of the resources still available. If so, there is an opportunity to plan for deliberate legacy-based community goals. We can call this a "Truly Generous" approach to financial planning.

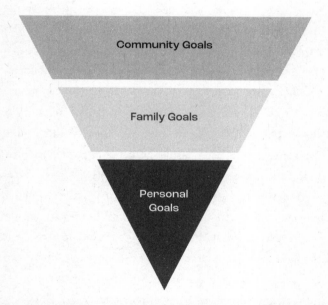

A "Truly Generous" Progression for Using Wealth

Such situations present great opportunities for generosity. I love being involved in this process. Regardless of the amount of money involved, the motto for my advisory practice is: "Helping successful people be even more generous and generous people be even more successful."

Giving Beyond Money

As noted in chapter 6, Possessional Giving is the lowest level in the giving progression. What about Personal Giving? How many minutes of every hour do you spend focused on others? How many hours of every day? How many days of every week or month? How do you "spend" your time and talent? Of course, the measure of Personal Giving is not limited to what we give to strangers. It also applies to what we give to the people around us: our families, our friends, our colleagues, our neighbors. How much of ourselves do we give to others?

Asking all these questions eventually led me to a new appreciation for the old concept of tithing. When you think about it, tithing seems like a good start for WISEgenerosity. If you are challenged in terms of any resources or habits, try to focus on giving 10 percent of them away. From my observations, you will be amazed by the positive impact this giving has on yourself and others. Intentionally dedicate 10 percent of time to your spouse, children, parents, siblings, friends, coworkers, neighbors, and people in your community.

You may already be dedicating more than 10 percent of your time, talent, and treasure to others. If so, great! Then you have the opportunity to see whether your generosity capacity has the potential to grow even further, which takes us back to the lottery question.

After years of wondering what I'd do if I were to win the lottery, I have come to the point where my first thought no longer is about myself (usually, at least). I imagine all the people I could help and things I could do with the money. As that mindset has expanded, it has changed my perspective on my own need for money. Generosity—both in actual practice and in my imagination—can make us more secure in and content with our own circumstances.

With more security and contentment, we can begin to work toward a "reverse tithing" mentality. In areas where we have surplus time, talent, or treasure, we can aspire to give away more than 10 percent, maybe even to the point where we give away 90 percent and keep 10 percent.

I can imagine someone reading this and thinking it is unrealistic and naïve. We live in a demanding world. There are things we continually "need" to do that easily will consume 90 percent and more of our resources. But I don't mean for reverse tithing to seem impossible or intimidating.

Remember that my definition of generosity is expansive. It exists at the intersection of attitude and action and includes pretty much anything we do conscientiously and with others in mind. Relieving your spouse of a chore is giving to others. Being a dedicated employee at work is giving to others. Welcoming a newcomer to school is giving to others. Calling a friend who is going through a tough time is giving to others. Supporting an aging parent is giving to others. Playing a game with your kids is giving to others. Even letting someone in front of you in traffic is giving to others. There are many ways, large and small, of being generous all the time.

In the lottery example, reverse tithing that $100 million of cash down to $10 million seems sensible. Truly, $10 million is much more money than most of us will ever need or expect to have. And having $90 million to give away would be an amazing opportunity for generously transforming places and people you care about.

Whether it is starting with 1 percent, working to 10 percent, committing to half, or dedicating 90 percent, when approached WISE-ly, more is better when it comes to giving.

CHAPTER 20

→

Production: More Frequent Is Better

IN WISEGENEROSITY, MORE FREQUENT IS BETTER.

Velocity is a term in economics that refers to the speed at which money circulates. Faster circulation indicates a stronger economy because it means that goods and services are changing hands more rapidly. Such activity usually represents higher output, more jobs, and more wealth being produced.

I suggest that "generosity velocity," or Productive Generosity, has similar characteristics. Gifts of time, talent, and treasure are not delicate flowers to display in isolation but rather are robust seeds to be planted over and over again. Productive giving stimulates more of the same. Accordingly, there is the potential for exponential growth in generosity.

Readers of a certain age will remember a TV commercial for shampoo from the 1980s. The idea was that the product was so good that you'd tell two friends about it. "And they'll tell two friends. And so on, and so on...." At each phrase the screen would split until it was filled with many images of the same small-boned, big-haired spokeswoman.[253]

This was the first suggestion to me of what became known later as *viral marketing*. While clean, voluminous hair is well and good, it would be even better to have explosive social impact for kindness, charity, and philanthropy, yes?

Good deeds do tend to replicate. Unfortunately, bad deeds do likewise—and with disproportionate effect. It takes a great deal of productive generosity

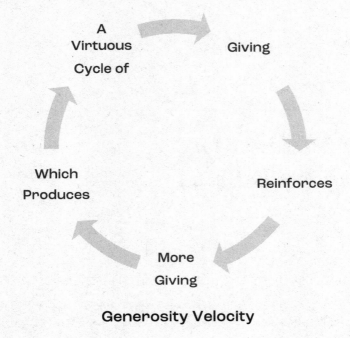

Generosity Velocity

to overcome the dead weight of accumulated malaise in individuals and much, much more for society as a whole. Even so, there is no other way I know to make the world a better place.

Productive Generosity in Action

An inspiring story of generosity is that of Hattie May Wiatt. If you visited the Philadelphia campus of Temple University some years ago, you would have seen Wiatt Hall, named after an important benefactor in the history of the school. Of course, this is not in and of itself unusual; institutions across America have buildings named after major donors. It might surprise you to learn, however, that Miss Wiatt was a local girl from a poor family who died young in 1886, around the time the school was founded. How did she come to be memorialized?

The answer is found in a sermon from the Reverend Russell Conwell delivered to the Grace Baptist (later the Temple) Church of Philadelphia in December 1912.[254] Reverend Conwell described the story of how the growing congregation he led years earlier had been short on space. One day, a little girl was among a crowd trying to get into a children's Sunday school class that was filled beyond capacity. She caught the minister's eye, and he carried her inside the classroom himself and found a place for her. Running into her the next day on her way to school, Reverend Conwell told her that someday there would be a larger space in which to gather, and he described a vision for what he had in mind to build if and when the money could be raised. This was a far-off prospect, and he was just making conversation, as far as he knew.

A short time afterward, Hattie May became sick and died. It came to light that she had taken the pastor's vision to heart and had managed to save fifty-seven cents, which she intended to contribute to the cause of the new church building. Her family passed along both the story and the money to Reverend Conwell. Inspired by her example, he changed the fifty-seven cents into pennies and auctioned each off to the congregation in her honor. Likewise inspired, the congregation paid around $250 for the fifty-seven coins. This was enough to buy a house near the church, where the Sunday school could expand.

The story would still be good if it ended there, but it continues. Fifty-four of the fifty-seven pennies sold were returned and displayed at the church as a testament to the generous spirit of young Hattie May. When the congregation again outgrew its space, Reverend Conwell went in search of more room. He used the remaining fifty-four cents as the symbolic down payment on a large lot. Over time, the congregation raised the rest of what was needed, and then raised funds to build a college and a hospital. These are now Temple University and Temple University Hospital. Thousands and thousands of people have been educated, healed, and blessed based on the inspiration of a small girl and her fifty-seven cents.

WISEgenerosity Example:
Good Coming from Adversity

Another powerful example of productive generosity comes from Children's Healthcare of Atlanta. My wife and I both have volunteered for years at Children's, one of the leading pediatric care and research hospitals in the world. A cornerstone of Children's Healthcare is the Aflac Cancer and Blood Disorders Center.

The story behind this program is remarkable. Vicki Riedel was a development officer on the hospital staff in 1995, when the treatment area for pediatric cancer patients was in need of $25,000 for renovations. Researching potential donors, Vicki identified Aflac, an insurance company, as a prospect. The company was located not far away in Columbus, Georgia, and they also sold insurance related to treatment of health issues, including cancer. Vicki hoped that was enough of a connection to encourage Aflac to donate the necessary gift, and she managed to secure an appointment and made the two-hour drive to meet with them.

It is important to note that Vicki's work meant more to her than just a paycheck. Vicki's then young daughter Ansley had suffered multiple battles with leukemia, from which she still was recovering. At a critical point in Ansley's disease, there was no place nearby that could perform the bone marrow transplant needed to save her. Vicki and Ansley had to move to Seattle for three months of intensive treatment. Drawing on these experiences as a mother, Vicki was a passionate advocate as well as a professional fundraiser.

Meeting at Aflac with Kathelen Spencer Amos, who was responsible for sponsorships and donations, Vicki told her own personal story and explained the need for support at the hospital. Realizing that more than $25,000 should be at stake, Kathelen then introduced president and CEO Dan Amos to Vicki. As Kathelen put it later, a "transformation" took place.[255]

Moved by Vicki's story and the need for a local facility capable of delivering the full range of care to kids with cancer, Dan asked how much it would cost to create such a program. Not long after, the company donated the necessary $3 million, and the Aflac Cancer and Blood Disorders Center was born.

The transformation didn't end there. Dan and Kathelen became deeply committed to this cause, but they knew that more was needed to perform the necessary research and provide the needed treatments. They started making connections inside and outside their company with the goal of inspiring as many people as possible to join them.

In the years since, the Cancer and Blood Disorders Center has become foundational to Aflac's culture and corporate purpose. More than 15,000 of the company's 20,000 field agents from across the country deduct money directly from their commissions to support the cause. The total of this exceptional collective generosity is now more than $400,000 per month.[256]

The combined individual and corporate efforts from Aflac and its associates have provided more than $165 million to Children's and to the cause of treating and ultimately eliminating childhood cancer. As a result, the Aflac Cancer and Blood Disorders Center is one of the preeminent institutions of its kind.[257]

Thinking back to the story of Ansley and her illness, Dan Amos talks about the lives that have been saved and believes the giving relationship that Vicki Riedel began provides at least one answer to the question, "What good can possibly come from adversity?"[258]

There is one last part to this amazing story. Little Ansley was grateful for and deeply attached to the wonderful nurses who cared for her at Children's. Fast-forward to today, and Nurse Ansley provides the same kind of comfort and care to her patients at Children's, on the same campus as the Aflac Cancer and Blood Disorders Center she inspired.[259] That is productive generosity!

CHAPTER 21

Power: Stronger Is Better

IN WISEGENEROSITY, STRONGER IS BETTER.

Strong and effective giving comes from aligning three forces: passion, opportunity, and impact:

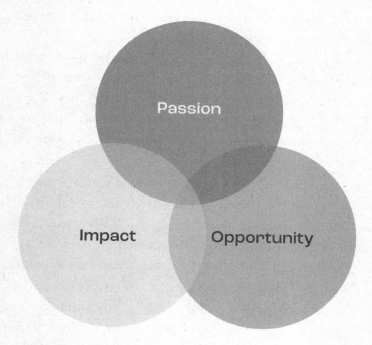

Alignment for Powerful Giving

Passion provides us with the internal drive to deploy ourselves on behalf of others. Opportunity finds situations where we can engage in the causes we care about. Impact is the positive result achieved from our efforts. The "sweet spot" in the center of this diagram is where the three intersect. This is where we have our highest and best prospects for powerful generosity.

Generosity Risk

There is a concept related to generosity power that I'd like to explore: *generosity risk*. When asked, 30 percent of potential donors say the largest single reason they don't give more money away is because they are not confident it will be used well.[260] The same surely is true for time and talent. If we are sharing precious resources, we can hesitate if we're not sure about the outcomes involved.

Consider your personal inclinations. Are you aggressive or cautious when it comes to giving? In other words, how much assurance do you need before you make a decision to help someone or something?

There is a trade-off involved. Being careful and reducing the potential risk that your gift won't be as productive as you'd like inevitably reduces the impact it might have. By contrast, aggressive giving has a wide range of potential outcomes, ranging from great to dismal. Cautious giving narrows the possible results. You are less likely to get a superlative outcome, but you reduce the likelihood of waste and frustration as well.

There is a parallel from the world of investing. Depending on your age, the amount of time until you need to spend money from your investments, and your natural inclination toward risk, you need to calibrate your portfolio. If you are cautious, you want to stick with safer holdings. If you are aggressive, you may prefer high-potential investments that have a large upside but also the possibility of disappearing. Your choices depend on your needs and goals.[261]

Giving is the same way. If you want to volunteer or contribute financially to a charity, for instance, what kind of nonprofit suits you best? If you are cautious, you will likely prefer a well-established, potentially larger group. Like a "blue-chip" stock, you are confident that it is well-run and that your involvement will support good results. On the other hand, your hours and your effort will have only a limited impact in proportion to the overall program size or budget of a large institution.

Conversely, if you put money and time into a small and struggling nonprofit, there is a significant possibility that the results may not be good despite your involvement. Even so, the potential positive result of the effort you apply as an aggressive giver will necessarily have a much larger relative impact. If the group succeeds, the "return" in terms of benefit for others and satisfaction for you will be that much greater.

Of course, these tendencies are not prescriptive. You can and should be as aggressive or cautious as you like when it comes to giving. Any giving done thoughtfully and with the right attitude is good. The key is making it as powerful as you can based on the approach that best suits you.

You also may want to "diversify" your giving like you would your investments. A balance of cautious and aggressive giving suited to your personality can be a great outcome.

One last related observation: As in investing, the more time, talent, and treasure you have, the more potential "risk" you can "afford." The rules of proximity (closer is better), proportion (larger is better), and production (more frequent is better) suggest that there is the potential for a "transformative" gift scaled to the size of the organization or the effort involved. Consider your ability to make a large and lasting impact when you give. We later will explore the potential exponential benefits to society from such an approach.

Overall, powerful giving is an important concept to WISEgenerosity. We will look at it further in chapter 24.

CHAPTER 22

$\longrightarrow$

Present: Now Is Better

IN WISEGENEROSITY, NOW IS BETTER.

A story to this effect comes from the now-ironically named New College, Oxford (founded in 1379), of which I am honored to be a member, dating back to my graduate studies there.

The college has a Great Hall worthy of the name. The massive oak beams supporting it are up to forty-five feet long, and the space has been used as a setting in television and films. A BBC TV series relates that, in the latter half of the nineteenth century, insects infested and compromised the Great Hall's wood.[262] Distressed about how such magnificent materials possibly could be replaced, a delegation consulted the forester in charge of timberland owned by the college:

> He pulled his forelock and said, "Well sirs, we was wonderin' when you'd be askin'."
>
> Upon further inquiry it was discovered that when the College was founded, a grove of oaks had been planted to replace the beams in the dining hall when they became beetly, because oak beams always become beetly in the end. This plan had been passed down from one Forester to the next for over five hundred years saying "You don't cut them oaks. Them's for the College Hall."[263]

The foresight to plant trees centuries ahead of their being needed and then the patience to nurture them for generations is generous. Such sacrifice indicates the importance of giving today—even if the benefits won't be realized until far in the future.[264] This example further relates to an observation about giving that I once heard from a wise man: "The best time to plant a tree is seventy years ago. The next best time is now."[265]

The "Middle" Squeeze on Generosity

This section may seem pretty straightforward at first. Giving is an area in which the adage, "No time like the present" should apply strongly.

Yet, our human tendency to procrastinate affects generosity as well. Moreover, there can be compelling rationalizations behind the idea of waiting to give or even avoiding it altogether.

- **You are busy.** Your time is limited and already allocated. You'd like to help others, but you're already maxed out with your own responsibilities.
- **You are focused elsewhere.** You do have talents that can benefit others, but they're more needed at home, at school, at work, or wherever you spend your time.
- **You are stretched financially.** Giving is nice, and you will drop some cash or write a check here and there. For now, though, you have other pressing needs. Giving sounds good in theory but will have to wait in practice.

There is an antigenerous "squeeze" that tends to come hardest for folks in the middle realm of income or the middle stage of life. The wealthy have surplus money in search of a home. The poor may deliver richly in personal kindness and proportional giving for what they lack in material goods. The young and the old may have more time available to share with others. It is easy to get caught in between and to miss out on the benefits of generosity as a critical and beneficial blessing for the present.

When COVID-19 swept the world in 2020, financial giving among Americans rose in response to the pandemic difficulties many of their fellow citizens were experiencing. Nonetheless, IRS data from that year shows that giving was lowest as a percentage of income at around 3.5 percent among those with incomes between $200,000 and $1 million per year. In contrast, earners at $10 million or above gave away nearly 8 percent. Not surprising, you might think.

Compellingly, however, the highest percentage of giving was among the lowest earners. Tax returns filed for earners under $50,000 record percentages of giving comparable to or higher than the mega-wealthy. In fact, the averages increase at each lower threshold. *Earners under $5,000 gave away more than 24 percent of their incomes!*[266]

This relationship of a "missing middle" in giving is consistent over many years. Income over $200,000 is well above average and may seem more than ample. However, it may not feel so, depending on where you live. Work that produces such income tends to be concentrated in expensive urban areas. Factoring in the higher cost of living, higher home prices, higher taxes, and expenses like private school can make for tight budgets among the middle class and upper-middle class. The temptation can be to cut out donations. WISEgenerosity suggests strongly, however, that such an approach is self-defeating.

On the topic of socioeconomic status and giving, one of the more interesting observations I received in the course of this project was this one: If you ever get into trouble, you better hope that you have some poor friends.[267] The point was that many of us are too distracted to focus fully on others in need.

My colleague Kelly Johnson shared a related example with me. A professional nonprofit fundraiser for many years, Kelly described how she once visited the local factory of a large company partner participating in the annual United Way campaign. This particular appeal was during a late-night shift of hourly wage earners. Concerned that her request might be an imposition, she was blown away by the enthusiastic response of generosity. The rate of participation was nearly 100 percent and at an exponentially higher percentage of

income than other employee groups, including those from the corporate office
who were earning much higher salaried incomes. After inquiring what motivated this high level of engagement and giving, the reply was consistent: "We've
been there. We know how important this money may be to someone else. We
are happy to help."[268]

Giving disparities like this one should be a challenge for any of us tempted
to prioritize financial comfort and security over generosity. What is the cost
of missing out on the happiness, enlightenment, and fulfillment that giving
provides?

Giving Now and Not Waiting for a "Better Time"

Generosity is comprehensive—it involves all of who we are and what we have.
It also is a mindset and a mode of living that begs to be part of our lives today
and not at some vague future time.

An investment in others is an investment in ourselves as well. Like exercise, healthy eating, or anything else we can and should to do improve our lives,
giving is something that needs regular practice and promotion.

A friend of mine owned a successful heating and air conditioning business.
Inspired by their involvement in community activities, he and his wife decided
to dedicate a portion of their efforts to charity when they started the venture
in 2003. From day one, they put 1 percent of all revenue aside into a "donor-
advised fund" at the Community Foundation for Greater Atlanta. This program
works like a charitable bank account: You put in cash, investments, or other
resources. Like other forms of saving, money builds up and becomes available
to support good work in which you are interested whenever you wish.

Putting aside $1 out of every $100 that came in the door quickly became
a habit for my friend. He didn't notice the money "missing," since it never hit
his bank account. He said that this was one of the best personal and business
decisions he and his wife ever made. There was no "suffering" involved—
having an "engine of opportunity" to do good was just an established part of

the enterprise. He described it as "paying rent" to the community in which his business operated.

Even after years of making many gifts, there still are ample resources in the fund that the couple uses to support causes they care about. The keys to success were to start at the outset and to remain consistent ever since. It would have been easy to say, "We'll wait to give until we are established." Yet the positive impact on them—and on the causes they care about—would have been much less without an initial focus on present generosity.

One takeaway from this example is that we should not be intimidated by generosity. We wouldn't run 26.2 miles on the first day we started to train for a marathon. Like my friend and his wife, we should find a starting point. Once we are engaged in the act of giving, we then can look to build our contributions of time, talent, and treasure from there.

Generosity Compounding

There is a likely apocryphal story where Albert Einstein was asked what he thought was humanity's greatest invention. The answer was "compound interest."[269] An aspect of generosity relates to this principle.

In a financial plan, typical growth projections imagine the value of assets growing substantially, or compounding, over a lifetime. When giving presentations to participants in 401(k) plans, I challenge the younger employees to start saving early. Based on the effect of compounding at a reasonable rate of return, waiting for ten years to start saving can mean that you end up with around half as much money in the end!

The root of this is the difference between "exponential" (compound) versus "arithmetic" (simple) growth. Simple growth is linear; compound growth is parabolic. The difference is the effect of the reinvestment of the interest earned in the process.

If I have $100 and it grows arithmetically at 10 percent, I have $110 in the second year, $120 in the third year, $130 in the fourth year, and so on. If the growth is exponential, however, I have $110 in the second year, $121 in the third year, $133 in the fourth year, and so on. What starts as a small difference in the early years explodes as the cumulative interest grows on itself in addition to the original principal.

Here is a graph providing a visual of a similar relationship:[270]

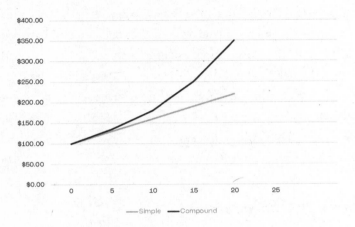

Generosity Compounding Is Like Compounding Interest

The exponential potential of generosity overall is a topic we will explore in chapter 25. For now, I hope to make the point that, like any other investment, the fruits of giving expand dramatically when they are pursued in the present rather than later.

● ● ●

Five P's Reflections

My great-grandmother was a hardworking, no-nonsense farmer's wife with a dry sense of humor and a battery of wise old sayings. While my favorite is, "That's using your head for more than a hat rack," it is hard to argue here with, "An ounce of prevention is worth a pound of cure." Applying the same ounces-to-pounds concept to Possessional, Personal, Social, Emotional, and Relational Giving, I think that "Great-mom" was right, as usual.

The world around us teaches that there are tensions between building more and acting now when it comes to sharing ourselves and our resources with others. Wisdom and experience show that the future benefits far outweigh any current costs. Act now. Giving in the present is generous.

In sum, when it comes to WISEgenerosity:

- Closer is better (Proximity)
- Larger is better (Proportion)
- More frequent is better (Production)
- Stronger is better (Power)
- Now is better (the Present)

Hopefully, these five P's will help you to evaluate where you can give with the most meaning and impact, now and going forward.

WISEgenerosity Example: Fully Engaged Giving

LET'S LOOK NOW AT AN INSPIRING EXAMPLE of how these five P's—Proximity, Proportion, Production, Power, and (the) Present—can come together in attitude and action.

John and Teresa Croyle have raised more than two thousand children. Two are biological; the rest come from an amazing commitment to kids who have not experienced even the most basic levels of care and concern from the other adults in their lives. These youngsters *are* troubled and *in* trouble with nowhere good to go. To serve them, John started Big Oak Ranch in Gadsden, Alabama, in 1974. It has been the center of life for John and Tee (as Teresa is known to friends) ever since.

John's life as a young man was the stuff of fantasy for many boys. A great athlete, he was an All-America defensive end for a national championship football team at the University of Alabama in the early 1970s. His coach was the legendary Paul "Bear" Bryant. John was primed for success, and many expected that his logical next step would be playing in the National Football League followed by a lucrative career in business.

There was much more to John than football, however. His childhood was marked by loss when his four-year-old sister was killed in a tragic accident when John was five. Rather than turning inward in grief, his family turned outward and engaged strongly in community activities. Following his father's example, John was active while growing up as a role model for younger kids. He played and coached and engaged positively with others around his own love for sports. Continuing in similar roles, he worked each summer during college as a counselor at a camp for troubled boys in Mississippi. Even in his football career, John had to overcome adversity. After suffering a serious knee injury during his freshman year of college, it was uncertain if John would ever play football again.

These challenges and experiences molded John's character. Over time, he realized that he was determined to commit his life to helping young people in need.

Having come to this conclusion during his senior year at Alabama, John went to see "The Man" (as Coach Bryant was known to his players). John told his coach that he planned to play pro football, but only as a means to an end. He wanted to make money so he could return home to start a ranch for boys in need. This idea to provide a safe home and opportunity for boys to develop in a work-focused family setting had been growing in his head and his heart for some time, and John was determined eventually to pursue this dream. Coach Bryant surprised him by telling him to forget football. He knew John's heart wasn't in it. Instead, the coach offered to help John by sharing his own name and support for the ranch.

The critical moment came in 1974, as John was preparing to graduate. His father had found the ideal piece of property on which to build the vision: 120 acres ready to go. The owner met John and liked his story, but only up to a point. He gave John forty-eight hours to find $48,000 to buy the property. John had about $5,000 saved. He had some additional money already committed from family and friends who wanted to help him. Still, he was $30,000 short. They needed a miracle.

One recurring theme in many of the stories I've heard is what I've come to call the *generosity catalyst*. "Aiding angels" help overcome an obstacle or reach a goal at a critical time for those looking to be generous. Usually, this requires a sacrifice on the part of the catalyst.

One of John's friends was an Alabama teammate named John Hannah, who was an outstanding player pursuing his own pro football prospects. (Hannah eventually joined the Pro Football Hall of Fame in 1991 as one of the top offensive linemen in NFL history.) John Hannah found out through a chance conversation about John Croyle's situation. Amazingly, not only was Hannah willing to help, but the signing bonus he had received as the first-round draft pick of the New England Patriots was exactly $30,000. Deal done. Ranch secured.

John Hannah was a newlywed with plenty of needs of his own. Professional football is not the most secure job. His willingness to help John Croyle realize his dream is one of my favorite generosity catalyst examples. (The fact that I grew up as a Patriots fan and have Hannah's autograph from a boyhood visit to their training camp may have a little to do with this.)

Through support from Coach Bryant, John Hannah, and others, John Croyle's dream was coming true. He and Tee married and settled into life at Big Oak Boys Ranch as the surrogate parents for group after group of boys. They raised the boys in their own home, as their own children, and worked beside them doing all it took to run the ranch. In time, they added more houses (the first fittingly named the John Hannah Home) and recruited others to take on the role of father and mother figures to the children they brought in.

Of course, this work has not been easy. The Croyles sacrificed in every way to provide for their charges. They exemplified the five types of generosity—Possessional, Personal, Social, Emotional, and Relational—and lived with failure and sadness alongside joy and success. But all the adversity simply made them try harder.

John was somber when he told me the story of a girl named Shelley. I could tell it still deeply hurt this imposing but tender man, even more than thirty years later. Only twelve years old, Shelley had endured a life that I can't and don't want to imagine. Her own parents—the people who were supposed to love and protect her—tortured her instead.

John and Tee had been rescuing boys from abuse and neglect for years, often appearing in family court to seek custody of them. The horrible details of Shelley's case had come to light as the same court considered her situation. John and Tee were desperate to take her in, but the court was concerned that their experience was with boys only, and Shelley was sent back to her parents—despite John's plea and prediction that she would be dead in six months if she were sent back home. It didn't take that long. Shelley was beaten to death by her own father three months later.

As in his early life, John didn't let tragedy turn into despair. He and Tee and their many supporters vowed to create a place for girls so there would be no more Shelleys if they could help it. As a result, the Big Oak Girls Ranch opened in 1988. John's office is there on a hill overlooking a beautiful valley, but every day he drives down the road on the ranch named after Shelley—the girl they so badly wanted to save.

Today, Big Oak includes both the Boys Ranch and Girls Ranch along with a school the Croyles founded to further support the children in their care. Westbrook Christian School is itself an impressive facility, where nearly seven hundred kids learn and play and grow. About 20 percent of these students come from Big Oak Ranch and about 80 percent from the local community. It is an energetic and happy place, where I personally saw John greet each boy and girl by name as we walked the halls of the school together. They all lit up when they saw "Mr. John." As we explored, we looked in on Tee teaching algebra and calculus. She seemed at home as well.

"Familial" is the way I describe Big Oak Ranch. The kids, the staff—everyone is friendly and connected. There are lots of smiles and jokes. Everyone is natural and unforced. I'm sure that there are serious moments as well. It is like the Croyles took a regular family and magnified it—well, about one thousand times.

The Croyles' son Brodie was a standout athlete and student at the University of Alabama. He was raised in his parents' work and has been passed the torch of leadership.

Consistent with the attitude of the other inspiringly generous people with whom I've spoken, the Croyles try to deflect attention away from their accomplishments. Attempts to focus on their own efforts is redirected to others—especially to God along with their supporters and the boys and girls they serve.

With apologies to John and Tee, then, I am going to call attention to how comprehensive their giving has been across all the WISEgenerosity elements we have been exploring.

Possessional Giving

For most of us, our homes and finances are central to our lives. This is true for the Croyles as well. They have shared all they have with boys and girls in need, raising their two biological children alongside all of their surrogate ones.

Personal Giving

Forgoing opportunities for more worldly success in pro football and business, the Croyles have dedicated their time and talent to others full-time for nearly fifty years.

Social Giving

As noted, Big Oak Ranch is like a large family. Adults and children live and work in community there side by side. This deliberately provides security, belonging, and love to children who have experienced little or none of either previously. The success of the environment speaks for itself. The national average tenure for the house parents of foster children is six months. At Big Oak Ranch, it's ten years. The boys and girls refer to the adults who work as house parents at Big Oak as "mom" and "dad" and the other residents in their houses as "sisters" or "brothers." The ages are staggered so the older ones help the younger ones. There are twenty-four of these homes spread across the Boys Ranch and Girls Ranch. They are impressive to see.

Emotional Giving

John still looks every bit the All-America football player. You would not want to get on his bad side. Through his generous nature, he turns that potential intimidation into reassurance. For fifty years, every child has received four personal promises when they arrive at Big Oak Ranch — originally from John and now from Brodie. The promises are the bedrock of Big Oak:

1. I will love you.
2. I will never lie to you.
3. I will stick with you until you are grown.
4. I will provide boundaries that you can't cross.

John referred back to Shelley at one point, saying, "Imagine never having slept well." That innocent girl was afraid every night of what would happen to her in her own house. John added a special extra promise in situations like Shelley's: "As long as I breathe, no one will ever hurt you like that again." I take him at his word, and I am sure those frightened children have as well.

Relational Giving

The point of boundaries in #4 of the last section is an important one. John Croyle is a devoted Christian and sees his work as a reflection of his faith that God is *loving* but also *just*. In our human view, these two qualities can seem incompatible at times. John bridges them as well as anyone I have ever met. Providing rules and sticking to them is part of the process.

John is known for saying, "Rules without relationship lead to rebellion." That is a marvelous parenting motto. John's boys and girls know that he loves them and wants what is best for them. At the same time, though, there is a firm consistency at Big Oak Ranch. There must be consequences for a disobedient child who rejects the rules adopted by the rest of the community. John sees such an approach as hard but necessary.

Giving Purpose

John and Tee find ultimate purpose in their faith. They believe they are doing what Jesus requires of his disciples: love God and love each other. They find fulfillment in their service to others. The life they've chosen clearly produces a great deal of happiness as well, for themselves and for the people around them.

Giving Proximity

John and Tee embody the idea that generosity is most productive when it takes place close to us. Before I met the Croyles, it would have stretched my imagination to think of people being able to provide a parent's loving support and encouragement to hundreds and hundreds of children, each of whom they have held close, encouraged, and walked through the ups and downs of life. I know better now.

Giving Proportion

It's clear that John and Tee are living examples of "Kingly" or "Diamond" giving. They strive to give others even more and better than they use or receive themselves across all the generosity dimensions. The impact of their dedication is large, but it starts small. The boys and girls learn good manners. They see from John and Tee the importance of hospitality. They are surrounded by kindness, charity, and philanthropy.

In my own case, I was treated royally during my visit. John spent the better part of a day driving me around, introducing me to people, and patiently explaining his life's work to someone he had never met before and to whom he was connected only by a mutual friend suggesting that we speak.[271] This generosity extended all the way to the gourmet four-course lunch the chef at Westbrook Christian made for us to enjoy while we observed the hustle and bustle of students coming in and out of the cafeteria for their own midday meals.

John told me that he has turned down Hollywood offers to film his and Tee's story, refused large contributions from well-meaning donors suggesting changes to his approach, and disregarded anything he sees as distracting from his single-minded focus on the kids in his care. John says that he "only is good at two things: clear focus and delegation." That seems like too short a list to me, but I don't dare dispute him.

Giving Production

The sum of what Big Oak Ranch has accomplished is impossible to calculate. The "Generosity Velocity" generated from the children served, community inspired, volunteers engaged, and staff employed is amazing to consider. John understands this. Each relationship is an opportunity to plant a seed that can grow into a mighty tree. Some of his charges will reach their potential. Some will not. That is outside of his control. His perspective is that the value of what he does today will be known in the years to come. He doesn't trouble himself with worrying about it, instead choosing to focus on the moment and opportunity in front of him. A magazine article about John some years ago quoted a local judge: "If everyone had as much interest in their *own* children as John Croyle does in *any* kid, we wouldn't have delinquency in this country. It's that simple [emphasis in original]."[272]

Giving Power

The "fruit" of John and Tee's work is the individual children they love. When I visited, preparations were underway for a reunion weekend. More than three hundred former residents and their own families were coming back to appreciate each other, Big Oak Ranch, the staff, and John and Tee. These now-grown people—each of whom was changed by what John and Tee provided for them—are the human outcome of this couple finding the perfect intersection of their own generosity passion, opportunity, and impact in ways that are Well-grounded, Inspired, Satisfying, and Effective.

Giving in the Present

John told me, "If I had one year left to live, I still would be here doing just what I am." He has felt that way since 1974. This series of commitments and relationships—minute by minute, person by person—has compounded into an incredible record of lives transformed for the better. If John hadn't taken Coach Bryant's advice to get right to work as a young man on what mattered most to him rather than waiting for "success" elsewhere, who knows what would have happened? Even more importantly, what would have *not* happened?

Giving Wisely: My Reflections

Thomas Edison is reputed to have said that "genius is one percent inspiration and ninety-nine percent perspiration."[273] When it comes to generosity, I believe that the scale is balanced more evenly between a considerate attitude (inspiration) and caring action (perspiration). Having robust motivation is essential to sustain service and support for others. Moreover, W.I.S.E. giving must be based on a well-grounded understanding of its underlying components, as outlined in this section around the *what*, *when*, and *where* elements of giving.

Reflecting upon this, I have come to appreciate that two of my primary practical gifts are synthesis and communication. I was trained as an historian, and my brain likes digesting large amounts of information and distilling it down to more manageable concepts, frameworks, and models like the ones you have been exploring. I also love to write and speak and to get others excited about the things that excite me.

To put it into the terms we have been using, my *heart drivers* and my *head drivers* aligned during this project like they never have before. WISEgenerosity then became a sustainable *habit* in my life.

My *Expressive* personality was triggered fully as my lesser *Discipled* and *Considerate* sides also had opportunities to develop. I can be un-*Focused*, and that was a challenge to manage throughout the project. Fortunately, my wonderful wife and others provided inspiration and direction.

The realization I had in 2016 that the five types of generosity I identified aligned with Maslow's hierarchy of needs was a milestone of confidence that the principles behind WISEgenerosity were more than just my own untethered musings. That the system also connected with my friend Pastor Bruce Deel's "Four P's Prayer" spiritual framework provided further reassurance. There certainly have been many situations over these past ten years when danger, deficiency, difficulty, and distraction in my life—and in this project—have been overcome by the protection, provision, power, and peace that I gratefully received.

Lastly, the "five P's of effective giving" anchored my own efforts toward WISEgenerosity. I felt a desire for *Proximity*—focusing largely on things that

I had learned and experienced myself. I developed a bold sense of *Proportion*—daring as a novice author to produce something comprehensive on this topic. I was continually supported in *Production*—benefitting from the help and encouragement of many other people. The effort required was based on *Power*—aligning my own passions, opportunities, and interests. Moreover, the work was grounded in an urgent sense of the *Present*—embarking on the project when I was first inspired to do so in 2013, when I had a young family and a still-underdeveloped career, rather than waiting until my life was quieter or more secure.

You may have similar elements at work in your life. *What* breaks your heart or lights you up? For myself, I hate to see people not being able to fulfill their spiritual, practical, emotional, and relational potential. WISEgenerosity is meant to help address the tragedy of unachieved human promise. *When* does it make sense for you to engage in W.I.S.E. giving? As noted in the introduction, I felt a calling to pursue this project that I could not ignore. I also wanted to see the blessings of generosity realized in my relationships with family and friends, in my professional work, and in my community service. *Where* does it make sense for you to engage? This book and the resources built around it were central to my own answer. Moreover, the effort brought an amazing group of talented and capable people into my life, for whom I will be forever grateful.

In sum, WISEgenerosity matters only insofar as the principles behind it are applied meaningfully in our lives. Section 3 aims to provide further guidance toward doing so.

SECTION 3

Experiencing WISEgenerosity— The Path to Your Best Life

Section 3, Part 1

Generosity That's Meaningful and Effective for the Giver and Receiver

While each of us lives a unique life with characteristics and circumstances all our own, we share common elements that can help align our relationships and resources in beneficial ways.

First, a W.I.S.E. approach to generosity generates more powerful outcomes than giving that lacks purpose and practical application.

Second, WISEgenerosity relates importantly to different ages and stages of life. Understanding these dynamics positions us to better give in ways that are meaningful and effective.

Third, in a broader context, WISEgenerosity offers the potential to align existing generations in service to positive community dynamics and social engagement—and to improve our world in the process.

CHAPTER 24

Giving Through Life's Ages and Stages

A CENTRAL BELIEF OF WISEGENEROSITY is that giving is essential at every age and in every stage of life from youth to elderhood. Applying some of the frameworks we've explored will help to show how generosity best applies to you and others in your life across generations.

Recall the pattern for Powerful Giving in chapter 21:

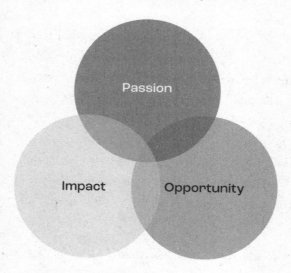

The Pattern for Powerful Giving

The central intersection of all three circles represents the place where the things that light you up (Passion) overlap with the places where you are able to do good (Opportunity) in order to provide the greatest potential benefits for the people and situations involved (Impact).

These elements align with the four W.I.S.E. components like this:

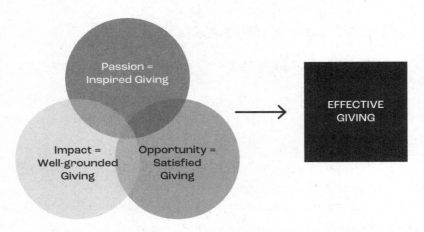

Powerful Giving Connected to W.I.S.E. Giving

Ideally, these elements are considered before a gift is made. In order for generosity to be W.I.S.E., you must be Inspired and have the resources at your disposal to do something Well-grounded on behalf of others. The resulting opportunity then needs the potential to be Satisfying to your internal and external goals. Meanwhile, a gift ultimately is Effective if it is used fully by the receiver in ways that well reflect the inputs that produced it.

Put another way, the first step in WISEgenerosity is making sure you have thought through the situation. Planning is essential for good giving, and an optimal gift is made only after considering these elements.

Giving in Each Age and Stage of Life

While a W.I.S.E. approach to giving is beneficial in any situation, there are elements that align naturally with different ages and stages of life. A key to purposeful and productive gifts is to understand what approaches will be most beneficial and useful to you, depending on where you are in life.

Part 2 of section 1 explored the *Why* of giving. Let's now segment how the purposes apply at different points in our lives:

Age of Life	Natural Focus / "Why"
Youth	Knowledge / Development
Growth	Accumulation / Happiness
Success	Awareness / Enlightenment
Significance	Wisdom / Fulfillment

Explaining further, there are four general stages of life:
- Youth
  Childhood and young adulthood—from birth to starting full-time work
- Growth
  Early adulthood—developing a career and establishing foundational relationships
- Success
  Midlife—peak engagement in career, family, and community
- Significance
  Elderhood—sharing resources and preparing legacy

Each of the eras has a different natural focus aligning with one of the "why" elements.

In Youth, we acquire knowledge and engage in a process of development. Ideally, we discover who we are in nurturing and supportive environments at home, at school, and in the community (activities, sports, church/temple/mosque, etc.). We also are introduced to social interaction and to the ways in which giving and receiving are central to our lives.

By the time we reach Growth in early adulthood, we are accumulating resources and seeking the elements of life in which we can find lasting happiness and fulfillment. We build on our self-awareness and harness our capabilities in service to our personal objectives and to others around us. We hopefully find work that suits our skills and interests while we nurture friendships and find a life partner.

Progressing to Success, we become more self-aware and conscious of how our lives intersect productively with those around us. Midlife brings heightened opportunities in our careers, in our families, and in our communities. We take on leadership roles and produce greater impact in the areas toward which we dedicate ourselves. We also can feel weighed down and may hope to lighten the loads we bear by offloading unproductive responsibilities and resources.

Significance likely is a transition over time during which our day-to-day activities reduce while we take on the role of guide and counselor for others. Ideally, we have the financial and practical freedom and flexibility to engage in projects that move us. At the same time, we take stock of our circumstances and plan for the ways in which our resources ultimately will be applied toward the legacies we want most at work, at home, and in the community.

Framing the Ages and Stages of Giving

Thinking back to chapter 11, let's revisit heart giving, head giving, and habit giving:

- Heart-driven generosity is emotional and determines *whether* you will give.
- Head-driven generosity is intellectual and determines *how much* you will give.
- Habit-driven generosity is sustainable and transformational and determines whether you will *keep* giving.

You also may recall the four categories of giving motivation from chapter 11:

- Compulsion—generosity is the best alternative compared to other choices.

- Connection—generosity is the result of positive engagement with others.
- Conviction—generosity focuses on specific results.
- Compassion—generosity is produced by strong attachment and commitment.

Adding in these elements from prior passages, we can see a more complete pattern of giving emerge for the different ages and stages of life. That model looks as follows:

Stage of Life	Natural "Why"	Heart Giving	Head Giving	Habit Giving
YOUTH	Learning / Development	Cares	Causes	COMPULSION Network
GROWTH	Accumulation / Happiness	Admiration	Affinity	CONNECTION Community
SUCCESS	Awareness / Enlightenment	Experience	Strategy	CONVICTION Focus
SIGNIFICANCE	Wisdom / Fulfillment	Love	Investment	COMPASSION Legacy

Giving Through Life's Ages and Stages

Here's a little more explanation:

Youth Giving
- The emotional (heart) aspects of giving are based on caring and connecting with others in your contact circle and where you yourself feel most engaged.
  Examples: crowdfunding; social media campaigns
- The intellectual (head) aspects of giving are based on causes that arouse your concern and incite your engagement with others who are

like-minded.

Examples: campus activism; religious revival

- Habit giving often is based on compulsion—first requirements imposed by your elders (parents, teachers, mentors); then group efforts to which you are drawn by collective impulse.
- Networking—coming together physically and virtually with others who share your commitments—is the primary channel through which you engage.

Growth Giving

- The emotional (heart) aspects of your giving are based on the example of peers and mentors whom you admire.
  Example: getting involved with a group soliciting money for a well-known charity
- The intellectual (head) aspects of your giving are based on affinity to entities of which you are a part (schools, local groups).
  Example: joining an event-planning or fundraising committee
- Habit giving often is based on connection—you are introduced to many different organizations and efforts by friends and colleagues.
- Community—the underlying theme of your involvement is drawing closer to others who share your general interests and circumstances.

Success Giving

- The emotional (heart) aspects of your giving are based increasingly on your own experience.
  Example: responding to a childhood illness experienced by a loved one by getting involved with your local children's hospital
- The intellectual (head) aspects of your giving are more strategic and well-defined.
  Example: joining a board of directors and serving in a leadership role
- Habit giving often is based on conviction—you narrow commitments down to your most important issues.

- Focus—you go from wider engagement to just a few causes in terms of time, talent, and treasure.

Significance Giving

- The emotional (heart) aspects of your giving are based ideally on love for the people and programs that matter most to you.
  Example: making meaningful gifts to the place of worship that has nurtured you and your family for decades
- The intellectual (head) aspects of your giving help to determine that your investments of money and effort are well-spent and enduring.
  Example: structuring your giving so that it uses appreciated assets and is aligned effectively with needs of the organization now and in years to come
- Habit giving often is based on compassion—you feel deeply about the causes that have captured your efforts and engagement over many years.
- Legacy—you want to ensure that the commitments you make now have a lasting and effective impact.

While each situation is different, people are likely to share at least some of these traits and characteristics with their peers. Moreover, individuals in each age range commonly are categorized as part of a wider "generation." Let's now consider how generations and giving align.

Generations and Giving

The concept of generations can be simplistic. Grouping an entire cohort of people together based on when they were born glosses over the inherent individuality of every person living during that era.

Even so, I believe that the concept of generations is useful if appropriately applied. Regardless of how we feel about generational labels or their application to us personally, the way in which everyone sees the world is influenced by their phase of life and by the cultural forces they have experienced alongside their peers.

With this view in mind, the best work I know on the topic of generations was done by social historians William Strauss and Neil Howe. Their sweeping 1991 book, *Generations: The History of America's Future, 1584 to 2069*, organizes American history into a repeating pattern of four generational types: Idealistic, Reactive, Civic, and Adaptive.[274]

Using these terms, here is the current landscape of primary generations:

Generational Type	Contemporary Example (and Birthdates)[275]
Currently Active Generations	
Idealistic	Boomer (1943–1960)
Reactive	Gen X (1961–1981)
Civic	Millennial (1982–2003)
Rising Active Generation	
Adaptive	iGen[276] (2004–)

Idealists are inspired youths, principled but moralistic midlifers, and potentially visionary elders guiding younger generations through difficulties. As a group, their giving tends to be self-confident, large in scale, and ambitious in desired impact.

Reactives are risk-taking and somewhat alienated in youth, pragmatic leaders in midlife, and respected but reclusive elders. Their giving is individualized, practical, narrowly targeted, and outcome-focused.

Civics come of age during a crisis and are drawn together by common experiences. They build institutions as powerful midlifers and end up status quo targets as elders for the next Idealists. Their giving is collaborative and trust-focused.

Adaptives are protected during a crisis in their youth and grow into risk-averse adults. They remain acutely attuned to their environment through life and prefer connection to confrontation. Difficulty making commitments in middle years gives way to the desire for calm in elderhood. Their giving seeks consensus and prioritizes problem-solving.

Applying a Generational Framework to Generosity

Returning to our earlier chart and considering current ages and stages of each generation:

Stage of Life	GENERATIONAL ALIGNMENT	Heart Giving	Head Giving	Habit Giving
YOUTH	iGens	Cares	Causes	COMPULSION Network
GROWTH	Millennials	Admiration	Affinity	CONNECTION Community
SUCCESS	Gen Xers	Experience	Strategy	CONVICTION Focus
SIGNIFICANCE	Boomers	Love	Investment	COMPASSION Legacy

Current Generations Aligned With Ages and Stages

Especially within families, companies, or other multigenerational environments, these distinctions are important. Effective giving—and interacting in groups generally—depends both on understanding the individual preferences and priorities of each member of the group and putting their age and stage of life into perspective.

Let's imagine a family foundation as an example. The Boomers involved likely think of their legacy while attempting to engage in larger, broader giving. In contrast, their younger Gen X cousins probably are skeptical of grand plans lacking clear rationale and well-defined objectives. The Millennial children of the Boomers can advocate passionately for causes that may not sit well with everyone. Meanwhile, the iGen children of the Gen Xers might look silently at their phones while messaging each other concerns about why their elders can't agree on anything along with complaints that the seemingly pointless discussion is taking so long [insert appropriate emoji].

Lacking thoughtful mediation, this situation has the potential to end frustratingly for everyone. That said, while the example may make these differences seem inherently problematic, our current national situation actually offers a positive generational alignment, which has been seen previously at times when America has risen to overcome its greatest challenges.

The Opportunity Presented by the Current Generational Alignment

Strauss and Howe wrote a later volume in 1996 applying their research to what they projected would happen in the late twentieth and early twenty-first centuries. *The Fourth Turning: What the Cycles of History Tell Us About America's Next Rendezvous with Destiny*, has proven to be remarkably accurate.

The book recasts the same four-generation pattern as a series of "Turnings." Just like seasons in nature (spring, summer, fall, winter) or in life (childhood, young adulthood, middle age, elderhood), history follows a regular progression, even as there is variation from year to year or from person to person. The Four Turnings are:[277]

1. High
2. Awakening
3. Unraveling
4. Crisis

According to this model, we are in a "Fourth Turning"—or "Crisis"—period. During such times, institutions are destroyed and rebuilt in response to grave threats. Like winter, conditions are cold and challenging but with the hope of positive change in the end. Fourth Turning societies are deeply unsettled and volatile. They also have underlying positive impulses that are community-focused and purpose-driven.

The two of the greatest American historical successes—the American Revolution and World War II—happened during Fourth Turning periods when a specific pattern of generations occurred:

- Elder Idealists
- Midlife Reactives
- Early Adult Civics
- Youthful Adaptives

In the American Revolution, the Ben Franklin generation provided moral vision, the George Washington generation provided pragmatic leadership, and the Nathan Hale generation provided the physical and social sacrifices needed to succeed.

Similarly, overcoming the Great Depression and the challenge of World War II involved the Franklin Roosevelt generation of Idealists, the Dwight Eisenhower generation of Reactives, and the Greatest Generation of heroic Civics.

In both cases, the young Adaptives provided motivation on the home front and learned during their upbringing about what it took to address great social upheaval and international conflict.

Fast-forwarding to the present:

- Boomers are an Idealist "Opportunity" generation looking to Satisfy their life concerns.

  They have time, talent, and treasure to use in service to causes they care about.
- Gen Xers are a Reactive "Impact" generation determined to be Well-grounded.

  They collectively have a practical, pragmatic approach to life and want to get things done.
- Millennials are a Civic "Passion" generation seeking a better, Inspired future.

  They are community-minded, morally engaged, and impatient for progress.

- iGens are an Adaptive "Outcome" generation who ultimately will determine the Effectiveness of all current projects and programs. They are the cohort whom our current circumstances will most affect.

Using the earlier "W.I.S.E. and Powerful Giving" model:

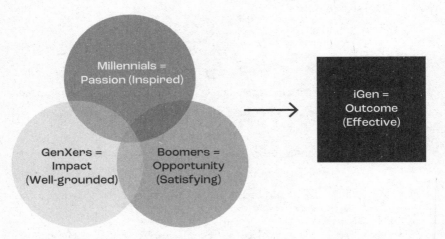

Generational W.I.S.E. and Powerful Giving

WISEgenerosity applies not only to us individually but to our society as a whole. An optimal future must engage our individual and collective perspectives and commitments.

This is a time of great challenges to our society. However, I believe that the seeds of a successful future already have been planted in current generations and through the individuals who comprise communities across America and the world. The necessary catalyst is a common purpose born of generous attitudes and actions. This book is designed to help provide the framework for such a new "Age of Generosity." I invite you to work together toward that end.

CHAPTER 25

Exponential Giving

IF WE TREAT OTHERS AS WELL AS—if not better than—we would like to be treated, then we increase the odds that they will do the same to us. That reflected generosity comes back to us and is radiated to others in our orbit. Generosity can start small and multiply if everyone touched by it is willing to take it in and pass it along. A connection is then made between our Personal Giving and the welfare of the community around us. Personal and collective goals are connected and aligned in giving. We will explore this thought more in the book's final chapter. But first, consider these examples.

"Viral Growth": Why not Generosity?

Exponential Generosity Spreading from a Single Act of Kindness

I interviewed the head of a successful faith-based private K–12 school in the western US known in part for its innovative and effective partnership with a local public school serving primarily disadvantaged students.[278] The head of the school shared a marvelous example of Exponential Generosity in action. (I am not sharing names in order to protect the desired anonymity of the people involved.)

A few years ago, the private school accepted a student's midyear transfer into the eighth grade. The girl had been so unhappy at her previous school that she was willing to be dropped into a new middle school where she knew no one. Imagine how nervous she was.

Empathizing, a boy raised his hand in class on the new student's first day and asked that they all say a prayer for the new girl. That gesture helped to break the ice, and other students engaged with her kindly as well. She ended up enjoying a good initial experience and a positive transition.

Using the Maslow framework from chapter 15, the fellow students applied Personal Generosity to help the newcomer feel more secure. Likewise, their Social and Emotional Generosity provided a sense of belonging and welcome empathy. Ultimately, their Relational Generosity led to an opportunity for the girl to self-actualize—and to settle into a happy and productive place at the school.

Relieved and pleased, the girl told the story of her warm welcome to her family at home. Among those who heard it were a wealthy uncle and aunt. This couple had been looking unsuccessfully for a compelling way to support education. Intrigued by their niece's story and by their own research, they made an appointment to see the headmaster on the first day school was back in session following Christmas break.

The couple made it clear right away that they were not Christians or even religious in any way. Nonetheless, their investigation of the school had revealed strong programs in academics, arts, and athletics delivered with a sense of purpose and innovation that they admired. They were considering offering significant financial support to the school.

Selflessly, the headmaster then introduced the couple to the principal of the local public school that had partnered with the smaller private school to help provide resources and mentoring for some of the public school's disadvantaged students. Facilities and activities at the private school were shared with the public school students to mutually enrich academic and extracurricular opportunities. In the process, friendships were built, and a broad community of learning was created.

Applauding this collaboration, the wealthy couple asked what they could do to assist the public school. The principal identified several of his best students with great potential. He wished that there was funding for them to attend the private school full-time. The benefactors agreed and committed to paying the way of the five students not only through high school but through college as well.

It is exciting to imagine what the ultimate impact of the expanded opportunities for these five students will be. Their lives will be transformed, along with the lives of everyone with whom they come into contact. The effects will radiate out over generations, and the potential impact is enormous.

Amazingly, this wave of transformation began with a single ripple of kindness by an eighth-grade boy. Most of the people ultimately affected will have no idea of this fact, but that does not diminish in any way the huge impact of the seemingly small gesture. Exponential Generosity happens when engagement leads to expansion leads to exponential impact. Here is a visual expression of the story to reinforce the point:

EXPONENTIAL: Impact of kindness rippling across people and time

EXPAND: Adoption of kindness by others

ENGAGE: Act of kindness

E³: Exponential Generosity Progression

Imagine what similar efforts by millions of people could do. Every day, each of us is able to produce small acts of giving. In turn, our efforts can be replicated and multiplied over and over again. That wave of WISEgenerosity would change the world.

An Exponential Example of WISEgenerosity

This project has connected me with many amazing and inspiring people, perhaps none more so than Bruce and Rhonda Deel, the couple I introduced in chapter 15. In the interest of full disclosure, I have been in awe of Bruce and Rhonda for two decades—years before I consciously started this generosity journey. In many ways, they are the most fully generous people I know.

In 2004, a friend introduced me to a growing program addressing the needs of people in crisis in Atlanta.[279] The group, City of Refuge, was run by Bruce and a dedicated team. I started volunteering, and they haven't been able to get rid of me since.[280] In more than thirty years of service to nonprofits as a staff member, volunteer, and consultant, I have never seen an organization more driven by passion and excellence and more effective at using its resources productively than City of Refuge. It has been a great honor and privilege to serve there.

There is an old saying about "walking the walk" versus "talking the talk." No one walks the walk like Bruce and Rhonda. Not only that, but their story is a perfect way to show how all the themes we've been exploring come together.

The City of Refuge Story

City of Refuge takes its name from the Bible. In the earliest days of Israel, thousands of years ago, there were tribes but no formal government. Punishment for crimes was delivered by whomever was wronged or their representatives. This was the original "eye for an eye, tooth for a tooth"[281] justice system.

In the case of murder or manslaughter, the family of the deceased was charged with finding and immediately executing the killer. This presented at least one problem: What if the death was accidental or wrongly attributed? There was no court system to determine guilt or innocence. And the angry, grieving family could not be expected to soberly evaluate whether or not their loved one was being avenged correctly.

In response to this problem, Israel created "cities of refuge."[282] These were places where someone accused of murder could flee and would be protected from immediate retribution. A special system then provided for adjudication and appropriate action. It is an historical footnote but a fascinating attempt to introduce a formal justice system into a period when there was little or none.

Bruce chose the name City of Refuge deliberately. As in ancient times, the organization was designed to be an oasis where those fleeing the scourges of society—poverty, addiction, and despair—had a place to recover, reorient, and restore hope and opportunity to their lives.

City of Refuge (COR) occupies eight acres in the middle of Atlanta's 30314 ZIP code. Using any statistical measure of poverty, this is one of the most challenged neighborhoods in America. The two vast former warehouses on the property provide 210,000 square feet of opportunity to serve people in this troubled community, including homeless women and children, schoolchildren needing a safe haven and enriching activities, sick neighbors with no other access to primary or specialized medical care, and rescued victims of sex trafficking. By design, City of Refuge has planted itself at the "center of need" in my city.

Why did the Deels take on this mission in the first place? In 1997, Bruce and Rhonda were living a comfortable life in Atlanta's suburbs. Bruce was the associate pastor of a church there, and they had their slice of the American Dream: rewarding work, a house they loved, and a great environment in which to raise their family of four, and eventually five, girls.

Then Bruce received an assignment that changed their lives and the lives of thousands of other people. His denomination owned a "mission church" at the edge of the inner-city Midtown neighborhood in Atlanta. The program was failing. The decision had been made to close the church and to get rid of the property. Bruce was given a six-month assignment to go to the church, sell the property, and then come home.

You need to know that Bruce is charismatic. He radiates a rare combination of energy and accessibility. You can tell immediately that he cares about you and that he wants to help you if you are in need. He also is "all in" on everything he does. When he went to that run-down property on Fourteenth Street, he did what he does best: minister to others. From that point on, things did not go as he expected.

Soon after relocating, Bruce delivered a Sunday sermon to a nearly empty sanctuary. Afterward, a woman I'll call "Tanya" (not her real name) approached him. She was a longtime stripper, prostitute, and drug addict who was desperate for hope and change in her life. Bruce promised support, and a connection was made. Tanya returned to the church the next week with "Martin," one of her regular clients and a drug addict himself. One thing led to another, and soon the Midtown Mission Church was attracting hundreds of lost and needy people. This was a crossroad in Bruce and Rhonda's lives.

Rhonda is a woman of strong faith, and she always had supported Bruce's ministry career. She and Bruce met and fell in love while attending Lee University in Cleveland, Tennessee. Bruce is a pastor's son and fits the stereo-type: he was bold and rebellious earlier in life. Rhonda is steady, compassionate, and wise. They were a great match from the start.

Bruce came home one day and broke surprising and unsettling news to Rhonda. What had started as a temporary assignment was becoming a calling to serve his new congregants that he could not ignore. After prayer and reflection, Rhonda suggested to Bruce that they sacrifice the white-picket-fence life they were comfortable with and the security it offered them and their children for the sake of an unknown and seemingly dangerous urban venture dedicated to others.

That is how the Deels ended up living in the upper rooms of the run-down church in Midtown. How they raised their young girls surrounded by people they sheltered off the street. How their residence was broken into thirty-four times, and how they had three cars stolen. How Bruce was threatened with guns and knives, and how he chased off would-be robbers in the middle of the night in his underwear—a story he tells with innate comic flair. How Bruce found himself in court facing someone who had tried to kill him. How Bruce and Rhonda sacrificed the comfortable life they expected for the life of generosity to which they were called.

Midtown Mission Church outgrew its space after several years of expanding programs and clients. A new home was needed. Bruce's vision was to move a couple of miles west to an even more dangerous and needier neighborhood. A Realtor friend found a great property in the area known as "The Bluff."[283] The large warehouse facility was decrepit but huge. It was owned by a local real estate developer named Maylon Mimms and was for sale at $1.6 million.

We've explored how catalysts are needed to make generosity happen, often at a sacrifice to themselves. Maylon Mimms was just such a catalyst for Bruce and Rhonda and for the by-then-renamed City of Refuge.

Bruce agreed that the warehouse was perfect. There was one problem: City of Refuge had no money to buy it. An initial offer of $0 was politely declined. Bruce was persuasive, though. After six months passed, Mr. Mimms agreed to donate the property outright to City of Refuge. Mr. Mimms later told Bruce that this gift was one of the most meaningful acts of his life. Thousands of people since have had their lives changed as a result of Maylon Mimms and his family's Possessional Giving.

Courageous Generosity

One of the things I most admire about Bruce is his courage. He is absolutely unafraid to do whatever he thinks is needed in service to others.

Generosity requires bravery to enable us to commit to helping others without assurances that our efforts will be rewarded. Not all giving stories end well. For every person at City of Refuge who has regained dignity and opportunity, there have been others who weren't able to overcome their demons.

Put another way, Exponential Generosity requires risk. A marvelous web of virtuous giving inevitably will have broken strands and unrealized potential. The commitment necessary to effect real change in people's lives comes at a cost, both physical and emotional.

Bruce's brother Jeff likewise has been dedicated to COR and to the cause of helping others for many years. Jeff wrote a powerful book about their experiences called *The Garden and the Ghetto*.

One chapter shares the story of Vanessa, who is described as a "horror story of abuse, neglect, alcoholism, prostitution and cocaine addiction."[284] Even for a seasoned counselor like Jeff, it was "a life of injustice unlike anything I have ever heard. A few minutes into the interview...I was a pitiful, emotional heap of human flesh, and I could not speak without my voice quivering and breaking."[285]

Vanessa moved to a special program at City of Refuge that helps transition women with special challenges from homelessness and hopelessness to restoration and opportunity. The keys are caring and compassion. "When roommates, COR staff persons and Mission Church family members treated her like a sister instead of an item...she transformed before our eyes."[286]

Vanessa graduated from the program and got a job and an apartment nearby. Whenever she met a visitor on campus, she would point to Bruce and say, "See that man right there...That man saved my life."[287]

Whenever I visit COR, I enjoy seeing people I love and admire. One is Greg Washington, who ran the "Level Up" youth program and now leads an amazing mentoring and support effort for "returning citizens" coming out of prison. His road to that job was winding, to say the least.

Greg was a cocaine trafficker on a route from Miami to Atlanta. He went by "G" on the street. Originally from Orlando, he discovered that, for a guy with a lot of talent but seemingly limited opportunities, drugs paid a lot more than working at Sea World.

As Jeff wrote, Greg's "story contains the themes movies are made of: The foolishness of youth, high speed chases, second chances, crime, violence and horror, a mother's love."[288] Greg first went to jail after crashing his motorcycle at 130 miles per hour while trying to evade the police. He was sentenced to federal prison a few years later after drugs and an unregistered gun were traced to him at a house he owned.

In prison for the second time, his life changed again, but this time for the better. He decided to bury "G" and to reembrace the "Greg" who had been there all along.

City of Refuge became a place for Greg to work out his body in the gym while working on himself after being released from prison. Over time, he became part of the family. He started to participate in the feeding program out on street corners and parking lots. One day, a homeless man in the line kept staring at him: "'G', is that you?...Wow! If you can change, *anybody* can."[289]

Greg, his beautiful wife, Malika (also an amazing COR staffer), and their wonderful children all have made a mission—and a life—of service to others. It is an amazing story of transformation and redemption.

There are Vanessas and Gregs at City of Refuge, but there also are Jakes. Bruce sent an email to the COR board of directors at 9:09 p.m. on a June evening a few years ago. "Tough Day in the hood" was the subject. The message seized my attention immediately: "As I peered into the back window of the broken-down truck sitting on our property earlier today, I knew immediately that the older gentleman lying in the back seat was my buddy Jake. I knew, just as immediately, that Jake was dead."[290]

Jake had been part of City of Refuge for thirteen years. He first walked into a COR men's shelter on Christmas night when it opened. Bruce wrote: "Soon after, he started calling me 'Ghetto Rev' and not long after dropped the 'Rev' and just called me 'Ghetto,' a term of affection from an old African American crack addict to a middle-aged white guy from the mountains...still one of my favorite things to have happened in my [then] 16 years in the city. The cover of my Bible is embossed proudly with the word, 'Ghetto.'"[291]

The pain was raw when Bruce put the situation into perspective with an Emotional Generosity I still find amazing:

Within an hour of Jake's death I heard 3 people use the same phrase, "he came home to die." At the end of the day isn't that what City of Refuge is supposed to be...home for those with no home, help for those with no help, hope for those who have lost all hope. It is tragic that Jake died in a broken-down pickup truck but not near as tragic if he had died under a bridge, in a ditch, on a street corner where no one knew his name, had no history of laughter and tears with him, didn't know that his daughter lives in Atlanta and other family in Macon. If he had not come home to die, he would have been buried in a pauper's grave, no name marking his final resting place, no songs at his funeral, no one to tell the stories of his life.

So, life is what we desire at City of Refuge but, if necessary, we also submit to being the place of death ... if home is where they wish to come and die.[292]

Exponential Generosity at Work

City of Refuge is recognized today in Atlanta and across the country as one of the most successful and influential social impact organizations anywhere. The impressive scope of its work is hard to describe with mere words. It involves care and support, ranging from education to health to housing to vocation, for people in crisis. I recommend that you explore their ministry for yourself at www.cityofrefugeatl.org.

I could go on and on about City of Refuge, but my purpose here is to use Bruce and Rhonda as an example of how generosity can work on an individual, relational, and community level.

We've been considering various aspects of generosity: what it is, how it is done well, and the impact it can have on us and on those around us. There are five elements we've identified at work in each of these areas:

What is generosity?	How is it done well?	What impact can it have?
Possessional	Proximity	Physical Needs
Personal	Proportion	Security Needs
Social	Production	Love/Belonging
Emotional	Power	Esteem
Relational	(the) Present	Self-Actualization

The Deels live these interactions every day.

- They focus Possessional giving on meeting the immediate needs of people living in one of the most challenging parts of America. Their willingness to physically move where they were needed allowed Proximity to amplify their service.

- Their Personal gifts of time and talent provide a sense of security for those who have been buffeted by the fiercest storms life can inflict. They have been "all in" on their work for twenty-five years and have demonstrated Proportional giving that is "Kingly" in every way.
- Their Social Generosity is grounded in love and creates a sense of community that radiates outward from their immediate work. The Production or "generosity velocity" produced by this energy has transformed many lives.
- Their Emotional giving delivers empathy and compassion to those for whom suffering and abuse have been constant nemeses. The Power of aligning their passion, opportunity, and quest for impact is measured in tears, laughter, and hope far more than it is in statistics or program ledgers.
- Ultimately, their Relational generosity and willingness to strive for the best in all people and in all situations has led to transformation and the opportunity for self-actualization in thousands of lives. They have approached each day since 1997 with a sense of urgency and a commitment to being in the Present. This sustained commitment and courage continues to drive them forward to improve more lives.

The exponential power of what Bruce and Rhonda have done overcomes darkness with light and will radiate out for generations to come.

Connecting the Threads of Generosity

"God has a sense of humor," says Bruce. As a product of rural western Virginia, Bruce imagines that he could have been installed at a small country church that left him ample opportunity to go fishing. Instead, he is leading the transformation of an urban neighborhood, helping and healing thousands of lives, and providing a model by which people in need can positively receive care and support.

In that vein, City of Refuge is far from unique in terms of opportunity. No doubt, there is unused or underused commercial and industrial space in challenged neighborhoods across America. The strategic plan for COR includes a deliberate effort to extend its impact beyond its campus—into its own neighborhood, across its home city, and then to communities all over the country and even the world. The goal is to provide light and hope for as many lives as possible—an exponential vision that starts with individuals walking in through the front gate today and extending to everywhere across America where there is need. It is an inspiring effort of which I am excited to be a part.

Lessons to Consider

Bruce and Rhonda will tell you that being willing to live generously has transformed their own lives. They and their children have built bonds of love and trust forged during twenty-five years of hands-on service together. Doing so has made them more capable of weathering inevitable challenges in their own lives.

Bruce and Rhonda's personal focus changed over the years from "success" (an external measurement driven by the perception of others) to "impact" (an internal measurement driven by adherence to their own values and priorities). Most of all, sacrifice and struggle have strengthened their relationship with each other. Their common purpose has reinforced compassion and service inside their marriage as well as outside of it.

Bruce and Rhonda aim to live life with an "open hand." A scarcity mindset would balk at the cost of "giving away" so much of themselves. In contrast, their abundance approach has led to greater peace and freedom. They work harder than ever now, but with powerful purpose. They enjoy life more and feel unburdened by its inevitable ups and downs due to their fulfillment in doing what they feel they are meant to do.

If you want to hear Bruce in his own words, check out an interview he did at the wonderful program "Crazy Good Turns"[293] (a podcast filled with stories about amazing people engaging in incredible acts of service to others). You also should read Bruce's memoir, *Trust First: A True Story About the Power of Giving People Second Chances*. It is inspiring.

The Commonness of Exceptional Generosity

Bruce and Rhonda Deel are exceptional. They inspire me constantly with their example of how to live generously.

That said, what truly amazes me is not only how remarkably generous people can be, but how many such people there are. The heroes of giving like Bruce and Rhonda featured in these pages are just the ones I have met personally, or people whose stories I have come across. You know others in your own life. There are countless more spread across every community in this country and around the world. The commonness of exceptional giving is yet another marvelous generosity paradox.

Along the same lines, I hope that these examples of purposeful and productive giving do two things. First, I hope that they show us how important altruistic service is and demonstrate the vital impact it can have. Second, I hope that they inspire us to take steps forward in our own WISEgenerosity journeys.

Whatever our age and situation, there are acts of kindness, charity, and philanthropy that we can undertake. Each helps to change lives—those around us as well as our own. Building out from these individual acts, the potential effects of Exponential Generosity are limitless.

Optimal Giving and Successful Living

At the outset of this book, we posed two fundamental questions:

- What human attribute leads to the best life regardless of situation or circumstances?
- What human behavior is surest to produce happiness, enlightenment, and fulfillment?

The answer presented has been *generosity*, but not just any sort of generosity. For giving to achieve its full potential, it must be W.I.S.E.—Well-grounded, Inspired, Satisfying, and Effective.

Along the same lines, the goal of WISEgenerosity is *Optimal Giving*, with optimal defined as "producing the best possible results."[294]

Given the scope of topics we have covered, there are many aspects to Optimal Giving:

- WISEgenerosity enables us to live abundantly.
- WISEgenerosity delivers inward and outward benefits to us and to others.

- WISEgenerosity supports our personal purposes for happiness, enlightenment, and fulfillment.
- WISEgenerosity harnesses Possessional, Personal, Social, Emotional, and Relational giving in service to the people and priorities around us.
- WISEgenerosity provides insights into our own and others' personalities, motivations, perspectives, and circumstances.
- WISEgenerosity aligns human needs with the ability to achieve our own potential and to enable others to achieve theirs.
- Ultimately, WISEgenerosity enables us to experience and produce meaning and impact in our own lives, in the lives of those around us, in our communities, and in the world.

In sum, WISEgenerosity hopes to identify and align the objectives and activities you are called to pursue in order to experience a purposeful and productive life.

CHAPTER 26

Changing the World One
Relationship at a Time

I HOPE THAT THE INSPIRING STORIES OF AMAZINGLY GENEROUS
PEOPLE in this book will have a strong impact on you, as they have had on me.
Here is one last example drawing together the ways in which W.I.S.E. giving
can produce a meaningful impact in two people's lives and ultimately in the
wider world.

We recognized the Civil Rights Movement in chapter 8 as an historic,
large-scale act of Social Generosity. For the cause to succeed, many courageous
people had to act in difficult and dangerous situations. Reacting graciously to
hatred was a critical part of changing the hearts and minds of other Americans.

The generous goal of integration was meant to knit together a country
broken apart for generations by racism and segregation. The most important
efforts were conducted not only in marches and sit-ins but also in one-on-one
encounters between people who were determined to be the positive change they
wanted to see in the world. One such relationship involved a schoolteacher and
a young girl whose quiet determination on the front lines of history helped to
change our nation for the better.

Ruby Bridges was six years old in 1960 when she was asked to single-
handedly integrate a previously all-white elementary school in New Orleans.
Reflecting back years later on the angry mob that gathered outside the school,
Ruby recalled: "I saw barricades and police officers and just people everywhere.

And when I saw all of that, I immediately thought that it was Mardi Gras. I had no idea that they were here to keep me out of the school."[295]

Quintessential American artist Norman Rockwell powerfully depicted the scene:

"The Problem We All Live With," © Norman Rockwell, 1964[296]

The painting shows the brave girl purposefully striding forward while flanked by US Marshals, who were providing Ruby with protection while she passed by evidence of hatred and violence. It is a powerful image.

Ruby's story was part of the chain of change that led eventually to integration. It wasn't just her actions that were remarkable, however; her attitude was remarkable as well.

Protesting her court-mandated arrival, white parents pulled nearly all the children from the William Frantz Public School and showed up every day thereafter to loudly express their displeasure. For the rest of the year, Ruby and a lone white teacher were a classroom of two.

Revisiting the experience years later, Ruby wrote:[297]

I couldn't have gotten through that year without Mrs. Henry. Sitting next to her in our classroom, just the two of us, I was able to forget the world outside. She made school fun. We did everything together. I couldn't go out in the schoolyard for recess, so right in that room we played games and for exercise did jumping jacks to music. I remember her explaining integration to me and why some people were against it. "It's not easy for people to change once they've gotten used to living a certain way," Mrs. Henry said. "Some of them don't know any better, and they're afraid. But not everyone is like that." Even though I was only six, I understood what she meant. The people I passed every morning as I walked up the school steps were full of hate. They were white, yet so was my teacher, who couldn't have been more different from them. She was one of the most loving people I'd ever known. The greatest lesson I learned that year in Mrs. Henry's class was the lesson Martin Luther King, Jr., tried to teach us all. Never judge people by the color of their skin. God makes each of us unique in ways that go much deeper. From her window, Mrs. Henry always watched me walk into the school. One morning when I got to our classroom, she said she'd been surprised to see me talk to the mob. "I saw your lips moving," she said, "but I couldn't make out what you were saying to those people." "I wasn't talking to them," I told her. "I was praying for them." Usually I prayed in the car on the way to school, but that day I'd forgotten until I was in the crowd. *Please be with me*, I'd asked God, *and be with those people too. Forgive them because they don't know what they're doing.*

The contrast could not be more striking. Angry adults screaming and threatening. A small child calmly praying for herself and for them. Ruby Bridges was amazingly generous.

Likewise, her teacher, Barbara Henry, demonstrated a corresponding generosity and courage of conviction that was necessary in order for Ruby's determination and bravery to be effective. The two of them set an example of moral leadership that resonated across the nation and continued in later years.[298] More recently, Ruby Bridges Hall has traveled around the country, sharing her story and reaching a new generation of children with a message of social inclusion and racial harmony. [299]

In his 1963 book *Strength to Love*, Martin Luther King Jr. exhorted: "Darkness cannot drive out darkness, only light can do that. Hate cannot drive out hate, only love can do that." [300] Ruby Bridges and Barbara Henry shone light and shared love and helped to change history for the better. They exemplified the power of WISEgenerosity.

CHAPTER 27

WISEgenerosity Ripple Effects

THIS PROJECT HAS HAD A PROFOUND EFFECT ON ME. It has deepened my personal purpose and made me more conscious about how my attitudes and actions affect others. More broadly, WISEgenerosity has provided me with the opportunity to live better and to help those around me do likewise. The potential impact is limitless.

Recall John Croyle from chapter 23. As someone with two thousand children, John is a very busy man. Yet he spent the better part of a day with me patiently explaining his life's work and showing it in action.

As we finished the delicious lunch he and his colleagues kindly provided, I asked John what had prompted him to lavish so much time and effort on a stranger. His first reply was practical. A mutual friend he respects had connected us, and that recommendation was enough for him.[301]

More importantly, he said that he had learned not to focus on outcomes in terms of what he does. He is planting seeds—in the children's lives he serves and in the people around his work. He doesn't know which will take root and which will not. He has learned to accept that and to dedicate himself to the tasks at hand with all his talent and energy.

I was struck by John's humility and wisdom. Then, he turned to me seriously and said, "I don't know fully why we are together today, but something good will come of it. It may be that people read your book and are inspired by this story. It may be that you go home today and treat your son or your daughter differently and better than you would have otherwise. Large or small, there will be a ripple effect from our conversation that may not be felt for years and years."

None of us knows what will come in life, but everything we do today affects tomorrow for the better or the worse. WISEgenerosity strives to make our ripples positive and meaningful. This generosity journey has inspired me to care and give and love as best I can. I hope that the same will be true for you.

Experiencing WISEgenerosity: My Reflections

Ideally, life is a journey of improvement based on the purposes we considered in chapter 2: happiness, enlightenment, and fulfillment. I am thankful for the opportunity to improve at my own living and giving. Along these lines, I was encouraged to offer my own reflections after each *WISEgenerosity* book section to share how this project has affected me personally.

Reflecting on the ages and stages of life framework presented in chapter 24, I felt compelled to care about others when I was young because my parents and those around me expected me to, and because I had an inner sense of obligation to serve others. My youth was a time of new experiences and testing who I was and where I felt most comfortable and capable.

In the growth phase when my wife and I married and settled in Atlanta, we were concerned primarily about being happy and productive as we developed our life together. Engaging in our new community, we connected by proximity with many people and organizations through our church, our children's schools, and worthwhile causes in our city.

Now, in midlife, our time commitments are increasingly focused. Having accumulated opportunities and belongings through the years, we are more concerned about enlightening our circumstances—paring back to essentials—than we are about acquiring more. In our community engagements, for instance, we tend to commit more time and money to the causes where we have the most conviction. Using the Power concept from chapter 21, these are the places where our passion, opportunity, and potential impact intersect most clearly. My own passions are to remove barriers to human flourishing for those whose circumstances have not been as fortunate as my own and to build a stronger society by nurturing connections across barriers of race, class, politics, religion, and other areas. In my view, we all are children of the same benevolent God, and all of us should be able to experience the blessings and benefits of love and justice, which are the foundation of WISEgenerosity.

Looking ahead, I imagine at some point that Courtenay and I will reflect back upon our lifetime of priorities and pursuits. My hope is that when we do, we will feel a sense of empathy, gratitude, and love. We will have compassion for the people and groups who have meant so much to us, and we will aim to leave a legacy across all of the WISEgenerosity dimensions: Possessional, Personal, Social, Emotional, and Relational. Ideally, we will have fulfilled as much of our potential to benefit this world as we were able. That would feel right and good.

Continuing on a Path of WISEgenerosity

THE BOLD HOPE OF THIS BOOK AND RELATED MATERIALS is to add momentum to a growing movement of people living meaningful and effective lives of generosity. I hope that what you've read here supports and encourages your own willingness to direct attitude and action in productive and positive ways. Toward that end, additional resources are available.

First, there is a "WISEgenerosity Key Concepts: Companion and Journal" accessible on the platform website:

This tool is meant as a complement to this text and as a place for you to record your own thoughts and questions. I hope that you'll download and use it as you reflect on this material and your personal generosity opportunities.

Second, there are other WISEgenerosity resources including blogs, videos, and additional materials available here:

Of course, the ideas and stories herein represent one person's perspective. I sincerely want to hear your own thoughts and visions and for our individual generosity journeys to align.

Here are connections to ongoing conversations about WISEgenerosity:

https://linkedin.com/company/wisegenerosity

https://instagram.com/wisegenerosity

https://www.facebook.com/wisegenerositybychrisgabriel

I invite you to join in, and I welcome your thoughts.

In addition, the WISEgenerosity website hosts a forum for everyone to share their own examples of generosity, large and small. These are collected and displayed to provide inspiration as we all look to grow in our own positive engagement with the world. Please go here to see these stories and to share your own:

Thank you in advance!

Additionally, I am traveling around the country engaging with groups and having discussions about WISEgenerosity. Perhaps we will meet at some point. If so, I'd love to hear your story in person. Likewise, please connect via www.wisegenerosity.com/contact if you are interested in my visiting your community or organization.

Three Short Questions to Answer Now

If you will permit, I have a final request. Below is blank space in which you can write answers to these three simple but provocative questions:

- What breaks your heart and troubles your mind?

  _____

- What lights you up and makes you come alive?

  _____

- What is your next step of WISEgenerosity?

  _____

The first two questions help to indicate where you should be looking to be generous (attitude). The third question points toward what you should be doing to be generous (action). As we've explored, Generosity = Considerate Attitude + Caring Action.

Putting something to paper is a first step toward making it real. Find a pen and write down whatever comes to mind. It can be tiny or huge, a momentary gesture or a lifetime commitment. Don't wait and don't fret over what you put down. Record something now. Then follow wherever WISEgenerosity leads.

WISEgenerosity Today, Tomorrow, and Always

One of my historical heroes is the seventeenth-century British reformer John Wesley. Wesley cofounded Methodism to correct what he viewed as stagnant and elitist religious practices and to engage fully with all segments of society toward personal betterment and positive change.

Wesley's world was not unlike our own. Technological progress due to the industrial revolution had increased overall prosperity but upended long-standing social conventions and institutions. The information revolution is doing much the same today.

Wesley lived a generous life. He made a fortune from book royalties but dedicated himself to the welfare of others. He said repeatedly that if he died with more than a token sum of money to his name, he would be a fraud and a hypocrite. He was true to his word and left the world poor in funds but rich in purpose.[302]

One of my favorite quotes is known as Wesley's Rule: "Do all the good you can. By all the means you can. In all the ways you can. In all the places you can. At all the times you can. To all the people you can. As long as ever you can."[303] This exhortation is a beacon toward which to steer on our own journeys of WISEgenerosity. Onward and upward!

Acknowledgments

———————————————————————————————▶

IT SHOULD COME AS NO SURPRISE that a book about generosity depended on more people than can be thanked fully in a limited space. To everyone who has played a part in this production, please know how much I appreciate you.

This work would not have been possible without the stories that enliven it. My deep gratitude goes to those profiled in these pages for their willingness to share their experiences and perspectives. The heroes of WISEgenerosity are those who personify the considerate attitudes and caring actions referenced.

For a first-time author, experienced guides are essential. My dear friend, Sunday school teaching partner, and *NYT* bestseller Randy Street provided a first orientation and stepped in countless times thereafter with wisdom and support. Randy introduced book maven Clint Greenleaf who, in turn, brought in Kelsey Grode, content muse and kindness personified. Clint's and Kelsey's consultations over multiple years helped steer a wandering "manifesto" toward something more engaging and productive. In turn, their colleague Whitney Gossett offered gracious guidance and invaluable introductions to both the marketing team and the publishers behind *WISEgenerosity*.

Jayson Teagle and Collideoscope have been a literal answer to prayer. I knew absolutely nothing about building a platform in service to generosity (or anything else). Jayson, Natalie Tsang, Jessica Freeman, Abany Bauer, Sarah Mollus, Natasha Davis, Rachel Jarrard, and their whole team provided branding structure, process, design, content, and seemingly limitless quantities of faith, talent, and support. Photographer Mary Claire Stewart, videographer Daley

Hake, and stylist Kyle Vickers made me look better than I deserve. They all are leaders in their fields, and I can't thank them enough.

Working with Jonathan Merkh and Forefront Books has been superb. They have resolved the longstanding tension between self-publishing and traditional publishing by providing authors with freedom and control on the one hand while supporting them with highly professional and powerful delivery on the other. I am tremendously grateful to Forefront for signing on to this ambitious project from an unproven author. Kia Harris and Landon Dickerson are exceptional publication guides. Jen Gingerich, Justin Batt, and Lauren Ward have provided wonderful counsel and direction. Allen Harris with Harris Editorial was an excellent developmental editor. Janna Walkup contributed impressively as copy editor.

None of this could have happened without support from my amazing colleagues at work. Firm policy prevents me from naming names, but please know how much I appreciate all of your dedication and efforts. It truly is a pleasure and a privilege to serve with each of you.

WISEgenerosity references "generosity catalysts"—people who step in at crucial times to meaningfully support the giving of others. Of the many folks who have blessed this project with their ideas, encouragement, and connections, the following stand out for special mention: Terry Balko, Syd Walker, Ryan West, Mike Blake, Susan O'Dwyer, Jason Franklin, Jared Homrich, Larry Harris, Allen Sells, Randy Hicks, Sally Finch and Stan Moor, Bonnie Harris, Thompson Turner, Gaia Marchisio, Joshua Seftel, Randy and Holly Street, Bill and Lacey Jordan, Page and Amanda Woodall, Buck and Ellen Wiley, Kris and Alison Dickson, Neal and Rosa Sumter, Rich and Becky Matherne, George and Katie Mori, Peachtree Road UMC clergy and congregants, including Rev. Bill Britt, Susan Marshall, Janet Joiner, Scott Alexander, John and Cindy Ethridge, Pam Sansbury, Rev. Josh Miles, Rev. Carolyn Stephens, Rev. Elizabeth Byrd, Rev. Leslie Watkins, and Rev. Julie Wright, the Open Door class, City of Refuge colleagues past and present, the Legacy Advisors Leadership Council at Children's Healthcare of Atlanta, fellow trustees and staff at Trinity School, my

Simeon tribe, and the God Quad crew. In addition, Ryan Bailey of Liros Group has been a coach and guide for whom I am deeply grateful.

My two best friends from growing up have their fingerprints all over *WISEgenerosity*. Rob Fletcher provided meaningful perspective and guidance throughout. Theo Michelfeld and I encouraged each other during weekly phone calls for several years while we were penning different projects. Theo and my dad, Harold ("Gabe" to my mother and friends), then served as personal editors honing and refining several drafts up until the "final" manuscript that went to the publisher in the spring of 2023.

Naturally, my greatest debts are to those with whom I am closest. The earliest lessons I learned about giving came from my late grandparents, Richard and Eleanor Jordan and Harold and Violet Gabriel. Perhaps the most generous person I've ever known measured by delight for sharing with others was my wonderful aunt Sandy Campbell.

Jack and Mary Jane Westall have treated me with all the love and support that any son-in-law could imagine. Cami Westall Sargeant and her husband, David, provided some of my most important inspiration through their example and by introducing me to great teachers and ideas. Likewise, Wiley Westall and nephew Jay demonstrate the energy and personal dedication at the heart of giving.

My parents, Harold and Jill Gabriel, have exemplified generosity in ways large and small my whole life. It is obvious but no less true to say that I would not be here in any way without them. My brother Jon has been superlatively supportive, and I am deeply thankful for our relationship. Likewise, my sister-in-law Frances and my niece Maia and nephew Jack model hospitality and many other generosity virtues.

Closest to home, rescued tiny dogs Baxter and Franklin have taken over from dear, departed beagle Princess in providing unending (if unpredictable) furry affection. My daughter Ellie's compassion for others and my son Reed's determination to do good are superpowers that illuminated this effort. My wonderfully loving and superbly sensible wife, Courtenay, inspired *WISEgenerosity* through to its completion over more than a decade of my musings and meanderings.

Her willingness to tolerate my idiosyncrasies and her determination that I make good on any potential in the project truly made it possible.

Last but certainly not least, this book is a product of faith. I believe that the God of perfect justice and perfect love is the source of all generosity and is the maker, the model, and the means for us in pursuing it. *Soli Deo gloria.*

Notes

1. Sermon series, "Be Rich," by pastor and leadership author Andy Stanley, North Point Ministries, originally delivered in four parts during the fall of 2012: https://berich.org/messages.

2. Seneca, *Minor Dialogs*, "Of a Happy Life," Book XXIII, tr. Aubrey Stewart, George Bell and Sons, London, 1900.

3. Simon Sinek, "Start with Why — How Great Leaders Inspire Action," YouTube, September 28, 2009, https://www.youtube.com/watch?v=u4ZoJKF__VuA.

4. Simon Sinek, "The Golden Circle," Simon Sinek, Accessed August 7, 2023, https://simonsinek.com/golden-circle/.

5. Alan Pratt, "Nihilism," Internet Encyclopedia of Philosophy, Accessed August 7, 2023, https://iep.utm.edu/nihilism/.

6. Acts 20:35.

7. American Heritage Dictionary of Idioms by Christine Ammer. © 2003. Appeared as far back as Sophocles c 408 BC.

8. John Spacey, "3 Origins of This Too Shall Pass," Simplicable, November 1, 2019, https://simplicable.com/storytelling/this-too-shall-pass.

9. Adam Smith, *Theory of Moral Sentiments* (Gutenberg Publishers, 2011), 3.

10. David M. Levy, and Sandra J. Peart, "The Secret History of the Dismal Science. Part I. Economics, Religion and Race in the 19th Century," Econlib, June 8, 2018. https://www.econlib.org/library/Columns/LevyPeartdismal.html.

11. Walpola Sri Rahula, "The Noble Eightfold Path: Meaning and Practice," Tricycle, May 9, 2023, https://tricycle.org/magazine/noble-eightfold-path/.

12. "Maitrī," Encyclopedia of Buddhism, July 11, 2023, https://encyclopediaofbuddhism.org/wiki/Maitr%C4%AB.

13. Bhikkhu Bodhi, "The Virtues of Giving—Dana," Bodhi Monastery, January 14, 2004, https://bodhimonastery.org/the-personal-quality-of-generosity.html.

14. Galations 6:7.

15. Lily de Silva, *Giving in the Pali Canon*, in *Dana: the Practice of Giving*, ed. Bhikkhu Bodhi (Kandy, Sri Lanka: The Buddhist Publication Society, 1995), https://www.accesstoinsight.org/lib/authors/various/wheel367.html#pali.

16. "Samsara," New World Encyclopedia, accessed August 10, 2023, https://www.newworldencyclopedia.org/entry/Samsara#Origins

17. Viktor E. Frankl, *Man's Search for Meaning* (Boston: Beacon Press, 2014), 92.

18. Ibid., 129.

19. Ibid., 129-130.

20. Ibid., 125.

21. Harry Hansen, *The Stories of O. Henry* (New York: The Heritage Press, 1965).

22. Ibid., 20.

23. Paraphrased from the Bible: Proverbs 11:24.

24. Matthew 6:38 (New Living Translation).

25. David Freund, "It's a Paradox #1," *MACNY*, April 5, 2023, https://www.oxfordreference.com/display/10.1093/acref/9780198609810.001.0001/acref-9780198609810-e-5221.

26. Christian Smith and Hilary Davidson, *The Paradox of Generosity: Giving We Receive, Grasping We Lose* (Oxford University Press, 2014), 2.

27. "Aldous Huxley," Wikiquote, June 29, 2023. https://en.wikiquote.org/wiki/Aldous__Huxley.

28. https://www.hinri.org

29. "Ross Mason," Georgia Tech Student Alumni Association. Accessed August 8, 2023. https://www.gtsaa.com/s/1481/alumni/17/interior-wide.aspx?sid=1481&gid=39&pgid=5514.

30. Simon McCormack, "Ross Mason Fosters Health Care Innovation," *HuffPost*, December 7, 2017, https://www.huffpost.com/entry/ross-mason-health-care__n__931896.

31. Kelcey Caulder, "Ross Mason to host 'Super Bubble Sweat for Charity,'" *The Morgan Country Citizen*, June 25, 2015, https://www.morgancountycitizen.com/news/ross-mason-to-host-super-bubble-sweat-for-charity/article__4d9b7026-7526-5817-82b8-03310c3d2080.html.

32. Thank you, Ken Churchill!

33. Melanie Greenberg, "How Gratitude Leads to a Happier Life," *Psychology Today*, accessed August 8, 2023, https://www.psychologytoday.com/intl/blog/the-mindful-self-express/201511/how-gratitude-leads-happier-life.

34. Interview, Ross Mason, December 7, 2015.

35. Lynne Twist and Teresa Barker, *The Soul of Money: Reclaiming the Wealth of Our Inner Resources* (New York: W.W. Norton & Company, 2017), 17.

36. Ibid. 18.

37. Ibid., 120-143.

38. Ibid. 142.

39. Ibid.

40. Ibid.

41. Thanks to Joshua Seftel for introducing me to Rais. Josh is an award-winning filmmaker in New York. He made a series of short-films called *Secret Life of Muslims* documenting un-generous behavior towards Islamic-Americans. Josh told CBS News that he was bullied for being Jewish in the small town where he grew up. That experience made him empathize with others suffering mistreatment for their faith and want to tell their stories. Rais is one of the main protagonists: https://www.youtube.com/watch?v=704XVwzLFNc. The full series is available here: http://www.secretlifeofmuslims.com.

42. Kari Huus, "A Victim of 9/11 Hate Crime Now Fights for His Attacker's Life," *NBC News*, June 3, 2011, https://www.nbcnews.com/id/wbna43241014.

43. Michael J. Mooney, "Could You Forgive the Man Who Shot You in the Face?" *D Magazine*, October 17, 2022, https://www.dmagazine.com/publications/d-magazine/2011/october/how-rais-bhuiyan-forgave-the-man-who-shot-him-in-the-face/.

44. *The Secret Life of Muslims*, episode 4, "This Muslim American was shot after 9/11. Then he fought to save his attacker's life," featuring Rais Bhuiyan, (New York: Seftel Productions, Inc., 2016). https://www.youtube.com/watch?list=PLJ8cMiYb3G5dIu76T008smkqjHOz1-kUo&v=dMlvidnkEwY.

45. Richard A. Serrano, "Finding Forgiveness on Death Row," *Los Angeles Times*, October 21, 2011, https://www.latimes.com/world/la-xpm-2011-oct-21-la-na-muslim-forgive-20111021-story.html.

46. Ibid.

47. *Secret Life of Muslims*, episode 4.

48. Ibid.

49. Timothy Williams, "The Hated and the Hater, Both Touched by Crime," *New York Times*, July 19, 2011, https://www.nytimes.com/2011/07/19/us/19questions.html.

50. Serrano, "Finding Forgiveness."

51. *Secret Life of Muslims*, episode 4.

52. Mark Greenspan, "The Primacy of Hesed: What We Learn from Abraham," Rabbinical Assembly, accessed August 8, 2023, https://www.rabbinicalassembly.org/sites/default/files/public/resources-ideas/source-sheets/tol-parashot/genesis-18-1-22-24-va-yera.pdf.

53. "Talmud," Wikipedia, August 3, 2023, https://en.wikipedia.org/wiki/Talmud.

54. Greenspan, "Hesed."

55. Shaunti Feldhahn, *The Kindness Challenge: Thirty Days to Improve Any Relationship* (New York: WaterBrook, 2016), 1.

56. Ibid., 17.

57. Thanks to Steve Gunderson, former congressman, one-time head of the Council on Foundations, and then president and CEO of the Association of Private Sector Colleges and Universities for his insights into these ideas as I first was developing them.

58. Kim Bearden, *Crash Course: The Life Lessons My Students Taught Me* (New York: Simon & Schuster, 2015), 118.

59. The Ron Clark Academy, May 4, 2023, https://ronclarkacademy.com/.

60. Kim Bearden, *Crash Course.*

61. Robert E. Buswell and Donald S. Lopez, *The Princeton Dictionary of Buddhism* (Princeton, NJ: Princeton University Press, 2014), 551.

62. Steve Bradt, "Wandering Mind Not a Happy Mind," *Harvard Gazette*, May 2, 2019, https://news.harvard.edu/gazette/story/2010/11/wandering-mind-not-a-happy-mind/.

63. "Gita: Chapter 3, Verse 5," Bhagavad, accessed August 8, 2023, http://www.bhagavad-gita.org/Gita/verse-03-05.html.

64. https://www.hafsite.org/media/pr/yoga-hindu-origins (link doesn't work)

65. "Antoine de Saint Exupéry," Wikiquote, January 12, 2023, https://en.wikiquote.org/wiki/Antoine__de__Saint__Exup%C3%A9ry.

66. Thanks to Jon Bridges for originating this framework!

67. Observation from my friend Rob Fletcher.

68. Taleb, Nassim Nicholas, *Fooled By Randomness: The Hidden Role of Chance in Life and in the Markets* (New York: Random House, 2005). The story of the lottery winner and the dentist appears in chapter 1.

69. Thank you, Chris Johnson.

70. Email exchange with Betsy and David Glass, ending May 21, 2017.

71. Thank you Jaynie Dominguez and House of Cherith!

72. *Webster's College Dictionary* (New York: Random House, 1991), 1312.

73. "David Rubenstein," *Forbes*, accessed August 8, 2023, https://www.forbes.com/profile/david-rubenstein/?sh=1e17ebfd792f.

74. Interview with David Rubenstein, January 2, 2014.

75. Daniel Kahneman and Angus Deaton, "High Income Improves Evaluation of Life but Not Emotional Well-Being," PNAS, September 7, 2010, https://www.pnas.org/doi/10.1073/pnas.1011492107.

76. Ed Diener, "Income and Happiness," APS, April 24, 2005, https://www.psychologicalscience.org/observer/income-and-happiness.

77. Raj Raghunathan, *If You're So Smart, Why Aren't You Happy?: How to turn career success into life success*, (London: Penguin Random House UK, 2016), 53-54.

78. Ibid, p. 53 and p. 284.

79. Ibid, p. 54 and p. 284.

80. Ibid., p. 54.

81. Paul Piff, "Does Money Make You Mean?" TED, October 2013, https://www.ted.com/talks/paul__piff__does__money__make__you__mean.

82. Kirsten Weir, "More Than Job Satisfaction," APA, December 2013, https://www.apa.org/monitor/2013/12/job-satisfaction.

83. Ibid.

84. Ibid.

85. Ibid.

86. Ibid.

87. Ibid.

88. Richard Alm and W. Michael Cox, "Creative Destruction," Econlib, May 12, 2023, https://www.econlib.org/library/Enc/CreativeDestruction.html.

89. Miral Sattar, "Gadgets Then and Now," *TIME*, November 29, 2010, https://content.time.com/time/specials/packages/article/0,28804,2033483__2033504__2033433,00.html.

90. "Atlantic Station," Wikipedia, July 25, 2023, https://en.wikipedia.org/wiki/Atlantic__Station.

91. J. Scott Trubey, "Atlantic Station Retail Core Sold," *The Atlanta Journal-Constitution*, October 1, 2015, https://www.ajc.com/business/atlantic-station-retail-core-sold/3qLut6a1nZAMUV-V7w61yJL/.

92. "Yale Endowment Earns 40.2% Investment Return in Fiscal 2021," *YaleNews*, October 22, 2021, https://news.yale.edu/2021/10/14/yale-endowment-earns-402-investment-return-fiscal-2021.

93. Full disclosure: I am a Yale alumnus and admired Swensen personally and professionally. Critics believe that it is questionable for Yale and other large nonprofit universities to control such large amounts of capital. That is not a debate for these pages. Swensen's Personal Generosity relates to what he could have earned in the private sector.

94. Notable structures on the Yale campus include Harkness Tower, Sterling Memorial Library, Beinecke Rare Book & Manuscript Library, and the Yale Center for British Art (founded by Paul Mellon).

95. Marc Gunther, "Yale's $8 Billion Man," *Yale Alumni Magazine*, July/August, 2005, http://archives.

yalealumnimagazine.com/issues/2005__07/swensen.html.

96. "Yale CIO David Swensen Tops University Pay at $4.7 Million," Pensions & Investments, May 16, 2019, https://www.pionline.com/article/20190516/ONLINE/190519888/yale-cio-david-swensen-tops-university-pay-at-4-7-million.

97. Gunther, "Yale's $8 Billion Man,"

98. Yale Investments Office, accessed August 8, 2023, https://investments.yale.edu/.

99. Actually, this is an oversimplification. An accurate figure would involve calculating 2% per year based on the annual endowment asset value during Swensen's leadership and then adding 20% per year of net growth (whenever applicable). However calculated, the point is that Swensen's private sector income potential was vastly larger than his actual pay.

100. David Swensen, "ECON 252 (2011): Lecture 6," 2011, Yale University, transcript and mp3, 5:40, https://oyc.yale.edu/economics/econ-252-11/lecture-6#transcript-top.

101. Brochure from The Georgia Cotillion, Alice W. Stephens, Director, "Thank you for taking classes with the Georgia Cotillion: Here's a snapshot of what you learned," February 2016.

102. Mark Griffith, The Language and Meaning of the College Motto, (New College, University of Oxford, 2012), https://www.new.ox.ac.uk/sites/default/files/1NCN1%20(2012)%20Griffith-Manners.pdf.

103. Brian Spooner, "Nomads in a Wider Society," Cultural Survival, accessed February 17, 2010, https://www.culturalsurvival.org/publications/cultural-survival-quarterly/nomads-wider-society.

104. We secretly did leave some cash behind when we left. It was a serious discussion among us. On the one hand, we respected the genuine hospitality being shown and did not want to undermine it with money. On the other hand, we did not want to take selfish advantage of such wonderful generosity.

105. Elizabeth Bernstein, "You're Not Busy, You're Just Rude," Wall Street Journal, March 12, 2019.

106. Ibid.

107. Taylor Lorenz, "Why It's Okay to Be 'Too Busy,'" Harper's Bazaar, November 2, 2021, https://www.harpersbazaar.com/culture/features/a21404/being-busy-defense/.

108. Bob Goff, Love Does: Discover a Secretly Incredible Life in an Ordinary World, (Tennessee: Nelson Books, 2012).

109. Ibid., 21.

110. Ibid., 24.

111. Ibid., 224.

112. "ECPA Milestone Sales Award Program," Christian Book Expo, accessed August 8, 2023, https://christianbookexpo.com/salesawards/.

113. Rita Fahy, Ben Evarts, and Gary P. Stein, "U.S. Fire Department Profile," National Fire Protection Association, accessed August 8, 2023, https://www.nfpa.org/News-and-Research/Data-research-and-tools/Emergency-Responders/US-fire-department-profile.

114. "Volunteering in the United States—2015," February 25, 2016, Bureau of Labor Statistics, https://www.bls.gov/news.release/pdf/volun.pdf.

115. "Sixth Amendment," Constitution Annotated, accessed August 8, 2023, https://constitution.congress.gov/constitution/amendment-6/.

116. Mona Chalabi, "What Are the Chances of Serving on a Jury?" FiveThirtyEight, June 5, 2015,

https://fivethirtyeight.com/features/what-are-the-chances-of-serving-on-a-jury/.

117. *Webster's College Dictionary* (New York: Random House, 1991), p. 249.

118. Ibid.

119. Cherie Harder, "Hospitality and Healing," *Trinity Forum Update*, March 30, 2017.

120. "Evening Conversation with David Brooks and Robert Franklin," YouTube, February 23, 2017, https://www.youtube.com/watch?v=eBLzbux3do8.

121. Over "5 million copies in print" according to the publisher: www.simonandschuster.com.

122. Matthew 5:44.

123. Dr. Martin Luther King Jr., "Love Your Enemies," November 17, 1957, Dexter Avenue Baptist Church, Montgomery, Alabama, mp3 audio, https://www.youtube.com/watch?v=522wcqUlSoY

124. Jonathan Rieder, *Gospel of Freedom: Martin Luther King, Jr.'s Letter from Birmingham Jail and the Struggle That Changed a Nation* (New York: Bloomsbury Press, 2013), 41.

125. Dr. Martin Luther King Jr. to open letter, "Letter from a Birmingham Jail," May 19, 1963, https://www.csuchico.edu/iege/__assets/documents/susi-letter-from-birmingham-jail.pdf.

126. Rieder, *Gospel of Freedom*, 24-25.

127. Dr. Martin Luther King Jr., "I've Been to the Mountaintop," April 3, 1958, Mason Temple, Memphis, Tennessee, transcript and mp3, https://www.americanrhetoric.com/speeches/mlkive-beentothemountaintop.htm

128. "Emotions Quotes," Goodreads, accessed August 8, 2023, https://www.goodreads.com/quotes/tag/emotions.

129. G.K. Chesterton, *Orthodoxy*, (San Francisco: Ignatius Press, 1995), chapter VI, "The Paradoxes of Christianity."

130. The late Professor Robert Plutchik of the Albert Einstein College of Medicine identified these eight core emotions in his 1980 study, *Emotion: Theory, research, and experience: Vol. 1.* The related "Wheel of Emotions" tool is powerful and explored further here: https://positivepsychology.com/emotion-wheel/.

131. Paul Mason, "Role of Emotions in Brain Function," Neuroanthropology, August 26, 2008, https://neuroanthropology.net/2008/08/26/role-of-emotions-in-brain-function/.

132. Personal Interview with Jessica Ethridge Chicken, March 2, 2017.

133. If you want to explore this topic further, Jessica recommends *My Grandfather's Blessings: Stories of Strength, Refuge, and Belonging* by Rachel Naomi Reymen, M.D. A cancer physician, Dr. Reymen tells how her grandfather (an Orthodox Jewish rabbi) taught her how "blessing one another is what fills our emptiness, heals our loneliness, and connects us more deeply to life."

134. Wise observation, Fletch.

135. Ron Greer, *The Path of Compassion: Living with Heart, Soul, and Mind*, (Tennessee: Abingdon Press, 2018), 48.

136. Guy Winch, "5 Ways Emotional Pain Is Worse Than Physical Pain," *Psychology Today*, July 20, 2014, https://www.psychologytoday.com/intl/blog/the-squeaky-wheel/201407/5-ways-emotional-pain-is-worse-physical-pain.

137. Ibid.

138. Fred Bronson, "Top 50 Love Songs of All Time," Billboard, February 9, 2023, https://www.billboard.com/lists/top-love-songs-all-time/.

139. C.S. Lewis, *The Four Loves*, (New York: Harcourt, 1991).

140. C.S. Lewis, *The Allegory of Love: A Study in Medieval Tradition* (United Kingdom: Clarendon Press, 1936).

141. Lewis, *Four Loves*, 32.

142. Ibid., 31.

143. Ibid., 53.

144. Ibid., 64.

145. Ibid., 58.

146. I owe a special debt of gratitude to my oldest friend, Theo Michelfeld. He and I spoke most Monday evenings for several years while writing this book, and he has encouraged and supported it in myriad ways large and small. Thank you, good sir.

147. Lewis, *Four Loves*, 91.

148. Ibid., 93.

149. Ibid., 106.

150. Ibid., 111.

151. Ibid., 128.

152. 1 Corinthians 13:13 (King James Version).

153. Lewis, *Four Loves*, 126.

154. Ibid., 121.

155. Marshall Hargrave, "Goodwill (Accounting): What It Is, How It Works, How to Calculate," Investopedia, July 16, 2023, https://www.investopedia.com/terms/g/goodwill.asp.

156. Lewis, *Four Loves*, 133.

157. Marcus Buckingham, *The One Thing You Need to Know ... About Great Managing, Great Leading and Sustained Individual Success* (London: Pocket Books, 2006), 22.

158. Ibid.

159. Feldhahn, *Kindness Challenge*, 17.

160. Ibid., 12.

161. Ibid., 120-21.

162. Ibid., 1.

163. Ibid., 59.

164. Ibid., 35.

165. Ibid., 15.

166. Ibid., 52.

167. Ibid., 50.

168. Wayne W. Dyer, "Success Secrets," Dr. Wayne W. Dyer, July 19, 2017, https://www.drwaynedyer.com/blog/success-secrets/.

169. "Fundamental Attribution Error," Wikipedia, July 4, 2023, https://en.wikipedia.org/wiki/Fundamental__attribution__error.

170. "Emotional Intelligence Works," Quixote Consulting, accessed August 8, 2023, https://www.quixoteconsulting.com/Training__descriptions/emotional__intelligence.html.

171. Greer, *The Path of Compassion*, p. 33. Also in PIXAR filmmaker Andrew Stanton's "The Clues to a Great Story," February 2012: https://www.ted.com/talks/andrew__stanton__the__clues__to__a__great__story

172. Proverbs 11:24-25 (New Revised Standard Version).

173. Thanks to Bill Boardman, retired senior fundraiser at Harvard, for providing the original basis for this list. Bill ran the first billion dollar nonprofit capital campaign in American history and has met and counseled with thousands of donors through the years.

174. Rick Bragg, "All She Has, $150,000, Is Going to a University," *The New York Times*, August, 13, 1995.

175. Ibid.

176. John Koten, "Giving: The Unusual Tale of Oseola McCarty," *The Wall Street Journal*, December 13, 2013.

177. "A Remarkable Woman, an Unforgettable Gift and a Legacy Beyond Compare," About Oseola McCarty, The University of Southern Mississippi, accessed August 10, 2023, https://www.usmfoundation.com/s/1149/foundation/index.aspx?sid=1149&gid=1&pgid=1287.

178. Ibid.

179. David Brooks, *The Road to Character*, (New York: Random House, 2015).

180. Rick Bragg, "Oseola McCarty, a Washerwoman Who Gave All She Had to Help Others, Dies at 91," *The New York Times*, September 28, 1999.

181. Ibid.

182. Ibid.

183. Oseola McCarty, "The Legacy of Oseola McCarty," interview by Aubrey Lucas, *University of Southern Mississippi*, https://www.youtube.com/watch?v=K8US__bQFAJs

184. Ibid.

185. The four types used here are based loosely on research pioneered by psychologist William Moulton Marston. His study, *Emotions of Normal People*, was published in 1928 and suggested that most people express themselves based on self-perception in response to their environment. These insights were developed by others over the years into what became known as the DISC model based on four behavioral styles: Dominance, Influence, Steadiness, and Conscientiousness. A good practical guide to these ideas is *The 8 Dimensions of Leadership* by Jeffrey Sugerman, Mark Scullard, and Emma Wilhelm. Thank you Eric Wilbanks for connecting me to this source material!

186. "Inspiring Giving to Your Full Lifetime Potential," Bolder Giving, accessed August 9, 2023, http://www.boldergiving.org/.

187. Kristi Heim, "The Inspiration Behind the Billionaire Pledge: Bolder Giving," *The Seattle Times*, August, 12, 2010.

188. Luke 21:1-4 (New Revised Standard Version).

189. Matthew 6:19-21 (NRSV).

190. John Irving, *A Prayer for Owen Meany* (New York: Ballentine Books, 1989), 616-617.

191. There are many versions of this story. The one quoted appears here: https://www.goodreads.com/work/quotes/503244-the-star-thrower. The original writing from which the story is derived can be read here: Eisely, Loren, *The Start Thrower*, Harvest/HBJ, New York, 1979, pp. 169-173.

192. Salwen, Kevin and Salwen, Hannah, *The Power of Half: One Family's Decision to Stop Taking and Start Giving Back* (Massachusetts: Mariner Books, 2010), p. vii.

193. Ibid., p. viii.

194. Ibid., pp. 225-26.

195. Adam Smith, *The Theory of Moral Sentiments* (Gutenberg Publishers, 2011), 301.

196. A caveat: both books center on God. The authors are dedicated to their faith, and it is front-and-center in their motivation for service and in their perspective on the world. They seek the alleviation of spiritual as well as material poverty. I respect and admire their commitments and do not intend to side-step them. At the same time, many of their observations are universal regardless of faith tradition or inclination. I am focused on these elements in the interest of engaging everyone who reads this book regarding the challenges they raise about giving.

197. http://documents.worldbank.org/curated/en/131441468779067441/Voices-of-the-poor-can-anyone-hear-us

198. Steve Corbett and Brian Fikkert, *When Helping Hurts: How to Alleviate Poverty without Hurting the Poor ... and Yourself* (Illinois: Moody Books, 2021), 51.

199. Ibid.

200. Ibid., 100.

201. Ibid., 99.

202. Ibid., 100.

203. Ibid.

204. Corbette and Fikkert, *When Helping Hurts*, 109.

205. Ibid., 140.

206. Ibid., 120.

207. Ken Callahan, *Twelve Keys to an Effective Church*, (New Jersey: Jossey-Bass, 2010).

208. Robert D. Lupton, *Toxic Charity: How Churches and Charities Hurt Those They Help (And How to Reverse It)*, (New York: HarperOne, 2012), 1.

209. Ibid., 5.

210. Ibid., 8.

211. Ibid., 147-148.

212. Idid, 148-149.

213. Ibid., 161.

214. "The Social Genome Project," Brookings, June 16, 2023, https://www.brookings.edu/the-social-genome-project/.

215. Rakesh Kochhar and Stella Sechopoulos, "How the American Middle Class Has Changed in the Past Five Decades," Pew Research Center, April 20, 2022, https://www.pewresearch.org/short-reads/2022/04/20/how-the-american-middle-class-has-changed-in-the-past-five-decades/.

216. Gary Hoag, "Give to Street People?," Christianity Today, January 13, 2011, https://www.christianitytoday.com/ct/2011/january/should-christians-give-money-to-street-people.html.

217. Ibid.

218. Ibid.

219. Courtney E. Ackerman, "What Is Positive Psychology & Why Is It Important?," PositivePsychology.com, July 6, 2023, https://positivepsychology.com/what-is-positive-psychology-definition/.

220. Ibid.

221. Ibid.

222. Saul Mcleod, "Maslow's Hierarchy of Needs," Simply Psychology, July 26, 2023, https://www.simplypsychology.org/maslow.html.

223. Ibid.

224. This list is adapted from Maslow's "Metaneeds and metapathologies" which is cited in *Theories of Personality* by Duane P. Schultz and Sydney Ellen Schultz, (Masachusettes: Cengage Learning, 2016), 257.

225. Matthew 5:16 (NRSV).

226. John Donne, *Devotions upon Emergent Occasions* (1624).

227. Mcleod, "Maslow's Hierarchy."

228. Thanks to my son Reed for his help with this section when I wrote it years ago. Realizing that I was going to have to look up all of these long-faded-from-memory formulas, he walked in and immediately told me what they were. Final score: then fifth grade math 1, Daddy memory 0. Here is the formula for the volume of a pyramid with a triangular base: V = 1/3 (AH). In words, the volume of one of our Generosity pyramids equals 1/3 of the area of the base triangle x the height of the shape from bottom to apex. The formula for the area of a triangle: A = (h x b) / 2. In words, the area of our base triangle equals the height from the base to the apex x the length of the base which then is divided by 2. For Givers, the base of the base triangle is the Satisfaction dimension, the height of the base triangle is the Sacrifice dimension, and the height of the whole pyramid is the Significance dimension. For Recipients, the base of the base triangle is the Sincerity dimension, the height of the base triangle is the Substance dimension, and the height of the whole pyramid is the Significance dimension. In the Master's example, the following applies for the Giver: area of base triangle = (Satisfaction x Sacrifice) / 2 or (5*4)/ 2 = 10. The volume of the Giver pyramid is that triangle area (10) multiplied by the height of the pyramid or Significance (5) and then divided by 3. (10*5)/3 = 16.6. For the Recipient: area of base triangle = (Satisfaction x Sacrifice) / 2 or (5*5)/2 = 12.5. The volume of the Giver pyramid is that triangle area (12.5) multiplied by the height of the pyramid or Significance (4) and then divided by 3. (12.5*4)/3 = 16.6. Adding the Giver and Recipient volumes provides a measure of the entire scenario. 16.6 (Giver) + 16.6 (Recipient) = 33.2.

229. Check out Syd's work at www.prosperispartners.com

230. Steve Hargreaves, "The richest Americans in history," *CNN Business*, June 2, 2014, https://money.cnn.com/gallery/luxury/2014/06/01/richest-americans-in-history/index.html

231. Two fascinating books chronicle the story of each family and enable comparisons between them: *The Rockefellers: An American Dynasty* and *Fortune's Children: The Fall of the House of Vanderbilt*.

232. David Horowitz and Peter Collier, *The Rockefellers: An American Dynasty* (New York: Summit Books, 1989), 183.

233. Arthur T. Vanderbilt II, *Fortune's Children: The Fall of the House of Vanderbilt* (New York: William Morrow, 2013), 13.

234. Vanderbilt, *Fortune's Children*, 25-26.

235. "History at Rockefeller Center: NYC's Historical Landmark," Rockefeller Center, accessed August 9, 2023, https://www.rockefellercenter.com/history/.

236. Horowitz and Collier, *The Rockefellers*, 173.

237. Antoine Gara, "M&A Flashback: Rockefeller Center's Japanese Takeover," Forbes, August 2, 2017, https://www.forbes.com/sites/antoinegara/2017/07/18/ma-flashback-the-takeover-of-rockefeller-center-capped-a-1980s-frenzy-now-a-new-mania-is-afoot/?sh=2ec8e8e6331b.

238. Vanderbilt, *Fortune's Children*, 183-184.

239. Ibid.

240. Benjamin Waldman, "Then & Now: The Cornelius Vanderbilt II Mansion," Untapped New York, May 18, 2021, https://untappedcities.com/2012/02/09/then-now-the-cornelius-vanderbilt-ii-mansion/.

241. Barbara Shubinski, "Evolution of a Foundation: An Institutional History of the Rockefeller Foundation," RE:source, August 3, 2022, https://resource.rockarch.org/story/rockefeller-foundation-history-origins-to-2013/.

242. The Rockefeller Legacy: Philanthropy and Conservation, accessed August 9, 2023, https://www.nps.gov/grte/planyourvisit/upload/Rockefeller__17-access.pdf.

243. "History of Vanderbilt University," Vanderbilt University, accessed August 9, 2023, https://www.vanderbilt.edu/about/history/.

244. Peter Churchouse, "How One of the Richest Dynasties in American History Lost Its Fortune," Business Insider, December 17, 2017, https://www.businessinsider.com/how-vanderbilt-dynasty-lost-its-fortune-2017-12.

245. "Thomas Fuller," Quote.org, accessed August 9, 2023, https://www.brainyquote.com/quotes/thomas__fuller__151889.

246. "Be the Change You Wish To See in the World," Quote Investigator, December 19, 2020, https://quoteinvestigator.com/2017/10/23/be-change/.

247. "Shantideva," Wikiquote, July 15, 2022, https://en.wikiquote.org/wiki/Shantideva.

248. Jacqueline Kramer, "Generosity in Buddhism," Tibetan Buddhist Encyclopedia, accessed August 9, 2023, http://tibetanbuddhistencyclopedia.com/en/index.php?title=Generosity__in__Buddhism__By__Jacqueline__Kramer.

249. Luke 12:48, New Revised Standard Version.

250. Dear CPA friends, I know that these numbers are not correct. Please humor me. CCG

251. See Leviticus 27:30, Numbers 18:26, Deuteronomy 14:22-23, and 2 Chronicles 31:5.

252. Lucy Brewster, "Warren Buffett Pledged to Give Away His $96 Billion Fortune. What Will His Three Children Get?," Fortune, July 9, 2022, https://fortune.com/2022/07/09/warren-buffett-pledged-to-give-away-his-96-billion-fortune-what-will-his-three-children-get/.

253. "'and They Told Two Friends'.. How Faberge Organics Shampoo Explained Virality," The Retroist, December 14, 2015, https://www.retroist.com/p/and-they-told-two-friends-how-faberge-organics-shampoo-explained-virality.

254. "The History of Fifty-Seven Cents," Temple University Libraries, accessed August 9, 2023, https://library.temple.edu/webpages/the-history-of-fifty-seven-cents.

255. Kathleen Amos, shared during the "Footprints" ceremony at the Aflac Cancer Center, Atlanta, GA, September 1, 2015.

256. 1. "Aflac Makes a Meaningful Difference during Childhood Cancer Awareness Month," CMN Hospitals, September 7, 2017, https://childrensmiraclenetworkhospitals.org/aflac-makes-meaningful-difference-childhood-cancer-awareness-month/.

257. "A Historic Partnership: AFLAC Inc.," Children's Healthcare of Atlanta, accessed August 9, 2023, https://www.choa.org/medical-services/cancer-and-blood-disorders/aflac-inc-partnership.

258. Dan Amos, "Footprints" ceremony, 2015.

259. "An Ally in Beating Childhood Cancer," The Atlanta Journal-Constitution, July 2, 2015, https://

www.ajc.com/lifestyles/ally-beating-childhood-cancer/WFDecg5pTje2IIPYVqpICJ/.

260. *The U.S. Trust Study of the Philanthropic Conversation*, October 2013.

261. Of course, this is a simple statement of how investments generally are managed. Nothing herein should be construed as investment advice.

262. Stewart Brand, "The Oak Beams of New College, Oxford," YouTube, June 10, 2012, https://www.youtube.com/watch?v=YqH4eWR7jDQ.

263. "Oak Beams, New College Oxford," Atlas Obscura, March 23, 2010, https://www.atlasobscura.com/places/oak-beams-new-college-oxford.

264. The New College archivist describes the story as more myth than reality (https://www.theguardian.com/politics/blog/2013/oct/02/david-cameron-oxford-college-trees-myth), but I love it nonetheless.

265. Thank you, Don Harp!

266. Data available from the IRS under "Individual Income Tax Returns with Itemized Deductions: Sources of Income, Adjustments, Itemized Deductions by Type, Exemptions, and Tax Items" at https://www.irs.gov/statistics/soi-tax-stats-individual-statistical-tables-by-size-of-adjusted-gross-income

267. I can't find the source of this observation from my early notes for *WISEgenerosity*. If it was you, please let me know!

268. Kelly herself is an excellent exemplar of possessional, personal, social, emotional, and relational generosity.

269. "Did Einstein Ever Remark on Compound Interest?," Stack Exchange, accessed August 9, 2023, https://skeptics.stackexchange.com/questions/25330/did-einstein-ever-remark-on-compound-interest.

270. "Reading: Compound Interest and Exponential Growth," Course Sidekick, accessed August 9, 2023, https://www.coursesidekick.com/mathematics/study-guides/finitemath1/reading-compound-interest-and-exponential-growth.

271. Thank you wonderful Susan O'Dwyer!

272. Roy Exum, "John Croyle's Speck of Heaven," *Reader's Digest*, May 1987.

273. "Genius Is One Percent Inspiration, Ninety-Nine Percent Perspiration," Quote Investigator, October 5, 2018, https://quoteinvestigator.com/2012/12/14/genius-ratio.

274. William Strauss and Neil Howe, *Generations: The History of America's Future from 1584 to 2069* (New York: William Morrow, 1991), 74.

275. Ibid., 36; 378-79.

276. I prefer iGen to the more common "Gen Z" as a label for this generation. With apologies to my own beloved iGen offspring, the term alludes to the Apple phone ubiquitous through this group's lives along with a hint of social-media driven self-absorption.

277. Adapted from William Strauss and Neil Howe, *The Fourth Turning: An American Prophesy* (New York: Broadway Books, 1998).

278. Thank you JH for this introduction! I am not identifying the school or parties involved due to the desired anonymity of some.

279. Thank you Tom Powell and Jeff Gray!

280. I've been on the board of directors for City of Refuge since 2006.

281. Exodus 21:24.

282. Four passages in the Bible cover this subject: Exodus 21:12-14, Numbers 35-9-34, Deuteronomy 19:1-13, and Joshua 20:1-9.

283. "The Bluff" is an unwelcoming acronym used by gangs in the neighborhood. It stands for "Better Leave U F*****' Fool."

284. Jeff Deel, *The Garden and the Ghetto* (Bloomington, IN: Westbow Press, 2011), 80.

285. Ibid.

286. Ibid., 83.

287. Ibid., 84.

288. Ibid., 117.

289. Ibid., 120.

290. Bruce Deel, e-mail to author, June 17, 2013.

291. Ibid.

292. Ibid.

293. "City of Refuge," Crazy Good Turns, August 16, 2016, https://crazygoodturns.org/episodes/city-of-refuge.

294. "Optimal," Oxford Advanced Learner's Dictionary, accessed August 9, 2023, https://www.oxfordlearnersdictionaries.com/us/definition/english/optimal.

295. "Ruby Bridges Goes to School," PBS, November 18, 2013, https://www.pbs.org/wnet/african-americans-many-rivers-to-cross/video/ruby-bridges-goes-to-school/.

296. The Problem We All Live With, 1964, accessed August 9, 2023, http://www.nrm.org/thinglink/text/ProblemLiveWith.html.

297. Ruby Bridges Hall, "In 1960 Little Ruby Bridges Bravely Entered an All-White School," *Guideposts*, accessed August 10, 2023, https://guideposts.org/inspiring-stories/stories-of-faith-and-hope/in-1960-little-ruby-bridges-bravely-entered-an-all-white-school/

298. Dr. Robert Coles was a child psychiatrist who served in the Civil Rights Movement and later became a Harvard professor and Pulitzer Prize-winning author. Dr. Coles was in New Orleans in 1960-61 and consulted regularly with Ruby Bridges during her first-grade experience. He later wrote a children's book about her—*The Story of Ruby Bridges*—and featured her in other works including *Lives of Moral Leadership*.

299. Ruby Bridges Hall, "Ruby was the first Black child to desegregate her school. This is what she learned," interview by Mary Louise Kelly, Elena Burnett, Mallory Yu, and Courtney Dorning, NPR, September 7, 2022, https://www.npr.org/2022/09/07/1121133099/school-segregation-ruby-bridges.

300. "Quotations," National Parks Service, accessed August 9, 2023, https://www.nps.gov/mlkm/learn/quotations.htm.

301. Thank you again Susan O'Dwyer!

302. Charles Edward White, "What Wesley Practiced and Preached About Money," Christianity Today, accessed August 9, 2023, https://www.christianitytoday.com/pastors/1987/winter/87l1027.html.

303. George Eayrs (ed.), *Letters of John Wesley: A Selection of Important and New Letters with Introductions and Biographical Notes* (London:Hodder and Stoughton, 1915), 423.

Index

Generation X / Gen X (reactive), 290-294

generosity

      benefits of, 25, 51-55, 90, 149-151, 171, 185, 212, 260-265

      catalysts, 118, 268-269, 301, 324

      definition, 25-28, 201

      essence of, 24-25, 53-55, 64-65, 180, 283-284

      excuses, 179-185

      importance of, 23-32, 72-74, 179-181, 185, 260-265, 274, 307

      normative impact of, 61-62

      paradox of, 53-55, 56-58, 167, 185, 211, 307

      "squeeze," 260-262

      velocity, 249-250, 273, 305

Generosity Dimensions tool, 213-221

generosity mindset (abundance vs. scarcity), 51-53, 55-58, 145, 180, 192, 306

Generosity Personality Types (considerate, disciplined, expressive, focused), 173-178, 198, 257, 275

generous exchanges, 105, 211-212

"The Gift of the Magi" (Henry), 48-49, 53

"Giving Pledge," 179-180

Glass, David and Betsy, 88-89, 90

God, 146, 181, 182, 207, 243, 270, 272, 305, 313, 317, 326

Golden Rule, 112, 240-241

gratitude, 57, 90, 166-167, 323-326

Greer, Ron, 141

grief, 137-138, 141, 267

H

Hannah, John, 268-269

happiness (life purpose), 37-38, 39-40, 45-47, 54, 97-99, 200-201, 212, 287

Harder, Cherie, 121-122

Harp, Donald, 95, 260

heaven / Promised Land, 84, 127, 147, 180

Henry, Barbara, 312-313

Henry, O., 48-49

Wesley's Rule, 322
When Helping Hurts (Corbett and Fikkert), 190-192, 200
Wiatt, Hattie May, 250-251
Winch, Guy, 143-144
wisdom, 26-27, 45, 57, 138, 190, 192, 201, 265, 285, 287, 315
W.I.S.E. giving, 28-30, 48, 186, 207, 213, 240-241, 276, 284, 311
World War II, 44, 123, 201, 293

Y
Yale Endowment Model, 108
Yale University, 108-110
youth stage of life, 42, 285-287, 290-291, 316

Z
zookeepers, 102-103